The Therapist and the Soul: From Fate to Freedom

Elisabeth Lukas

The Therapist and the Soul:
From Fate to Freedom

Elisabeth Lukas

Translated from the German by Waltraud Schulte

Purpose
Research
Charlottesville, Virginia

Published by Purpose Research, LLC
Charlottesville, Virginia
http://PurposeResearch.com
Contact us at charles@purposeresearch.com
Layout, typesetting, and cover design: Charles McLafferty, Jr.
Back cover photograph © 2014 Heidi Schoenfeld

Translated from the German (*Psychologische Seelsorge*, 1984) by Waltraud Schulte. Original manuscript corrected by Reid Sonner & Terence Pritchard. "Human dignity and psychotherapy" and "About love and work" also translated and corrected by Joseph Fabry; versions of these chapters were originally published in *International Forum for Logotherapy*. English translation corrected and copyedited by Charles McLafferty, Jr.

For more information about the work of Elisabeth Lukas around the world, please visit the Lukas Archives: http://elisabeth-lukas-archiv.de

For more information about logotherapy and existential analysis and to support the work of Viktor Frankl and Elisabeth Lukas, search for "Viktor Frankl Institute" and "Elisabeth Lukas Archives" on the web.

ISBN: 978-0982-4278-3-5

9 8 7 6 5 4

With gratitude
for generous support
to publish this book:

Anonymous

Mark and Beth Falkenberg

Ann Fangio

Deborah Paden-Levy

Rock House Center

Neil and Carolyn Segars

Sunshine Coast Health Center

CONTENTS

ABOUT THIS BOOK

[From the first German edition]

Life today is regarded by many people as empty and questionable. One no longer finds meaning in work, in the family, in the future. However, a life without meaning is, in spite of technical progress, a life without human dignity.

Logotherapy—Viktor Frankl's brilliantly inspired new orientation in psychotherapy—has therefore taken up the task of returning to a focus on meaning and human dignity in the psychological understanding of being and self. It is the aim of this book to demonstrate with numerous examples that this is possible, even under present circumstances, and that it can be applied to everyday problems of the individual. At the same time, it is an anniversary edition in honor of the 80th birthday of Viktor E. Frankl, a psychological counterpart to his world-famous book, *The Doctor and the Soul* (in German: *Ärztliche Seelsorge = Medical Ministry*). This is why I have titled it *Psychologische Seelsorge*: in English, *Psychological Ministry*.

PREFACE to the first German edition

When Viktor E. Frankl was interned in a concentration camp in 1942, he carried in his pocket the manuscript of a book which contained the fundamental ideas of his teaching, later called *logotherapy*. The title of the book was *Medical Ministry* (now known as *The Doctor and the Soul*), which was published after the war under this title.

Since then, a new generation has grown up; it has experienced more changes than the 10 previous generations put together. Traditions have collapsed, hierarchies of values have shifted, and ideas about freedom, responsibility, human rights, and human dignity have changed. These changes have had philosophical and psychological consequences, which have affected work in universities and consulting rooms of the medical profession all over the world.

It has always been the responsibility of philosophers to elaborate on fundamental principles according to which man can understand himself as a human being. Psychologists, on the other hand, have the responsibility of translating these principles into practical terms so that we remain healthy human beings. This book pursues both aims in an exemplary way. Therefore, it is appropriate that, as a counterpart to Frankl's first book, it has the title *Psychological Ministry* [now known as *The Therapist and the Soul* —Ed.]. Just as Frankl's first book marks the beginning of his pioneering career, this book rounds out the octogenarian's lifework. Nobody could have been better suited for this task than his most outstanding pupil, Elisabeth Lukas.

The ancient admonition of the Delphic oracle "Know thyself!" is obviously not adequate. In addition, today it is more than ever necessary to respect each other as beings of worth and dignity. The consequences of any kind of dehumanization affect not only the immediate victim; they also dehumanize whoever causes others to suffer. Whoever habitually hurts other people's worth and dignity, in the end hurts himself. Often it is just this lack of self-respect which leads to inhuman treatment of others.

As Elisabeth Lukas describes in this brilliantly inspired text, psychotherapists are in no way immune to the double-edged destructive power of disregarding human dignity. The problem seems to be rooted in a mistaken philosophical anthropology which she identifies as a regrettable chasm between the spiritual and psychological dimensions of the human being. Reductionist tendencies of traditional psychology have alienated this branch of science from the essence of human existence. On the other hand, there is a movement among the schools of psychotherapy, built on the humanistic theories of logotherapy, to remove these degrading tendencies.

The inviolable dignity of the patient plays a central part in Frankl's "psychiatric credo" and is at the same time the foundation for his concern with rehumanizing psychotherapy. According to Frankl, the doctor or therapist has to establish in each consultation a distinctive and unique person-to-person relationship with his patient, thus maintaining the dignity of both throughout the course of treatment. One could even claim that this is an essential part of treatment.

By means of an alliance with logotherapy, philosophy has found an additional opportunity to serve as a perfect complement to psychotherapy. Such profound themes as fate and freedom, conscience and responsibility, being and meaning, which Frankl introduced into his medical-psychological work, are now convincingly discussed by Lukas, and are, after all, the main themes of philosophy. The removal of existential blindness through logotherapy, therefore, goes hand in hand with the correction of metaphysical myopia in the philosophy of life and vice versa.

What is important is human participation in the conditions of reality instead of subjugation under them. It is exactly this different nuance in orientation that distinguishes a person who is able to see an area of freedom from another who regards himself as at the mercy of fate. Individuals, for instance, who live under the "slavery" of their feelings suffer their self-imposed tragedy and are forever dependent on environmental conditions. The truly free and wise person, on the other hand, can act despite the unavoidable burdens presented by life itself. Spinoza speaks of a person who is a slave to his feelings as someone who "ceases to live when he ceases to suffer."

Only the person who is free to act has energies available to investigate the meaning of the total situation. Doing this, that individual automatically turns away from destructive goals towards aims of a meaningful design. Elisabeth Lukas shows in tragic case histories how this tactic finds its psychological manifestation—where the surrender of freedom in favor of the tyranny of fate would have speedily caused emotional chaos if logotherapeutic help had not been available. She reaches a conclusion which becomes the essence of her statement: "Pointing out to a person the—possibly last—remaining area of freedom is, beyond any psychotherapeutic tactic, an act of human dignity!"

I would like to add one comparison. A game of tennis does not rob us of our dignity by forcing us to obey the rules and limitations of the game. Quite the opposite: These rules and regulations are the preconditions of the game and provide us with the opportunity to develop our individual skills. In a similar manner, we are not robbed by life when it imposes its unchangeable limitations. Our responsibility lies in accepting these limitations and integrating them into our freedom, so that we neither overestimate them nor underestimate our spiritual potential for dealing with them.

In logotherapy, and especially in this book, many opportunities for a positive and meaning-oriented confrontation with fate become apparent, opportunities that may spread into wider circles and thereby benefit humanity.

Dr. Sandra A. Wawrytko
Professor of Philosophy at the San Diego State University
Visiting Professor at the Chinese Culture University of Taiwan
San Diego
September 1984

A

TOWARD A PSYCHOLOGY
OF HUMAN DIGNITY

1. Finding Meaning and Psychological Health

Today, everyone is aware of the threat to the human race and the question mark which hangs over the future ecology of our environment. Young people have always opposed traditions and forcefully pushed towards new horizons. But never before have the young been filled with such dark forebodings as at present; so much so, that some members have called themselves the "no-future generation." However, this dark mood is only indirectly aroused by a fear of negative events in the future.

Even if the possibility of an atomic war that would put an end to all human endeavor can be envisaged, and even if there are more and more alarming prognoses concerning poisoned environments and insurmountable famines ahead of us, human beings are too short-lived and shortsighted to let it affect everyday business. No, fear of imaginary terrors is not the original deciding factor in this displeasure that can be observed worldwide and that grips both older and younger generations.

The hallmark of a no-future generation is a profound *feeling of meaninglessness*, a continuing loss of meaning which happens now—today—and saps the strength for facing tomorrow. A "no-meaning generation" is emerging, which is of more concern than that for the survival of the species; when the "wherefore" falls away as the existential basis, survival loses its value.

Viktor E. Frankl, one of the most insightful psychiatrists of the 20th century, was the first to prove a close connection between a person's inner meaning orientation and his psychological health. This idea was previously unknown in psychology, and with it he laid the foundation for a new approach in all the human sciences. Thanks to his research, we can now reconstruct the *vicious circle* that ominously affects individual lives as well as the fate of entire nations, and is, at present, active on several levels. Because we are aware of it, we can design proposals for breaking this vicious circle. Even if it hasn't yet found a satisfactory echo in world events, Frankl's theory gives a powerful impulse to individual psychotherapists, who are able to provide active support to the people of today who face this crisis of meaning.

What is this vicious circle? It is a causal chain of several links which cascade on each other in an uninterrupted chain reaction. Simplified, it looks like this: Factor A leads to factor B, and B again leads back to A, and A, now fortified again, leads to B, and so on. These circular effects have been known for some time in the theory of psychological disorders. In every case it starts with some feeling of insecurity. Let us look, for example, at examination anxiety. A well-prepared student fails a test. This is factor A. It may happen that a great fear of the next test develops—we call this "anticipatory anxiety"—this is factor B. As a consequence of an exaggerated negative expectation of failing again, factor A is fortified and the test taker is so blocked and frozen up that failure results on the next test. Thus B has led back to A. Examination fear is now solidly established—A immediately intensifies B—i.e., the vicious circle between anticipatory anxiety and failure is closed.

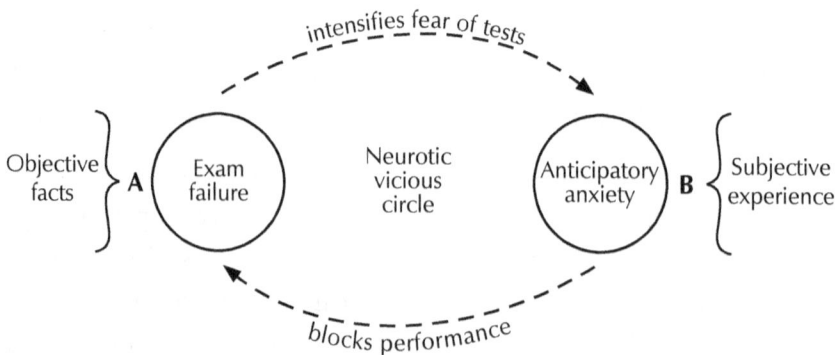

Naturally, this is merely a simple example of what can be said to be the origin of every psychopathological deviation. It is positioned—as the reader may have observed—on the tangent of the subjective internal and objective external world; anticipatory anxiety belongs to the subjective experiences of a person, while failing an examination represents an objective reality.

I would like to discuss a number of factors involved in the vicious circle, whose shadow can fall on any one of us. Yet it is the same pathological type of circular interaction between subjective experiences and objective events, and at its origin there is an insecurity that is existentially deep-seated and intense. It is the pervasive total insecurity of modern times and the overwhelming doubt as to the meaning of life. Viktor Frankl formulated its genesis:

> If you ask me to explain the genesis of this feeling of meaninglessness, I can only say that, in contrast to the animal, no instinct tells man what he must do, and in contrast to the person of former times, no tradition tells him what he ought to do and now he does not seem to know what he really wants to do. Thus it happens that he either only wants what others do—which is the case in conformism (Western world), or he only does what others want—which is totalitarianism (Eastern world).

We see that the human being no longer has the foolproof instincts of animals. Furthermore, the individual has lost—in this century more than ever—support from established traditions and value norms. The two World Wars and enormous technical progress have considerably contributed to this state of affairs. This caused a sudden *existential vacuum,* as Frankl called it. It is a loss of orientation and support, in which the question of meaning in any activity becomes suddenly acute and remains unanswered. Subsequent events simply demonstrate the neurotic vicious circle. The chronic feeling of meaninglessness upsets the balance of psychological health in a person and, once this balance is affected, social and individual maladaptive behavior is the inevitable result. This usually introduces *anticipatory anxiety*. The resulting pessimistically tinted, and by no means groundless, anxiety in its turn reinforces the resigned feeling that, in the final analysis, everything is meaningless anyway. This completes the vicious circle [see inner circle in figure on next page].

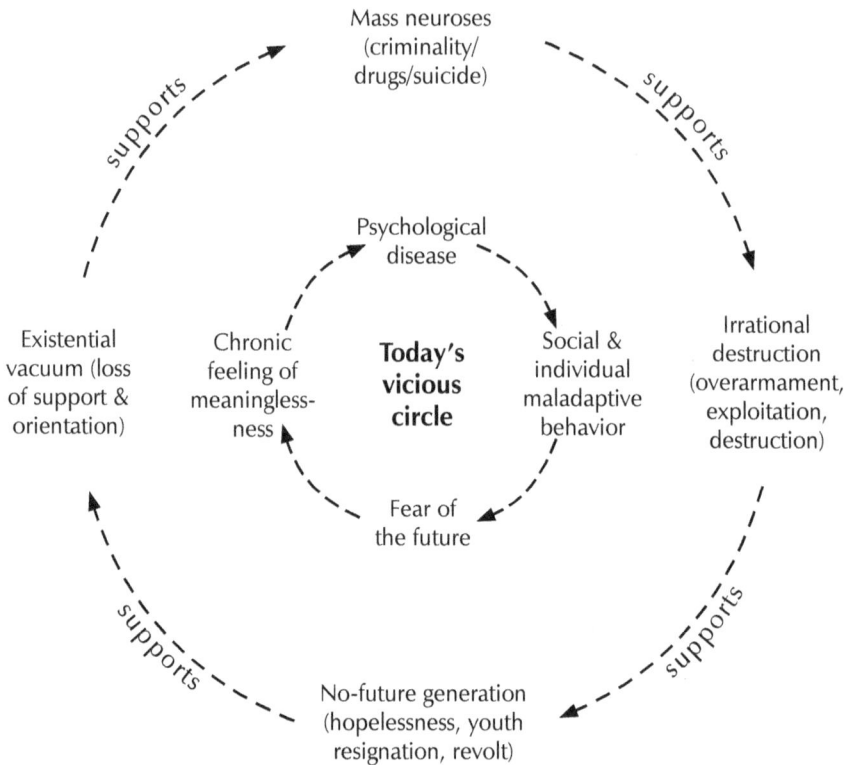

If we relate these four factors to world events at large, a specification can be assigned to each, indicating the complexity of its effects. The feeling of meaninglessness of the individual is analogous to the existential vacuum of a no-meaning generation on the level of the total population. The psychological illness of the individual parallels the mass neuroses of our time, with high rates of perversions, criminality, alcohol and drug dependency, depression, and suicide.

All those unsound deeds of humanity that have no other aim than irrational destruction, such as overarmament, exploitation, and the destruction of environmental and cultural treasures, can be understood as social and individual maladaptive behavior on a large scale. The fear of the future finds its expression in a generation of young people without ideals or compromise, a group that has named itself the "no-future generation" [see outer circle in figure].

If we disregard world events and turn our attention to the individual, we find clear parallels with the processes mentioned above. Here as well, all kinds of meaning frustrations attack the psychological stability of a person and tempt the individual to behave in a way that later boomerangs and removes future possibilities. Considerable influence is exerted by the interaction between objective external events and subjective internal events. This was discussed above in the basic scheme of the vicious circle. On closer inspection, we find that this vicious circle contains one objective and two subjective axes or, to put it differently, we encounter an objective reality in two places on its chain.

One place is self-evident and needs no explanation; it is the arc between maladaptive behavior and a fear of the future. Logically, maladaptive behavior results, in addition to all subjective failures, in actual mistakes, objective damage, and nonvalues in one form or another. When humankind, for instance, cuts down tropical rain forests, negative climatic and ecological consequences result as a matter of course. Or when an individual spends every last dollar on entertainment, debts and deprivation for the family are natural consequences. These are not just subjective feelings, but very real facts which lend a certain justification to emerging fears of the future.

The other point in the circle where objective reality impinges is not so evident and was (as far as psychology is concerned) overlooked for a long time. It is the arc between feelings of meaninglessness and psychological pathology. In order to explain this, a short digression into the general concept of the human being is needed.

What is the human being? For millennia, philosophers and thinkers have battled to portray human existence, but their models have remained incomplete. Still, they have progressed to the point of assigning a body and a soul to the person, although the area of contact has been shrouded in mystical darkness. According to Western thinking, the body represents the earthbound dimension that the human being—from the beginning of evolution—shares with the animals, while his soul was assigned a higher place, reaching beyond this world, as the "image of God." Early in the 20th century, as religious dogmas lost some of their credibility and the newly developed science of psychology entered medical practice and academia, the concept of the soul changed dramatically. The "image of God" became a demythologized "image of man"; psyche, in turn, became part of the naturalistic, conceptional framework. Just as the human body is supposed to have evolved from the animal organism, so the human psyche is interpreted scientifically as a developmental and structural refinement of animal drives, emotions, and subintelligent capacities for problem solving.

Using this interpretation as a basis, the fundamental psychological schools of psychoanalysis and behaviorism were developed. Both schools, in spite of considerable methodological differences, understand the person as a being primarily concerned with self-preservation, i.e., a homeostatic instrument oriented to balance well-being by satisfying significant needs while obtaining as much pleasure as possible. This perspective was very attractive because it precisely matched the drive for emancipation by modern, enlightened humanity and gave much-needed armor for the fight against the power of those old traditions that were about to be thrown overboard. It came to a massive break with traditions in the Western world and was not without a ripple effect on less-developed nations.

Apart from this general trend, there were critics of this exaggeratedly egocentric psychological concept of the human being. One of them, whose ideas must receive serious consideration, is Viktor Frankl. Even before the great break with tradition in the mid-1900s, Frankl repeatedly noted that the human being is not a homeostat whose sole task in life is self-satisfaction. In Frankl's opinion, the person does have a physical body that can be compared to other organisms and also has psychological dimension, which includes the differentiated human emotionality based on drives. However, beyond this, the person has a spiritual or *noëtic* dimension—the essential human dimension. The noëtic dimension raises the human being decisively above the animal not only quantitatively, but also qualitatively. The traditional view of the "image of God" had found a kind of symbolic expression, but this was lost in the scientific teachings of modern psychology.

Frankl reintroduced the spiritual dimension of the person into psychology Along with that, he fundamentally revised the concept of the human being.

The spirit does not strive after lust, it needs *meaning*. It does not seek satisfaction of needs but rather meaningful tasks and aims in life… and exactly at this point the environment emerges with its multitude of potentials for meaning, including all of its objective values, which are to be realized.

Only a concept of the person that embraces the spiritual dimension allows for transcendence of the homeostatically oriented inner self and for recognition of the person as a being who has one primary necessity beyond all need balancing, namely, to find meaning in the external world and to fulfill it. This search for meaning could become so important that a person could dedicate his or her life to it. Pascal, the great French philosopher, expressed this idea in the statement "man infinitely transcends man."

Let us return to our sketch of the vicious circle, which at present has innumerable people in its grip. We have established that after the break with traditions came an existential insecurity with a worldwide feeling of meaninglessness as its consequence. According to Frankl's findings, we now know that the feeling of meaninglessness of life can only be the expression of a spiritual frustration, because it is this potential that seeks meaningful existence independent of any "pressure of drives."

The contrast between the psychological dimension (with its continuous search for "self-actualization") and the spiritual dimension (with its equally continuous search for "value realization") is apparent from the fact that a virtual epidemic of meaning-frustration occurred just at the time when great economic progress emerged in the Western industrialized countries. The resulting prosperity made the satisfaction of innumerable desires possible, starting with the wave of sexual obsession up to the wasteful extravagance of an affluent society. Every imaginable wish for consumption could suddenly be fulfilled; only the spiritual longing of the person remained, the longing to live for something, to be useful for something. There was—as Frankl noted—more and more to live *from*, but less and less to live *for*. The present calamitous situation is, therefore, based on an enormous spiritual frustration that throws each individual back onto the self. It misleads the person into searching for happiness within the psychological dimension. As a result, the market for psychological prescriptions for happiness is boosted astronomically, but they in turn seduce the individual to neglect those value dimensions which are the only ones worthy of the human spirit: bringing positive values into the world, such as the good, the beautiful, and the positive; in other words, that which is meaningful. This neglect, however, demands its price, which is neither more nor less than psychological health.

Why is this the case? How can this vicious circle be broken? How can the process be reversed and health restored through finding meaning? First, let us add to the sketch three coordinates mentioned earlier:

1. *The objective axis*—which has to be drawn between the neglect of objective values and the creation of objective nonvalues.

2. The *two subjective axes* which are determined: a) on the side of "pathology," by psychological illness and inadequate social and individual behavior; b) on the "normal" side, by anticipatory anxiety and feelings of meaninglessness.

An example illustrates this theoretical framework. Suppose a son takes over his father's firm but sees no deeper meaning in the continuation of the business. He simply feels compelled to do so or just does not know of anything better to do with his life. Of course, it might be possible for the son gradually to grow into his task and to find a certain amount of satisfaction in accomplishing it. However, it could happen that the business never presents a meaningful task for him but simply remains a comfortable source of income or a prestige factor. Even if this is the case, the possibility remains that the young man has so many fulfilling life interests in addition to his occupation that, with them, he can balance the time and energy used for his business with that needed for his own inner satisfaction. We may assume that he will not overexert himself for his firm. From the point of psychological hygiene, everything may still be healthy.

If, however, the young man has few interests outside his business, has no hobbies, or is not capable of lasting interpersonal relationships, and in his leisure time is bored rather than engaged in something meaningful, then the situation would be conducive to starting the vicious circle. This would mean that he does not utilize his healthy spiritual energy for improving the situation; instead, he gets caught up in the chase after momentary pleasures and short-lived personal advantages, seeking artificial self-confirmation. Thus he seeks satisfaction on the psychological level, thinking that satisfaction cannot be found on the spiritual level. He might give less and less attention to the firm, start drinking, frequent nightclubs, have a string of girlfriends, show off with expensive cars, give himself thrills with dangerous adventures, and so on.

Ignoring opportunities for objective meaning goes hand in hand with the disintegration of psychological stability. The person concerned is intuitively aware of the situation and somewhere in the recesses of the spiritual existence regrets it deeply. Such individuals come into conflict with their consciences and become angry with themselves. They could increasingly react with depression or aggression or flee into drug-induced oblivion.

Without proper help, the son would be in danger of sinking into a pathological condition. He might slip into a neurosis or some addiction; he might come into conflict with the law or even attempt suicide. This would cause a scene with his family. At work, wrong decisions might be made and money squandered or embezzled. The maladaptive behavior becomes more obvious and its consequences become more drastic until something collapses that can affect the entire firm or family. The collapse could be another crisis or it could be the end, because it makes the hopelessness of a questionable future conscious and paralyzes any spiritual defiance, which alone would be able to build a new, meaningful existence out of the ruins.

Reflecting step-by-step on such an unhappy chain of events, of which there are countless variations, the question arises: How could one prevent them, how can help be offered? Therefore we will now leave the vicious circle and instead concentrate on the positive perspectives of finding meaning.

One thing is important to note: With a spiritual psychotherapy as represented by Frankl's approach, the young man can be helped at any stage of his crisis, not only at its beginning. The only condition is that he must be willing to accept help; psychotherapy cannot be effective without a person's consent. Prevention, however, is only possible in the beginning, when the struggle for meaning threatens to go awry and when the process of dehumanizing starts.

Having seen many people at this juncture and having learned how amazingly important and far-reaching even the slightest human support can be in the struggle for meaning, I know how crucial the right word at the right time can be—an encouraging book placed in someone's hand, an idea or suggestion which ignites the spiritual spark, even the flicker of a meaning potential that was not perceived by the person previously because it was obscured by a veil in front of his or her inner eye.

One has no idea how much misery could be prevented by seeming trivialities. Just as we know that small matters can have terrible consequences, so, too, can they have redeeming effects, sometimes even more so than grand schemes. Psychology and psychotherapy are not everybody's forte; neither is it everyone's task to heal psychologically afflicted people; but it is everyone's task to help wherever they can. *There is an opportunity for every person.*

How can helping support be given in the search for meaning, which every person faces sooner or later? One fact has to be kept in mind: *Meaning can never be given—it must be discovered.* What can be done is to describe the process of finding meaning and learn from these descriptions. Road signs for finding meaning can be constructed and used for orientation. In particular, that which is meaningful can be used as a yardstick for our actions, even if its measure does not apply exactly to our individual preferences. The purpose is to orient life towards a criterion which points beyond life, just as the compass needle points beyond the rim of the compass towards something outside of itself and is therefore independent of the compass's location. This example serves to explain the concept of meaning, which is likewise a permanently valid criterion for defining our location as it remains independent of any life situation from which bearings may be taken.

The compass reflects another insight because it shows that a direction contains no information about distance. North, as indicated by the needle of the compass, may be inaccessibly far or very near.

Similarly the meaning of life may be both infinitely abstract and exceptionally concrete. Generally, three levels can be distinguished.

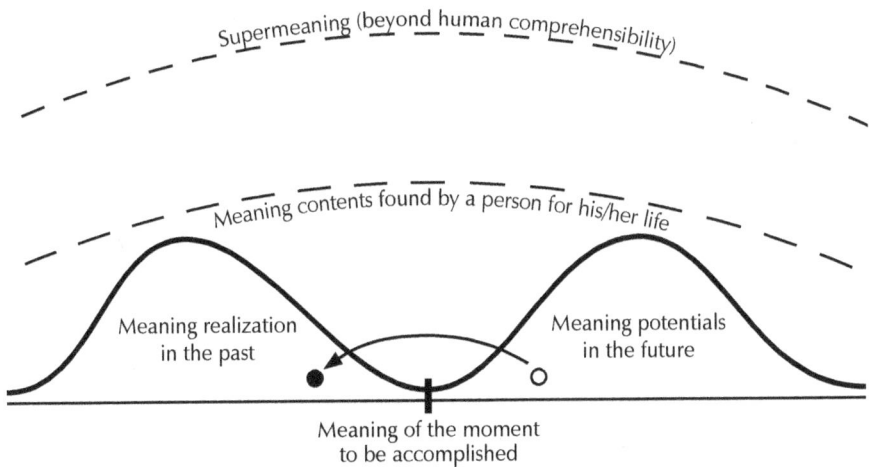

Supermeaning (beyond human comprehensibility)

Meaning contents found by a person for his/her life

Meaning realization
in the past

Meaning potentials
in the future

Meaning of the moment
to be accomplished

For the type of meaning that cannot be attained by the individual, except by reaching in faith into the transcendence of God, Frankl coined the term *supermeaning*. It is useless to speculate about this "supermeaning," which has nothing to do with the supernatural, because by definition it is beyond human comprehension. The theory of such a supermeaning simply affords a possibility that even those elements of this world which our intellect would have to declare "senseless"—e.g., the existence of evil, the occurrence of tragic accidents, the suffering of innocent people, or the inescapable fact of aging and dying—might, in a higher dimension, have meaning. However, humankind is barred from attaining or understanding this dimensional level.

What is open to human beings but closed to animals is the discernment and experience of special *meaning contents* of one's life. Such meanings may be, for example, the accomplishment of a self-chosen task, research into new frontiers, inventing something, creation of a work of art, production of new articles, or remedying of some grievance.

That means that purpose can be found in *being for something*. But it can also be discovered in establishing a family, in loving children, in working for a charitable cause, or in caring for persons in our charge, and thus find its crowning expression in *being for someone*.

It is essential to note that these meanings are not entirely identical with a person's aims for the future, although they may be very worthy pursuits. However, meanings penetrate the *total* span of a person's life. They flow from the future into the past; though a personal goal may fade with its accomplishment, the meaning of a positive creation, a beautiful experience, a fulfilled love, etc., remains—nothing and nobody can ever extinguish it. Contained in the future, and therefore beyond any subjective goals, are objective potentials of meaning awaiting realization. Once they are realized, they will be transformed into objective materialized meaning, into values created and formed by an individual and preserved safe and secure in the past. If, for example, a young doctor saw the meaning potential of the future and devoted years in developing a serum against a dangerous disease, and if this dedication was crowned with success, then the realization of this potential will forever be coupled to this life and nothing can take away the fact of the gift, a precious serum to humanity. This fact remains long after the death of the individual.

I emphasize this aspect of Frankl's theory because, within a lifetime, the two curves of meaning potential and meaning realization are continuously changing. A young person on the point of entering adult life has a huge mountain of potential ahead but hardly any realized meaning treasured in the past; while the future is rich for that individual, the past is poor.

Youth:

Meaning realization in the past

Meaning potentials in the future

Meaning of the moment to be accomplished

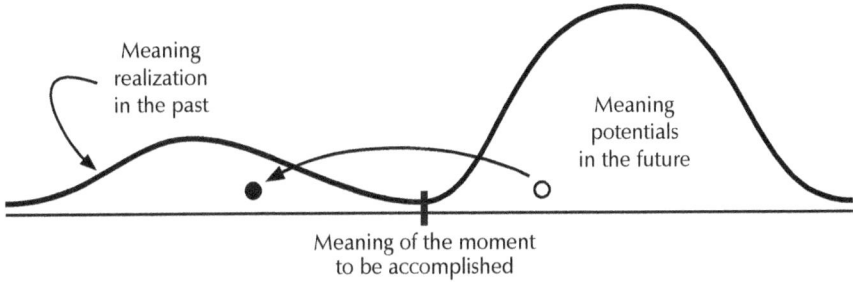

The older adult, in turn, if successful in living meaningfully, has already crossed the mountain. It lies behind, with an abundance of all those values that, by realizing them, have been safely stored in the past. The future of an older adult, however, has only limited potentialities; it is relatively empty compared to the riches of the past.

Older adult:

Meaning potentials in the future

Meaning realization in the past

Meaning of the moment to be accomplished

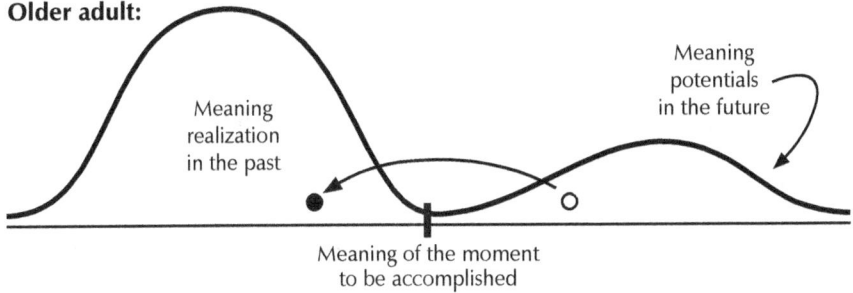

This illustrates why we should not only focus on immediate goals as meaning factors. The person near the end of life has hardly any goals left and, if they existed, that individual would most probably not be able to reach them. What exist are the goals reached, the aims attained, the sufferings and experiences harvested; in sum, the total of all that has made life worthwhile. These are simply realized potentials of that life, which belong to that person forever. We perceive that even old age has its comforts.

In our passage from the highest level of abstract meaning (the certainly timeless supermeaning) via the far less abstract future and past contents of a meaningful life, we want to venture on to the actual concrete level of meaning, which is located in the present. It is the *present meaning*, the *meaning of the moment*. Here we encounter, in Frankl's words, the "pacemaker of being." Any great meanings of life—individual goals, tasks, works, the total dedication to a cause or a person—can only be realized if they are taken in relation to minute entities, to moments, to specific situations, each of which is unique and cannot be repeated and contains its own unique and unrepeatable quality of meaning.

Indeed, it is impossible for the human being to snatch some meaning out of nothing and then to proceed with fulfilling it. Imagine what that would imply: One could think it "meaningful" to burn down a house; for another, to blow up a jetliner. Humankind is not the authority for defining meaning, just as we cannot define mathematical laws. We can discover that the square root of 169 is 13 but we cannot invent that fact. Likewise, the specific meaning of the moment must be discovered and decoded. This meaning is no less objectively assigned than the laws of mathematical operations.

I noted earlier the tangential point between subjectivity and objectivity in order to make it understood that the person is surrounded by the world and becomes human only to the extent to which he or she enters into a relationship with it. Further, any kind of self-actualization needs to take the long path via value realization. In this regard, fulfilling the meaning of the moment is a total fusion of meaning subjectivity and meaning objectivity, and if this fusion is disturbed, the very humanity of a person is upset. This is why continuous disturbances can cause such serious psychological disharmonies as were mentioned regarding the vicious circle.

Let us focus again on the young man in our example who took over a business without personally seeing a deeper meaning in this task. We agreed that permanent meaning frustration will drive him into sickness and maladaptive behavior. There is yet another factor that has not been discussed because only his subjective life situation has been under scrutiny. The very existence of the business is an objective fact and has meaning in itself, namely, an appeal to meaning to make it the best business possible.

At the moment the young man takes over the business, he is no longer confronted only with his own subjective ideas about the meaning contents of life, he is also confronted with the objective challenge to take over the business and to shoulder the responsibility for it. This implies that, if the young man did not feel called to take over the management of the business, he should not have accepted it at all but should have passed it on to more capable hands. Thus he would have answered the meaning of the moment. By doing what he actually did, he not only let his own search for meaning end in emptiness, he also acted against the challenge of the situation. The subjective and objective meanings of the situation at that time were in no way congruent, and thus he could not cope with the psychological consequences.

In contrast, turning to the example of the young doctor who undertook the self-imposed task of developing a life-saving serum, we see clearly that the hours spent in the laboratory conducting research may be counted as the most fulfilled of an entire lifetime, even considering that the work may have required a great number of sacrifices, resulting in exhaustion and burnout. However, the doctor will have to contend with being called away again and again from the research project by another current meaning of the moment when there is another call, in the role of parent or physician. These calls almost must be obeyed in order to maintain a sense of fulfillment; how could attention be given to this research with a clear conscience, knowing that tasks are being neglected for which there is a commitment and responsibility?

Therefore, to live up to the meaning of the moment implies harmonizing the superordinated aims and values that we perceive as our personal meaning of life with the specific responsibility for the actual, concrete situation. Or to formulate it more simply: To live up to the meaning of the moment means to follow one's own conscience, where conscience, according to Frankl, represents the human capacity to detect the unique and specific meaning which is concealed *in every situation*.

"In every situation...." Perhaps the reader thinks this may be an exaggeration? Can a situation of suffering, pain, or loss contain meaning? I would say "yes" and urge you to think seriously about it. Even moments of inevitable suffering have their potentials for meaning, although they are not reflected in the emotional world of the psyche. They can, however, be detected with spiritual probes.

Suffering challenges us to maintain our composure, to bear it with dignity and, through it, to grow and to mature and eventually to become a changed person. This is a kind of self-actualization by way of value realization: The values of a heroic example that a person radiates into the environment while bravely dealing with some dire distress enable that individual to grow beyond the self.

The person who believes the traditional psychologizing concept of the person, that the individual exists mainly to satisfy one's own needs, to grasp for happiness and success, to accumulate power and success, will be psychologically broken by suffering. Such a person has not yet understood anything about the essential value criterion of humanness, such as the meaning of the moment and, with it, the meaning of life. There is a saying which is 2,000 years old and contains wisdom that modern psychology is at present busy rediscovering as *the key* to psychological health. The saying comes from the apostle Matthew, who attributes these words to Christ: "Whosoever finds his life will lose it; but he that loses his life for my sake shall find it."[1]

If we replace the "for my sake" in these words of Christ with "for the not human bound," "for the objectively meaningful," "for the Being in the world," then we have exactly the same statement that the eminent psychiatrist Viktor Frankl will leave to our chaotic times as his legacy: If an individual wants to remain psychologically healthy, such a person must transcend the self by discovering a meaning to be fulfilled.

2. From Depth to Height Psychology

In the 1980s, there was a psycho-boom very much to the disadvantage of the population in our Western world and very distressing to all responsible psychologists. Every human (and inhuman) aspect was scrutinized and analyzed from the most peculiar psychological perspectives. The result was an intense irritation in normal life for the uninitiated layperson and a sectarian splintering and increased fanaticism among professionals.

To bring this harmful process of psychologizing to an end, we need no additional schools of psychology, nor new direction according to the latest fad, but rather a *rehumanizing of psychology in its entirety*. This means that we need to reinforce those healthy self-help resources within the population which can prevent vicious circles of all kinds without paying the price of psychologizing. We further require an optimization of the offer of therapeutic support from professionals who know the complexity of the human psyche without making the mistake of considering only one side. I know of only one theory which would make such an undertaking possible and that is the framework of Frankl's logotherapy.

It has now been 22 years since I entered this system of thought as a student, and—considering it metaphorically as a complete building—I have wandered through its many stories from the cellar to the attic, and again and again new passages have opened onto mysterious rooms hardly ever entered, which give the impression that the entire building is one huge shelter for the human spirit. Logotherapy is an anthropology that is not satisfied with illuminating psychological phenomena, but rather incorporates spiritual-noëtic phenomena of human existence. Suddenly doors which were closed to the emotional substrata of the psyche open up to the capabilities of the human spirit.*

Everybody knows that depth psychology was engaged in a protracted, tireless processed research to uncover the true nature of the human being, to interpret even the slightest psychological agitation; indeed, it succeeded in uncovering and explaining a large number of hitherto unsolved enigmas. However, there remained an inexplicable remnant, comparable to the blank areas on a map, that escaped the grasp of depth psychology. There is a threshold that cannot be crossed with the knowledge of drive dynamics because a yardstick beyond needs and satisfaction is required.

It was the indisputable merit of logotherapy to point out that, for the person on a spiritual level, the satisfaction of needs is not predominant; rather, it is the perception of tasks, the achievement of self-defined goals, and the realization of values. In short, the attainment of something like a personal meaning of life is essential. Each person is prepared to forego all kinds of need satisfaction in order to fulfill the *will to meaning*. The great work of depth psychology has been carried on, revised, and supplemented by the efforts of "height psychology," as logotherapy is often called.

Today, we are able to draw a fairly accurate picture of the human being that is true to life. If we can offer appropriate assistance for adjustment, which is necessary whenever a human being deviates pathologically from how he or she perceives the self, then we have to thank both depth psychology for illuminating the psyche of the person to its limits and height psychology for being able to break through these limits with the evidence that being human always reaches beyond the psychological dimension into the noëtic.

The following are some case studies where such boundary crossings are crucial, because traditional methods of psychology very soon reach their

---

* [Frankl noted that the human being lives in three dimensions. The *somatic* is the physical dimension, also noted as *soma*; the *psyche* is composed of our emotions and intellect. We share soma and psyche with the animals. The *noëtic* dimension is that of the human spirit, and involves free will, choice, responsibility, creativity, and the capacity to develop symbol systems such as used in science, mathematics, and music. The noëtic is the dimension that makes us uniquely human (and thus different from animals). —Editor]

limit of application. The examples are chosen from years of experience in dealing with people seeking counseling. Practitioners among readers will recognize the complex types of problems, which are most difficult and extremely resistant to psychotherapy and psychiatry.

First to be mentioned would be *hysteria*, which, in spite of endless theoretical papers about it, still belongs to the virtually incurable psychological disorders. The name "hysteria" is rarely used today because of its degrading connotation, and the manifestations of the disorder have changed considerably with time. Even today, one does not infrequently encounter those patients who, with theatrical perfection, enact tragic scenes of demonstrative character for no other reason than manipulating their environment or else eliciting specific reactions from it. These patients do not shy away from any means, not even from self-mutilation or similar weapons against themselves.

Pain, happiness, fear, passion, the wish to die, and the will to live—for them, everything is more or less counterfeit and used in the service of a goal which always takes the form of an appeal for help addressed to another person. For some, the usual theory may apply, that they were deprived of parental care and attention during childhood and as a result of a tremendous need to make up for it, they produce hysterical attacks for the rest of their lives, which at least for a short time, command the attention of the environment. However, the theory has seldom been proven that an exposure of these connections would automatically decrease the tendency to hysterical behavior.

The individual who has hysteric symptoms—to keep the label for the sake of simplicity—is a sick person who wants to be sick, who expects something from the affliction. The rewards are likely to the person's own advantage, or may give some perverse delight in someone else's disadvantage for whom something is spoiled with the hysterical outbreak.

How can therapy help, when every therapy has as a precondition a pressure of distress of the patient, that is, the genuine desire for recovery? The mere insight into the development of a disorder does not necessarily imply that the will to be healthy is aroused.

However, in logotherapy there is the concept of *meaningful renunciation*: the voluntary renouncing of something for a loved person or for something worthy of this renunciation. This is exactly the concept for treating hysteria, the only one of which I know that promises success. At the moment that one succeeds in bringing into the perceptual field of the patient a life task that has enough value for the person to surrender the hysteria and relinquish the performance of the next attack for its sake, when the affliction, in a manner of speaking, is offered as a sacrifice, then at that very moment the patient is cured. *To heal hysterics means to teach them to surrender their affliction.*

Without going into detail, I can confirm from my experience that true miracles happen when the boundary is crossed from the disturbed, affective part of a person lacking love to the untouched (in spite of all deprivation), spiritual part of a meaning-oriented person. One case involves a young mother who was brought before a judge for cruel child abuse. She was granted probation on condition that she undergo therapy with me for four years. In logotherapeutic dialogues she learned to surrender her hysterical outbursts as atonement for her guilt and today she is the most loving mother imaginable [see Case 19 in *Meaning in Suffering*, (Lukas, 2014, pp. 63-75)].[2]

Another example of a psychological problem that we can't handle without knowledge of logotherapy is *hyperreflection*.[3] Physicians, counselors, and priests know a great deal about it, and they are very concerned for those in their care, since hyperreflection makes a well-known mountain out of every molehill and never allows the patient to be peaceful or to be satisfied with anything. However small the worries of the patient may be, by continuously circling thoughts around them, they are blown up into an enormous load whose weight will finally cause a breakdown. Hyperreflection can therefore be defined as valuing as important some unpleasant matter which does not merit it, or alternatively, as a fixation of thoughts on an insignificant negative content which, by this very fixation, gains more and more negative importance.

Again, the question arises: How can therapy help if any worry that was reduced, perhaps with great therapeutic effort, regains massive proportions through the patient's tendency for hyperreflection? Who is going to break this vicious circle? The logotherapist has an instrument available which is applied from the start, aiming at reducing the unfortunate tendency for hyperreflection. This method is called *dereflection*.[4] The objective of this method is to redirect the attention of the individual in carefully measured doses toward some other event that is so positive, important, and meaningful that the person can temporarily let go of the hyperreflected worry, with the result that, due to lack of attention, it starts shrinking and eventually disappears altogether. Similar to hysteria (which, being itself psychological, frequently affects the somatic sphere of being and produces biological symptoms of illness), hyperreflection draws in its wake serious physiological consequences. Who doesn't know the typical stomach or heart trouble, headaches, sleepless nights, etc., caused by worrying and placing too much weight on everyday upsets and provocations? Small disappointments appear suddenly as insurmountable barriers and become a burden to the total organism. But what happens if, from the start, even before the exaggerations of hyperreflection have gained momentum, minimal physical defects were already present, as is the case with many people in our civilized world?

Won't these negligible defects, under the permanent pressure of hyperreflection, be aggravated into full-blown, chronic diseases with gigantic dimensions? In the *Deutsches Aerzteblatt* (September, 1982), it was reported that we live in the age of chronic diseases, something for which medical practitioners are in no way prepared. In 1901, 46% of all deaths registered were the result of chronic illness; in 1955, the percentage was 81%; today, the 90% mark has probably been passed. Furthermore, it was stated, "the concern of patients is more with their condition than with diagnoses, more with their subjective attitude to their disease than with its objective course!"

"The subjective attitude towards an affliction" could be translated as the personal decision of an individual as to whether unceasingly to focus on personal afflictions—that is, hyperreflect—or, in spite of numerous hardships, to turn attention towards fulfilling positive potentials and thereby mustering the strength for a healthy dereflection. In any case, a practitioner of logotherapy is prepared for numerous psychologically or physiologically chronic patients whom traditional medicine claimed for itself. The logotherapist knows effective methods for allaying dangerous hyperreflection and freeing individuals for the authentic and productive opportunities of their lives.

With this, we reach the next blank spot on our psychological map, which had escaped the attention of psychotherapy for a long time until it was mastered by height psychology. It is the drama of *egocentricity*. Only a person continuously thinking of him- or herself can fall victim to hyper-reflection. That person will never find happiness because happiness always goes together with some measure of forgetting oneself, a reaching beyond the self. This may be some accomplished task, a dedication to a loved one, living for something or someone—but not only for oneself.

This concept of *self-transcendence*,[5] which is the spiritual ability of a person to grow beyond a focus on the self, was first formulated by Viktor Frankl long before the concept of self-actualization circulated around the world. Today the self-actualization concept has become more than questionable. This will be borne out by colleagues who are, as I am, involved in counseling another "chronic patient," namely, the family.

Numerous struggles for self-realization end in the divorce courts. Often the frantic emphasis on one's own interests lead to an inability to love. How many family breakdowns must be assigned to a psychologically supported, exaggerated emancipation movement? How many children—and we tremble at the thought—have suffered under the immature egotism of parents who were taught to get rid of their sexual inhibitions but not to be responsible for their actions? Without returning to the logotherapeutic concept of self-transcendence, without knowing about *being for one another*, a family can neither be healed nor saved. Indications are increasing that it is high time for a change in our thinking if we want to pass on the achievements of Western culture to coming generations.

The phrase "coming generations" leads to another step in enumerating unanswered questions for which there is an answer in height psychology. Young people today are hardly inhibited, repressed, and neurotic; they rarely suffer from ego weakness and inferiority feelings. Only a small percentage have had to cope with authoritarian fathers and strict mothers from whose influence they were unable to free themselves for the rest of their lives. Our young carry a very different burden. It has, as it has been stated so expressively, "Nullbock auf Nichts" (which could be translated as "no desire for anything"). I don't know whether this slang is generally known. To have "bock" for something means one is interested in something, likes it, wants it. It is fairly easy to approximate what "Nullbock auf Nichts" means, where the double-negative does not mean cancellation but rather reinforcement. According to this, there is absolutely nothing of interest. Although this may be meant ironically and it may not apply to *all* young persons, it remains a bitter credo on young lips!

How is a psychotherapy, which is oriented to remove symptoms and discover causes, equipped to cope with such *motivation weakness* and total lack of interest? There is nothing traumatic to be traced back into childhood, there are no tangible symptoms and even fewer tangible causes to uncover.

On December 24th, 1984, a 17-year-old student from Munich wrote a letter to her parents saying they should not search for her. She then drove into the woods, poured methyl alcohol over herself and set herself on fire. She died on Christmas day. The laconic police report noted that the girl had no worries in school nor in love. Nothing untoward had happened at home to indicate a motive for the deed; there was talk of a sudden onset of depression without cause.

A "sudden depression without cause" in the life of a 17-year-old? Is psychotherapy equipped to cope with this? Young people who lack the zest for life? This is exactly the point where an uncovering psychology, as in depth psychology, must turn into a discovering psychology, as in height psychology. Psychology has to forsake *un*covering how everything came about and must start *dis*covering what meanings are latent in the life of a person. These are goals which nevertheless make life worthwhile and interesting and are worthy of being lived and experienced. Only a meaning-centered psychotherapy[6] has a chance to overcome this "Nullbock auf Nichts" and only a "discovering psychology" can uncover life structures which are not yet recorded in the book of the past but wait on the empty pages of the future for their realization.

Regarding considerations of "past compared to future," there is a further vast area of psychotherapy and psychiatry which needs to be complemented by height psychology. Hardly any other psychological deviation is as stubborn as abnormally exaggerated *anxieties and compulsions*, which, even when subdued, persistently return and plague their victims into exhaustion and despair. A layperson can scarcely understand how massive are the pathological anxieties that often accompany compulsive delusions. Above a certain intensity, they can render a person's reason and intellect virtually ineffective, even if the disturbance is purely emotional and neither cognitive nor intellectual.

The intensity of the disturbance is also the deciding factor for the type of treatment indicated. In the case of a minor affliction, an interpretation of its genesis might be helpful. In more severe cases, however, the chance for improvement through interpretation is small. Perhaps a parable may help to understand this statement.

Let us suppose that someone is lost in a labyrinth. If orientation was lost only a short time before, it may be sensible to stop and mentally retrace the steps into the labyrinth in order to find the way out. In this case, reconstruction of the past is useful. However, days and nights after having gone astray and after repeatedly and anxiously wandering around in circles, no reconstruction of previous steps will help. There is no chance of finding the crucial turns at this stage. Now is not the time to retrace the path to the entrance. The sensible thing is to employ all available faculties for finding an exit, if necessary even by tearing down the confining walls.

It could therefore be said categorically: The more critical a situation, the less useful is the knowledge of the "reason why" and the more important becomes the strength for a "nevertheless"! Seen from this angle, the development from depth to height psychology can be defined generally as a development from the *why* to the *nevertheless*; it is a progression from the minute reconstruction of psychological failures to the generous effort of the *defiant power of the human spirit* to tear down walls of psychological confusion.

The instrument that provides liberation from the labyrinth of pathological anxieties and compulsions is the logotherapeutic method of
paradoxical intention,[7] which is based on this defiant power[8] and has an
ally no less powerful than humor in anxiety. A person who has learned to
laugh in the face of anxieties every time others want to maliciously attack
will not easily fall prey to them. Each triumph over these weaknesses brings
an inner strengthening. This laughing at one's own symptoms really works,
as unbelievable as it may seem; it works by a trick that is as simple as it is
effective. The object of anxiety itself is consciously wished for in all possible
exaggerations as if that which was previously feared with panic is now the
most beautiful thing that could happen.

Earlier I noted that "doors which are closed to the emotional underground of the psyche will open up to the abilities of the human spirit."
When applying paradoxical intention, the therapist can directly observe the
process of opening doors that were closed for years. As soon as the feared
event or the object of compulsive battle can be sincerely wished for, even for
a fraction of a minute, all fear falls away; desire and fear cannot coexist with
each other and emotional stability is restored to the patient. In reality, the
individual with anxious or compulsive symptoms is not really imprisoned
in a labyrinth, but rather stands against a single wall, pressing his or her
face against it, not knowing the right direction. If, in a paradoxical manner,
such a person could decide to actually desire to be nowhere else but in this
large, magnificent labyrinth with all its romantic nooks and cul-de-sacs,
then he or she could turn around with a smile and suddenly discover that
what lies ahead is open country.

Of course, we have to add that the method of paradoxical intention
is only indicated when we deal with fears that have no basis in reality—
imaginary fears—and thus do not result from a real threat or a true case
of emergency. Psychotherapy refused for a long time to be concerned with
actual emergencies and acts of fate. It never wanted to be a comforter and
left this activity rather to priests who can look back on centuries of accumulated experience in this field. Because of this, the science of psychology
has had, until now, no idea of how to comfort. The most human of human

phenomena, such as justified concern or grief, were regarded merely as psychological disharmony factors which have to be "worked through." Psychology never accepted them as objective facts which belong inevitably to the human condition and have to be coped with psychologically.

If we did not have the logotherapeutic concept of medical ministry[9] which addresses the tragic triad[10] of *suffering, guilt*, and *death*, then we would be empty-handed facing those clients who are driven into our consulting rooms by the violent storms of fate. This would be catastrophic, considering the trend away from religious confessionals to psychotherapeutic centers.

It may be difficult to cure an anxiety or compulsive neurosis. However, they are curable. On the other hand, an unavoidable suffering or an irredeemable guilt or approaching death cannot be cured; they must be endured, and that is terribly difficult. These labyrinths are solidly built; the individual cannot defy these walls. Yet there is a freedom, one solitary freedom, which is ours to the last breath, even in facing these situations. It is the freedom of our noëtic attitude. Our attitude towards fate remains our very own affair.

Logotherapy has taken up this final freedom to make it available to its patients and to make it possible for them to become reconciled with their fate. It is the only discipline to do what no other psychological school has ever dared. An example may briefly illustrate such an *attitude modulation*.[11]

A Swiss couple came to Munich specifically to seek my advice. The wife asked me to help her husband, who had already consulted six Swiss psychiatrists without success. The couple had lost their only son and heir in the previous year through a car accident. Since then, the husband was submerged in total passivity. He let the farm go to ruin, talked to nobody, and sometimes would remark that life wasn't worth it any more and a bullet through the head would be the best solution.

The husband, who had only come to Munich at the insistence of his wife, sat stone-faced and detached at the table with us. I was aware that only one thing could reach him: "Tell me Mr. X, if there were something you could still do for your son would you do it?"

The man looked up, nodded his head and answered: "I would do anything for him."

I continued: "There is something you could do for your son that nobody else could do for him but you. You see, up to now, the death of your son has only caused unhappiness. You are sick from pain, the farm is neglected, your wife is in despair, every good thing your son might have wanted to achieve or accomplish by being alive was stopped short with his death, unless something good could arise even from his death, something which would in retrospect lend meaning to his life and death. But this no longer lies in his hands. Someone else will have to continue his good deeds, his father perhaps? In this way you will avert his having died in vain."

Tears welled up in the father's eyes and he whispered: "How can anything good come from his death?" But this answer he had to find himself. I could only indicate the general direction.

I said: "Suppose you could get your land to flourish again and could open your house to travelers and the needy. To all who enter your home, receive your gifts and, surprised, ask what is the source of your compassion, you can reply: 'It is the memory of my son. He was quite young when he left us, but I would like all to think of him with gladness and gratitude.'"

As I said this, the man put his head in his hands and for the first time in a year he cried bitterly for half an hour. Then he got up and helped his wife into her coat. "Let us go home," he said to her. "We have missed a lot, but now we shall honor the memory of our son."

This man was returned to life.

Logotherapy has taught us that *every* fate, as hard as it may be, can be endured psychologically if it can be embedded in a context of meaning that can be affirmatively accepted. Conversely, not even the most positive conditions of life are tolerable if life itself is perceived as meaningless. In this respect, we have undergone years of training during the times of prosperity and the years ahead will teach us just as much in the coming recession. I believe nobody has to be told that the curve of economic development in the last two decades reached a high plateau and is already on the decline. It is interesting that the curve denoting the population's psychohygienic health is not congruent with that of its economic development. Rather, there is a displacement in terms of time, more or less according to the figure below.

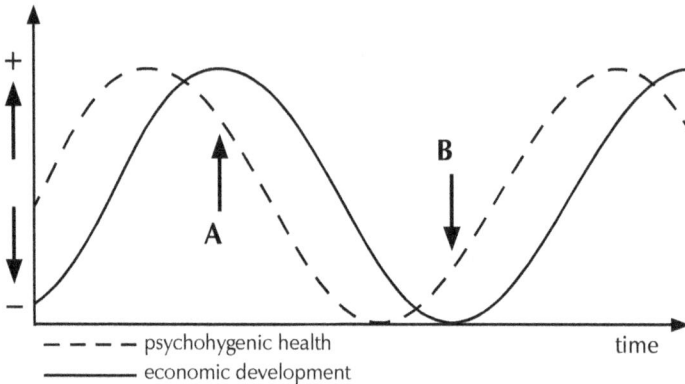

A indicates that when prosperity is at its highest the deterioration
    of psychological forces has already started.
B indicates that before the lowest level of economic development is
    reached the psychological energy has started recovering.

The curves show us that the psychohygienic health of a population is at its best when the economy is experiencing an upward trend. The people have an aim to which they aspire, and when everybody invests energy in progress, it advances forcefully. It is remarkable that psychological strength starts to increase even before the economy has reached its lowest level. Hardships certainly have a function in providing meaning for motivating readiness for greater efforts that, in turn, bear fruit.

The picture is different when economic development reaches its peak and enters the stage of prosperity. Suddenly psychohygienic health declines again because prosperity softens people and all too easily obscures the vision of further goals worthy of attainment. What is there to aim for if one has everything? Because possessions don't bring happiness in themselves, indifference and boredom arise. Money is there, free time is abundant, but what for? An *existential frustration*, as logotherapists call it, a feeling of meaninglessness, takes hold of a large section of the population and promotes typical excesses of prosperity, such as increasing criminal activity, sexual perversion, high suicide rates, and increasing drug consumption. Because we have witnessed all these aspects at close quarters and in some cases are still experiencing them, we don't have to go into detail.

When prosperity is beginning to wane, the psychohygienic health of the population is usually slightly damaged and there is a fear of economic decline. Economic superabundance can't be maintained, but the people have been spoiled by abundance and have never learned moderation. They are dependent on material possessions and suffer, with the decline of economic vigor, withdrawal symptoms similar to those endured by individuals diagnosed with addictive disorders. Instead of now concentrating on spiritual values, they are tempted into resignation and depression, and the feeling of meaninglessness is increased by the feeling of hopelessness. In this soil grow uncontrollable fear of the future and rash actions, which are inconceivable from the perspective of later generations. However, we know from history that most highly developed cultures declined and fell into ruin relatively soon after passing their highest economic level—that is, with the decline of their prosperity. This coincided with their psychohygienic descent, although they were far from actual misery.

Of course, these graphs do not represent an inevitable fate. Nevertheless, one can learn something from them, namely, that the psychological stability of entire nations is interconnected with their experience of meaning, and as long as this experience swings up and down with the economy, their psychological health is connected with it as well. According to this estimation, the Western world is bound to decline in the near future.

There is one important dissenting voice, that of logotherapy, which maintains that this does not have to happen. Experiencing meaning does not have to be determined by any prevailing economic situation. Quite the opposite. Meaning can be found in any situation, whatever it may be.

During the past period of prosperity, logotherapists incessantly fought the gradual, incipient weakening of spiritual and psychological strength by showing, with many examples and illustrations, that life contains rich potentials for meaning, especially when material affluence is available. One does not have to give in to existential frustration. One can put the positive realities in times of prosperity to meaningful use for creating positive works such as charitable works or works of art or scientific research which would not have been possible under different circumstances.

The same applies to the present time of emerging recession. Even arid stretches of unemployment, early retirement, bankrupt businesses, and increasing poverty contain positive potentials by teaching responsibility for oneself and by strengthening family ties. They point out the limitations of technology and re-establish humanness as a person's greatest treasure.

We may be helpless as far as economic recession is concerned, but we can actively fight against a recession in our spiritual and psychological condition. We can fight with the support of height psychology,[12] which made it our task to open our eyes to the meaning potential of every moment of every single day. Why do we have a *will to meaning*,[13] if not for applying it against the feeling of meaninglessness in an affluent society? Why do we have the defiant power of the human spirit, if not for fighting the feeling of hopelessness in an economic crisis? For what reason has psychology, after half a century of struggle, broken through from the "why" to the "nevertheless" if not to liberate human well-being from its dependence on emotional, economic, and social conditions and to place it exclusively under the guidance of the human spirit, the only element capable of perceiving and fulfilling the meaning of life?

These would be a number of problem areas in condensed form which we would face helplessly except for the knowledge and various techniques of height psychology; these are problems in which spiritual attitude has the final decisive influence. Hysteria, hyperreflection, and egocentricity are basically wrong and overemphasized attitudes towards the self. Lack of motivation in youth, depressive resignation, boredom, and weariness are mistaken attitudes towards the demand character of life, just as affluence crises, withdrawal symptoms, anxiety, and despair are fallacious attitudes toward inescapable factors of fate. Logotherapy has potential solutions for these problems that no other psychological system has had. It has found the entrance to the innermost center of all spiritual attitudes—the *conscience*.

This entrance leads into an area between two competencies, namely, psychology and ministry. This may be just the complement that was missing until now for the rehumanizing of psychology: not a new modern trend in psychology, but rather a meaning-centered psychological *ministry* based on a philosophical foundation.

3. The Healing Concept in Logotherapy*

There is a legend that goes like this: A modern man became lost in the desert. For days he dragged himself, without direction, across the sand dunes. Soon the merciless sun had him completely dehydrated. Just then he saw an oasis at some distance. "Aha," he said to himself, "this is a mirage which is making a fool of me."

He drew nearer to the oasis but it did not vanish. In front of his burning eyes appeared date palms, shimmering green grass, and, to crown it all, a murmuring spring. "Nothing but hunger fantasies and acoustic hallucinations," the exhausted wanderer sighed. "How cruel nature is!"

Shortly afterwards two Bedouins found him dead. "Can you understand that?" asked one of them. "The dates were almost growing into his mouth and next to him the spring is murmuring, and he dies of hunger and thirst! How is it possible?" "Easily," explained the other. "He was a modern man."

Of what does this legend remind us? Something genuine is held to be a fake with such conviction that it is not even tested for its genuineness. This reminds us of the science of psychology that, under certain circumstances, trusts its own hypotheses more than the obvious human phenomena confronting it. Thus it can happen that, when a grateful mother talks in a counseling session about the tremendous help her eldest daughter was in bringing up her younger twin siblings, the psychologist immediately accuses the girl of a serious mother complex caused by an excessive-demand syndrome.

---

* This chapter was presented by the author in the summer of 1984 as a lecture at a professional congress in Rome. Consequently, she was received in a private audience by Pope John Paul II, who gave recognition to her work.

This is what the legend talks about. Helpfulness and gratitude are far too simple an explanation of the situation in psychological terms. No! Mother-complex and excessive-demand syndromes sound much more acceptable. But as we heard, the legend has a tragic end, and that is exactly what happens in everyday psychological reality. A young person, persuaded that she has psychological complexes, stops being helpful and a mother, accused of excessive demanding, stops being grateful. It is easy to devalue something genuine, but this does not lend any value to fakes either. With this, we reach a cue that leads us into the center of the logotherapeutic healing approach: the concept of values. Logotherapy is a psychology that reinstates values, grants the existence of genuineness, and restores belief in a meaningful potential for being human, *a potential that is always available.*

When modern psychology began with Freud, one could describe it thus: For him, every oasis was a mirage. He wrote:

> The moment one asks for meaning and value in life, one is sick, for both are objectively nonexistent. After my death you will kindly let me go on living in your memory—the only kind of immortality I recognize. Heaven we leave to the angels and sparrows.

Freud has indeed remained in our memories as the founder of psychoanalysis, to whom we owe thanks; as F. W. Foerster described it, that to counterbalance its one-sided approach and exaggerations a psychologist like Viktor Frankl had to speak up.

In terms of the previous story, one could say that, for Frankl, an oasis would be thinkable even where eyes don't see it anymore. He writes:

> We can't see heaven even with the strongest searchlight. If we see something, perhaps a cloud, then this only proves that what we see is not heaven. And yet precisely those visible clouds are the symbol of an invisible heaven.[14]

While Freud was thus busy unmasking subjective fabrications and in the process devalued a number of genuine values, Frankl sought to find the authentic, the "specifically human" quality in the person and to orient it towards objective values. Indeed, for Frankl, human existence begins only when it is oriented towards a *logos* that is an independent entity which does not have its source in this same existence.

Now, I would like to select three therapy approaches from the multitude of concepts in logotherapy. They deal with values and can be adapted to practical psychotherapy without difficulty. The first approach could be called "the pointing out of values as such"; the second, "the increasing feelings of life worth"; and the third, "the handling of value conflicts and value losses." This discussion will demonstrate that, alongside these three therapeutic principles, one could place three collective concepts which circumscribe the envisaged goal like a headline. They are *reason*, *trust*, and *reconciliation*. Where therapy succeeds in anchoring the leitmotif of a patient's life on these three foundation pillars, it is successful.

Let us turn to the healing approach mentioned first—*the pointing out of values as such*. Logotherapy begins with the premise that living (as well as nonliving) existence has its own value. Plants, animals, and people, as well as objects, have their intrinsic value and not only some utilitarian value from the human perspective. Beyond that, there are abstract values which serve to maintain and promote being, such as positive thoughts, meaningful actions, and intellectual achievements, which are simply identified as "good." This goodness, as little as it can be made concrete, has its intrinsic worth and is good not only from a certain perspective. Without becoming a slave to absolutism, we must renounce any type of relativism which denies objective values and comment that they represent subjective concepts of a society prestamped by its own traditions.

Dealing with psychologically disturbed, unstable, misguided, or desperate persons, it is striking that one common factor affects all of them, whatever their individual problems, and that is a fixation on self or a subjugation to their own dispositions. Nearly all people who can't cope with their own lives place their own misery in the center of attention and continuously complain about it, fear it, avenge it, fight it, or bury themselves under it. In short, they themselves are virtually the center and extent of their own lives.

They hardly recognize values that exist *independently* of the life situation around them, and this makes their lives empty and devoid of values. The poorer and emptier their lives appear, the less happy they feel, and naturally their thoughts are more absorbed with their misery. In order to disrupt this cycle of interaction, it is not enough simply to introduce strategies for alleviating negative dispositions or for solving present problems. As an outsider, one may be able to get rid of one or more misfortunes, but one cannot introduce values if the individual concerned does not develop the ability to perceive them, values which were in any event existent all along, both internally and externally.

When, for instance, a depressed person walks through scenery in full bloom, it is highly probable that there will be no awareness of the beauty of the scenery because of the total enmeshment in sadness. It may be possible to reduce this sadness with appropriate medication, but this does not imply that the beauty of the scenery has touched the heart of that person.

Or another example: A youngster suffering from unrequited love may take out that disappointment on family members and remain blind to all the forbearance and patience on the part of the family. It may be possible to offer instruction to get rid of the excessive aggression, such as in some kind of competitive sport rather than on the family. But it does not necessarily follow that the person has a conscious awareness of the sanctuary offered by the family.

To some extent, maladaptive behavior can be corrected by means of therapy. However, as long as the person concerned remains fixated on the self and fails to recognize the intrinsic values that life offers, then the chain of inappropriate reactions will not end. The reason for this is that such an individual remains a *reacting agent* throughout, one who reacts to whatever happens, be it sadness, disappointment, etc. He or she will never mature towards becoming an active agent for independent and responsible behavior or establish an act of *spiritual intentionality*, as Frankl defined it: an *action* that takes place for the sake of realizing an objective value.

Only from the moment when the world can be perceived as largely independent of the prevailing condition of the observer can it be decoded in terms of those elements of meaning in it that await fulfillment, those which give meaning to a human life and, with it, enable the observer to answer the questions posed by life.

A person with symptoms of depression who, in spite of the symptoms, is able to recognize the harmony and loveliness of nature must be able to admit mercy along with the melancholia. And perhaps the melancholia can even be embedded in mercy. This would strengthen tolerance of life more than a one-sided use of medicine as therapy, which artificially vitalizes but ultimately weakens the individual.

Similarly, healing may be given to a young person who is disappointed in a relationship, if the eyes can be pointed beyond the personal turmoil, to the devotion and dedication of those who are always there in support. Not that one love can replace another, but it can offer consolation, and its comfort helps to ease the disappointment.

Thus, in logotherapy, an elementary approach to therapy is to strengthen the individual's ability to recognize values by bringing up and pointing out objective values. This procedure simultaneously facilitates the search for meaning that, according to logotherapy, is just as elementary for the person, and especially for the one burdened by problems or existential frustration. Individuals frequently have to answer the question of why they exist on earth at all. Existentialist philosophers have, with the slogan "existence before essence," pointed out that human beings must regard themselves as thrown into life: experiencing *being* before *knowing about individuality*. It will be each person's task to find this individuality.

If one translates these philosophical considerations into psychotherapeutic practice, one could define a psychologically afflicted person as one who has not yet found a true individuality. This individual is still stuck in a "bare existence" and still battles to find meaning in this existence. No therapist, counselor, or minister can tell a counselee the meaning of existence. Only by means of many examples can the healer demonstrate that every human existence has meaning in itself. It is a meaning that lets itself be found by the seeker as soon as the fixation on the self is overcome, through a spiritual opening up towards the world and its challenges.

One of the diseases of our time of epidemic proportions, and which has no chances of a cure if this opening towards the world does not take place, is *addiction*. It is generally defined as a "dependency" but basically it is not so much a dependency on some substance but rather a dependency of the individual on one's own disposition. In addition to this there is a gradual loss of all intrinsic values. The entire environment is reduced to two categories, namely, whatever serves the addicted person's needs and whatever opposes them. The drug itself becomes the regulator of prevailing moods; it shapes the yoke under which such an individual bends. It lifts the mood but increasingly prohibits the enduring of any bad mood. It conjures up imaginary values either in an intoxicated stupor or in drug-induced hallucinations, but it actually leaves the person who is addicted destitute of values. This is unbearable, which in turn keeps such an individual under its control. If, in addition to all the necessary measures such as physical and social rehabilitation and supportive family talks, the particular healing approach of logotherapy is not offered, then the success of therapy remains at risk. The logotherapist mobilizes a high degree of independence from prevailing subjective dispositions by pointing out objective values as well as by helping the person to find a spiritual refocusing—on true values in life.

For example, I remember a teenager who was in therapy for anorexia nervosa, which is an addiction in reverse, so to speak. We hardly mentioned the subject of eating. We used well over 20 hours of therapy together to investigate positive aspects of her personal life experiences. She loved to move gracefully and possessed a natural charm which had never been taught. Dance for her meant only clubbing. I took up the theme and theoretically explored with her what dancing could be, a rhythmic work of art, a medium of expressing oneself, a tool for delighting others, a striving for perfection.

She became inspired by these ideas and started taking up physical training. That was a real effort because she was underweight but at the same time it made her tired and hungry and helped to abate her antagonism towards eating. Coincidentally, it brought her into contact with a group of decent young people who had a far more salutary influence on her than the former nightclub companions.

Today she is a brilliant skier and a daring ice skater and, though she remains slender, there is no longer any thought of anorexia. A number of doctors had treated this girl for years. They all sought and found conflicts in her family that they saw as the cause of her condition. Perhaps they were correct. However, the pointing out of conflicts did not yield one-tenth of what was finally achieved by focusing on a single value.

Only recently have specialists in Germany discussed the alarming increase of a diagnosis that represents a combination of anorexia and bulimia: *bulimarexia*. Patients—usually women—eat huge quantities, then go to the toilet and induce vomiting, thereby throwing up everything they have eaten. This is repeated four to five times a day and causes deficiencies, stomach trouble, arrhythmia, and a variety of other organic afflictions.

Traditional discussions of this illness include attempts at interpretation, again tending in the direction that deep, internal conflicts probably prevent those suffering from these symptoms from allowing themselves to have good experiences and instead incite them to abnormal punishment. Excessive feelings of guilt, abandonment, self-hate, and so on are offered as explanatory factors. Nobody raises the question of whether such feelings must be obeyed automatically and as a matter of course. Nobody is surprised at the fact that the human being, who is after all an intelligent being, could become such a slave to feelings, utterly devoid of any willpower!

As long as the question remains—"What *emotional* potential causes this or that maladaptive behavior?"—we have not yet penetrated to the most important question in psychotherapy: "How is it possible that the spiritual potential of a person obeys, or is even subjugated to, some emotional deviation?"

In the example of bulimarexia, this means that it is far less interesting to research which negative state of self can reduce a person to such uncontrolled and unnatural eating habits, than to find out what type of spiritual immaturity or blockage modifies the vulnerability of the person concerned—a person whose intellect obviously does not prevent an "act against reason." In any case, the logotherapist does not focus on why the pathological component in a person is so strong, but rather on why the healthy, reasonable, and prudent component is not strong enough. Instead of a conflict theory which explains the pathology, the answer is found in a motivation theory of a will to meaning with which each person is endowed. It is this will to meaning that is the vehicle of a healing process, as long as an "intrinsic value" can be found, one that is worthy of the dedication of the person in a spiritual intentionality.

It appears to be the fate of our species to swing continuously between two extremes without finding a healthy balance. This also applies to the current psychological approaches that—in contrast to an earlier cycle of rationalizations and intellectualizations—predominately focus on the emotions. Undoubtedly, the affective component with its focus on feelings and moods is of great importance, but that is not the complete picture. It is time that we give more attention to the spiritual dimension and employ it for overcoming psychological problems; otherwise, our therapeutic efforts may ultimately result in a dead end. Only by an enormous effort of human reason that considers the prevailing ethical, ecological, and cultural values will it also be possible to consider universal problems of humanity; for example, third-world problems and the population explosion that cannot be solved by a reanalysis of the structure of emotions at all.

The logotherapist appeals to the inner wisdom of each person and is convinced that this spiritual power can be applied with an awareness of meaning, so that it is worthwhile to become healthy in order to fulfill this meaning. Sometimes I ask my patients—after they have described their manifold sufferings—what they would do with their lives if they didn't have any problems. Very few can answer spontaneously, and this is at the same time the central point of their suffering. *They have no reason for becoming healthy!* But this is also the very starting point of logotherapy. In addition to any elimination of suffering, we endeavor to illuminate such a reason by pointing to some intrinsic value. The decision of whether to become involved—and, if so, to what extent—belongs solely to the patient. Each must become aware that there are tasks in the world which await—and can only be accomplished by—that individual. Such tasks need the person's vigorous and total dedication. Individuals must recognize the value of these tasks and then go on to structure their lives according to the guidance of their consciences.

As logotherapists, we do not draw a world on a canvas as we imagine it to be. We want individuals to see the world as it is[15] with open eyes and then to paint their own picture with the most beautiful colors they can find. We only pull the veil from their eyes and thereby help them to lose their pernicious fixation on the self.

This cartoon symbolizes the "value-blindness" that afflicts a number of patients today; it also shows that the task of the logotherapist is to restore vision.

"I paint exactly what I see."

Let us look at the second therapeutic approach of logotherapy, which I described as the *increased sense of life worth*. The very concept of a "sense of life worth" proves that the logotherapist in no way neglects the emotional component of a human being, even if the emotions are not assigned the same superordinate importance as in depth psychology. The idea points to something else as well: the expansion of the concept of the feeling of self-worth. As such, it is an analogy for the general extending and complementing function of logotherapy in psychotherapy.

All psychotherapy aims at improving and balancing the feelings of self-worth in psychologically afflicted patients. There is no argument against that; self-respect and self-assurance are indeed important stabilizers of psychological and biological well-being. And obviously a value as such dwells in the self and must be perceived spiritually because it supports a person's self-confidence.

However, again one could say this is by no means the whole picture of the human being. Self-confidence by itself does not constitute humanness. A high level of self-worth is no guarantee of a good life. Feelings of self-worth reflect only the number and intensity of those works which let individuals regard themselves as successful but they make no statement as to whether these works are *meaningful*. A statement of that kind is primarily anchored in feelings of life worth—that means in feelings which precede every human expression—that life is worth living, that it is simply "meaningful."

Since feelings of life worth are very closely interlinked with the basic motivation of a person, a brief comparison of one action from two different motives may perhaps contribute to explaining the differences between a sense of life worth and feelings of self-worth. Let us suppose a boy meets an old woman carrying a heavy basket of invitingly fresh apples; on seeing them, he feels a great desire to eat one of them. Then he deliberates that surely the woman would give him a few apples if he were prepared to carry the basket home for her. This is exactly what happens. He carries her burden and she shows her appreciation.

So far everything is fine. Even if the motive of the boy was not quite unselfish, he still did a good deed and that is considerably better than not helping the old woman at all. He benefits, besides the few apples, from an increased feeling of self-worth; he was clever and his calculations worked out.

In contrast, let us think of another boy who also sees the old woman laden with the heavy basket. However, he doesn't see the apples but the woman. He sees how she is bent down, how she drags herself, how she labors. The boy becomes aware of a potential meaning of the moment, which consists in offering his dormant youthful strength where it is needed. He also offers to carry the basket home, does so, and gets a few apples as a gift. What will be the benefit for the second boy? He was in touch with "value as such," with the good and the meaningful, which were contained in his willingness to help without regard to how it would benefit him. As a result, his sense of self-worth and—even more—his feeling of life worth will increase through knowing about the meaning of his existence. While the one will applaud himself with "I have done that well!" the other will receive gratification from the thought "It is good that I was there!"

From this example, we can learn that a positive feeling of self-worth is the by-product of successful action and a positive feeling of life worth is a by-product of experiencing meaning. Naturally, in logotherapy we are happy if we can encourage an individual to successful actions. However, we see a certain danger in making this the aim of therapy. For example, what happens when our patients are not successful any longer and their feeling of self-worth suddenly declines? Will they not then begin to regress? We regard it as much safer to introduce them to meaning experiences that increase their feeling of life worth; meaning can be found at all times and places, even in failure.

To understand this idea better, let us return to the example of the boys carrying the apples and wonder what the consequences would be if the old woman should neither show gratitude nor give any fruit after she had been helped? Wouldn't the boy in the first example be extremely annoyed because his trouble was "all for nothing"; wouldn't his self-assurance be affected? The second boy has, however, a chance to find meaning even in this unsatisfactory situation, because nobody can take away the fact that he helped a struggling woman. No matter whether he was thanked or not, his act "is its own monument."[16] He can even improve the quality of his deed by following it up with forgiving her ingratitude. What he did was never in vain; therefore, his feeling of life worth is minimally affected by the woman's reaction.

One interference that totally obstructs the intellectual and personal development of a person and must be taken seriously, considering the above discussion, is *depravity*. Not infrequently it goes together with psychopathy, criminality, prostitution, and a debased lifestyle. In this case there is usually an amazing discrepancy between feelings of self-worth and feelings of life worth. While the self-worth can be strongly pronounced, sometimes even inordinately high, the latter sinks down to zero. This discrepancy finds its expression in an aggressive egotism following the slogan "What I need, I take!" together with a fatalistic nihilism: "Nobody needs me anyway!"

From the combination of both attitudes arises a careless and negligent handling of values; they are not identified as values, whether they are objects, people, or even oneself. High risks are taken that have no relation to the hope for short-term gains. Blood is shed over a ridiculous argument. Embezzlement and burglary bring transient riches. Body and soul are traded for an indiscriminate love relationship. Under this aspect of depravity, life isn't a value to be cared for, kept, protected, pondered, and shaped. There is nothing precious for which one is responsible, rather luck's dice are thrown either to gain or lose everything. The keenness for risks is no less an expression of self-assurance than indifference a lack of value awareness.

Until now, as is well known, all psychological schools, when confronted with the problem of depravity, have capitulated. Unfortunately, the slogan "therapy in place of punishment," which can be heard repeatedly in criminal psychology, has no solid, realistic foundation and has remained rather ineffective. I am convinced that this is related to the fact that traditional psychotherapy is oriented towards strengthening and stabilizing the feeling of self-worth in the patient. This may be appropriate with individuals who have neuroses or depression, but it is definitely not the problem of individuals with depravity or other psychopathy. With the latter, a treatment is indicated that raises the feeling of life worth instead. Logotherapy points out the direction that work with these clients would have to take.

As mentioned, both feelings are actually by-products. This implies that they cannot be directly intended; they need a detour and the detour by which feelings of life worth can be enforced is *finding meaning*. Depraved persons, however, are largely value blind so that indicating values by word or example has little transference effect on them, and furthermore their self-assured ego is so dominant that they are not even prepared to let advice or suggestions affect them. There remains only one alternative; they must be involved in meaningful projects, with the hope that gradually, perhaps even as an afterthought, the spark of finding meaning might yet catch alight.

This implies that, for example, youngsters who disfigure and vandalize public buildings should be employed in all kinds of work for beautification or, as is at the moment being discussed in Austria, drivers caught for drunken driving should serve at a hospital emergency department for several weeks. This also means that the pedagogic accent in institutions and schools of correction should not be confined to coping with everyday events such as the management of necessities. Courage should rather be mustered for challenging the inmates by confronting them untiringly with meaningful tasks within their scope, tasks that will foster inner growth.

Naturally, there will be conflicts in such confrontations, especially as it cannot be presupposed that the clients will volunteer. Yet everything related to coercion, even if it is therapeutic in nature, leaves a bitter aftertaste. From my experience as psychological supervisor of a number of institutions for children and youths, I can confirm that both the *must* and the *task* success-fully help to counter depravity. The "must" deflates the exaggerated feeling of self-worth and, with it, the aggressive egotism which seduces one into living according to one's mood, and the "task" lifts the low sense of life worth and thereby overcomes the fatal nihilism that prevents one from doing something meaningful.

Ask adults who spent part of their youth in educational institutions due to behavior problems for their best memory of that time and you will consistently hear reports about some community activity that was under-taken, such as a long-rehearsed carol sing in an old-age home or a carefully prepared climb of some mountain during a holiday. What is interesting is that, almost without exception, they describe how much the required preparation and effort was at first perceived negatively and had to be enforced by the group, but that, during the performance itself or sometimes even later, their hearts opened with enthusiasm for the event. This shows that involvement in meaningful objectives, even in the face of opposition by a child or adult with faulty development, may be more dignifying than the tolerance practiced of a laissez-faire attitude towards neglected children that is complemented by the intolerance of social contempt towards fallen or imprisoned adults.

We were introduced to feelings of life worth as a corrective to that fatal nihilism which claims that nothing has meaning anyway. In a positive sense, one could call it a level of "primal trust," that kind of trust in life which cannot arise from the self alone. Certainly a great self-confidence will induce trust in one's capacity for performance. However, if that capacity were to decrease, the self-confidence would also ebb away unless another factor comes into play that grants unconditional trust in advance. And this is the knowledge or belief that life is precious until the last breath.

I said "knowledge or belief" on purpose, for though the dividing line between them is normally clearly outlined, in the case of trust they overlap considerably. One could define it as "knowledge of the heart" as well as "belief of the intellect." It is a case of prereflexive trust that everything is somehow good as it is, that somehow it is all right, even if one can't understand why. For a religious person it is simply trust in God,[17] in a supermeaning beyond everything worldly.

This trust, which is supported by a person's feeling of life worth, is fundamentally different from any kind of fatalism which declares every event as inescapably predetermined; the result is that its followers put their hands in their laps and remain paralyzed in passive life expectation. In contrast to fatalism, trust remains quite active; it is not a discouragement but its opposite, an encouragement for action because those who act are on a foundation that cannot fail. They can make a mistake, can even fall, but life will keep its value. They can recompensate, they can get up again, and even if they could not make restitution or arise again, there remains the chance of inner change that can retrospectively fill whatever happened with meaning.

In the discussion of the first therapy approach of logotherapy I pointed out that many of our patients today have no *reason* for becoming healthy and this blocks their recovery. I would like to add that many of them do not have the *strength* to recover. They will only find a reason if they let themselves be guided by their inner wisdom which finds its ultimate expression in the will to meaning. And this strength they only find in an unshakable trust in life which rests in the knowledge of, and belief in, its worth. Thus the two main aims of therapy in logotherapy are to help the psychologically afflicted person find a reason and the strength to recover. Here it must be conceded that both can, in fact, only be discovered, but not be given, by therapy. The perfect cannot be created by human hands; whatever has been humanly made is not really perfect. This also applies to all psychotherapy.

Let us turn to the third therapeutic approach mentioned earlier, which is derived from the two former ones as a logical consequence. It should be noted regarding this trilateral approach that the anthropological foundation of logotherapy has such a multitude of methodological indications that, in its practical application, every individual case finds specific consideration. Since we are deliberating as well about the reconsideration of values in logotherapy, we have to face the fact that values can conflict and that values can get lost. Either demands reconciliation: reconciliation with a reality in which some things cannot be realized simultaneously and where nothing is available without limitations. Therefore we expect in our clients, besides inner wisdom, renunciation; besides trust in the future, reconciliation with the past; and besides the capacity for living, that for suffering.* If we can't summon these, we can't discharge the patient from treatment with reassurance, for there remains cause for concern. I would even go so far as to claim that a disposition towards reconciliation with self and with one's life is a fairly safe criterion for a positive prognosis in a patient with psychological problems. Conversely, there is no doubt that a lack of reconciliation keeps

---

* Frankl regarded the "capacity for suffering," (in addition to the "capacities for work and for enjoyment" that were postulated by Freud), as a further and no less important aim of therapy.

pathology alive. There is probably a considerable extent of psychological distress that has no other cause than this.

Let us begin our considerations with the therapeutic *handling of a value conflict.*[18] This does not refer to a conflict between a value and a personal weakness that prevents the attainment of this value; such a conflict could be solved by indicating the value that, as soon as the noëtic attention is totally focused on the conflict, will enable the overcoming of the personal weakness. Rather, value conflict denotes the actual conflict between two (or more) values which cannot be attended to simultaneously. It could be a conflict between occupation and family, between artistic inclination and work obligation, or between a given promise and a changed situation.

Logotherapy begins with the premise that what our personal conscience tells us is *unambiguous.* Frankl distinguishes very meticulously between what is called *superego* in psychology, which more or less represents the accumulated sum total of all traditional moral values and norms that have been instilled in us since childhood, and that other, innermost, voice in us which is inborn. This voice can be drowned out, ignored, or ridiculed, but it cannot be corrupted because it shows infallibly the most meaningful and responsible action that should be done at a given moment. "Conscience is the only mirror that neither deceives nor compliments" was succinctly stated by Christine of Sweden. Perhaps it might be too much to call conscience "the voice of truth," for every person can be mistaken. However, if anything human comes near to truth, then it is this "meaning organ" (as Frankl called it) in us which can evaluate even values by assigning rank order to them according to their significance in an actual situation. Very similar deliberations prompted Carl Friedrich von Weizsäcker to express the following thoughts:

> In place of instinctual direction, which dominates the
> animal—even social animals—man has social behavior norms.
> This gives to this freedom from instinct its first and, for
> average human behavior, dominant capacity. Freedom is, in
> its first approximation, the freedom to follow the norms of
> society.
> But how did customs originate? One can't believe that, at least

in highly-developed cultures, the blind process of trial and error was sufficient. Such a rich and harmonious structure needed insight, the insight of those ancestors, lawgivers, and wise men of antiquity who were later celebrated either historically or mythically. Whatever originated from insight can only be maintained with insight. Only insight into the meaning of customs maintains the elasticity of conformity and protects against falling into absurd idleness. In this way every society lives in a tension between blind adherence to moral precepts which determine some lives almost entirely and every life to a large extent and a free and reasonable attitude which is prepared to adapt spontaneously. This relation between automatism and freedom is repeated on a new level. As norm-adapted behavior indicates freedom from drives, so does reasonable behavior, freedom from norms. A reasonable, free person can say no even to conventions.

In so far as "reasonable" indicates insight into the meaning of an action and measures against objective criteria, one could condense the maxim for human action into one sentence:

> Live meaningfully
> and do what you like—
> your actions
> will be decent
> and morally justified!

Logotherapy, in dealing with value conflicts, therefore, does not strive to make the client's decision easy or to decide for the client, but rather to lead the individual to listen to the reasonable voice of the conscience and, as a consequence, to become aware of personal responsibility. In counseling conversations, the situation frequently arises that a counselee asks directly what choice should be made in a specific conflict situation, which does not imply that there would be implicit complicity with the answer. However, we logotherapists believe that we owe an answer to a question put to us. Therefore, we don't hide behind some obscure therapist mannerism.

One way of giving an answer without taking away responsibility is the logotherapeutic technique of the "common denominator," which is described in Frankl's books and which I would like to demonstrate in the following example. The conflict concerns the question of a married woman as to whether she should separate from her husband or give up her lover. As commonplace as this question may sound, and even if it has been the theme of thousands of novels and films, we must today attend to it more than ever because it is located at the cutting edge between marriage and divorce in a proportion of 1:1, which approximately corresponds to the actual proportions in Western industrial countries—for every functioning marriage there is at least one shaky or divorced one.

There were two remarkable things in the counseling talk that I had with the woman. First, it was an anonymous telephone counseling session because the client refused to come in person to our clinic, and secondly, just prior to phoning me she had contacted some telephone ministry, but that talk had apparently faltered. From her remarks, I understood that the telephone minister had applied a client-centered approach in which he had reflected the contents of her talk, reformulated with the hope that, by clarifying her statements, she would find her own autonomous solution. The clarification had taken place at the moment that the client-centered counseling came to an end. It had, as it were, become clear that on the one hand the woman valued the protection of her husband, his faithfulness to her, and the financial security he offered her.

Therefore she felt an attraction of "reason" while, in turn, she enjoyed the affection and erotic radiance of her lover and was fascinated by his adventurous, easygoing way of life. The attraction to her lover was emotional. The husband pushed for a decision and was unwilling to tolerate the triangle any longer but was willing to make a new start with his wife. The lover on his part had another lover as well but was quite prepared to keep the triangle (or quadrangle) going and refused to commit himself to any fixed future plans with the woman even should she obtain a divorce.

Here reason, there emotion; here solid relationship, there attractive noncommitment; in the middle, a person torn in two directions. What now? I suggested a special type of stock-taking to the woman, I said: "If I understand you correctly you have only two choices—or is there a third choice for you?" She answered, "No." She could either return to her husband altogether or separate from him and stay with her lover. The third option, a combination of both, would be like the present arrangement but could no longer be continued. "Thus," I answered "you are facing a momentous decision. Please tell me, how many people are affected by your decision?" The woman thought for a while and then she specified her husband, herself, her lover, and his lover. "Therefore," I summarized, "the fate of four people will change, depending on your decision. Let us write down how the change will affect each of the four. The one expected to be happy gets a plus, the one expected to be unhappy, a minus." The woman brought pen and paper to the phone.

First, we considered the decision pro-husband and then pro-lover. Each decision got four sections, one for each of those affected. In the column "pro-husband," the husband received a plus because he still loved his wife, the lover a plus and a minus because of his apparent indifference towards any decision. His own lover received a plus, for she would naturally be happy if the woman returned to her husband; the woman herself both a plus and a minus reflecting her indecision. Result: 4 plus and 2 minus.

The same calculation was done in the column "pro-lover." The husband got a minus as he would be sad to lose his wife, the lover again got both a plus and a minus due to his indifference, a minus was noted for his own lover because in this case she would fear for her own relationship. The

What does the decision of the woman mean:	Pro-husband	Pro-lover	Explanation
for her husband?	+	-	He still loves her.
for her lover?	+/-	+/-	He likes her compa but does not want be tied down.
for his lover?	+	-	She is anxious abou her relationship to the lover.
for herself?	+/-	+/-	She is ambivalent towards both men.
Sum	4+/2-	2+/4-	

counselee gave herself a plus as well as a minus indicating her ambivalence. Result: 2 plus and 4 minus.

Now only one thing was left to be done. I said to the client: "With your call, you wanted help in deciding and we balanced both your choices together. The last question, however, is still open and you must answer that yourself: How much happiness or misery do you want to cause from your actions?"

The woman was quiet for some time, then she replied softly: "I understand. You have shown me something that I had almost forgotten—responsibility. I don't know whether I am ready for it, but I will come to terms with it. I thank you. You have really helped me a lot."

Certainly such a "height"calculation is not always possible, but in principle in any value conflict, one of the alternative values must have the higher ethical value if we accept that the conscience is unequivocal. Logotherapy as a medical therapeutic system does not see itself as a moralizing agent which assesses good or bad. It sees its task only in pointing out this "height meter" for the patients who carry it as an organ within, which is able to detect the most meaningful choice, the *one* that is *necessary* here and now.

The parable of the "height meter" can also be used in another context involving something similar to a "height measure." This is the case with an *irretrievable loss of value*. There are blows of fate which leave no room for decision, which take any kind of action out of one's hand by inflicting inescapable suffering. Incurable diseases belong to this group, as well as amputations, loss of loved ones, and even desperate situations of all kinds such as poverty, misery, hunger, pain, none of which have any hope for a speedy recovery. Here, when the priority of helping and improving has reached its limits, the superiority of heroic suffering with dignity begins.[19] Where external circumstances weigh people down and force them onto their knees, they can still rise internally to their full height. In logotherapy, we speak in this context of *attitudinal values*. That means we can see from the manner in which a person assumes a spiritual attitude towards the inescapable facts of life and discovers yet a last opportunity to realize value, one which perhaps compensates on a higher level for the original loss of value.

Before, however, sharing such thoughts with a client, it must be determined whether there is perhaps still some chance for recovery from suffering that might be sought. Unnecessary suffering would be meaningless and is never the aim of therapeutic intention. Wherever, in the area of psychological suffering, we encounter a chance for change we must encourage bold *action* aimed at relieving the need. Only when we confront an unalterable situation may we call on courage for *suffering*, a courage to accept that which would remain unacceptable without a perspective of meaning.

Dealing with value losses, therefore, also results in a type of taking stock of one's life. However, this does not reveal the highest value among a number of values, but rather gives an indication of the deeper meaning of a nonvalue such as suffering. Indeed, even in the darkest hours, some meaning can be wrested from life if the sufferer does not get bogged down in the phase of revolting or resigning and thus become a victim of despair. In truth, one does not despair of suffering, but of meaninglessness in suffering.[20]

The deadly poison of despair is neutralized as soon as the entire misery one experiences can be turned into a sacrifice for something worthwhile, illuminating the horizon of understanding.

To help one of my patients understand this kind of thinking better, I told her about the oyster which happily lives at the bottom of the sea until the day when a sharp grain of sand enters its soft tissue and causes pain. Undoubtedly, the creature makes an effort to get rid of the foreign substance—but, alas, in vain. The pain is immovable. What does the oyster do in this inescapable situation? It works on itself, mobilizes resources, encapsulates the grain, and transforms it into a pearl. "This," I said to my patient, "you can do too. Transform your suffering into a human achievement and it will not have been in vain!" The patient, who suffers from a severe tremor, solely as a result of our talk bought herself a pearl necklace, which she wears daily. Whenever the anguish about her physical handicap overcomes her, she gropes with her shaky hands for the pearls and recalls that she is free to make something great out of this suffering, the triumph of the spirit over destiny. And every time when she removes her hands a tranquil smile lights up her face. People like her are witness to the fact that reconciliation is possible. This is why we can hope that even the most difficult reconciliation of all can be achieved: reconciliation between human beings.

From a logotherapeutic perspective, one of the obstructions to any kind of reconciliation is a tendency to talk too much about the negative aspects. This is a marked difference between logotherapeutical treatment and other psychological approaches, the latter of which sometimes see salvation in merely articulating all of the negative aspects. Naturally, there is a certain relief if one can pour out all one's troubles into a sympathetic ear. Logotherapists have no objection to that.

However, we believe that talking and crying about one's troubles is characteristically a precondition, insofar as the spiritual potential of a person could be obscured or blocked by the emotional stress of a given problem. It is possible that this spiritual potential can be released if the emotional stress is reduced with the help of words or tears. Our main concern is to address the spiritual potential in the human being, thus, any kind of "digging up," whether by means of discussions, floods of tears, relaxation exercises, or the use of tranquilizers, is merely a way to produce those conditions under which the actual therapeutic work can commence.

However, we consider it harmful if "talking it out" loses its precondition status and is chosen to play the main part in therapy. Patients who do not stop after getting problems "off their chest" and go on wallowing in their problems may end up by talking even more trouble "back onto their chest"! That is to say that such intensification and focus leads to emotional arousal and churns up the past tragedy that has already been worked through on a spiritual level, which provides kindling for emotional shock, which, in turn, finally smothers and paralyzes the spiritual dimension of a person more effectively than was the case before.

As early as 1931, Bumke stated: "There is far too much talk with psychotherapeutic intentions, especially on the part of the patients."[21] This is just as valid today, nearly 60 years later. It was supported, among others, by B. Horànyi of the neurology department of the university hospital at Budapest, who even spoke of *curative silence* and points out that affects and emotions follow the general law of inertia just as other phenomena in life. He concludes that repeated rehashing of problematic situations keeps a psychological trouble active. Indeed, repeating it over and over recreates it, while not talking about it inescapably lets it shrink, just as any other part of the human organism that has not been functioning for some time.[22]

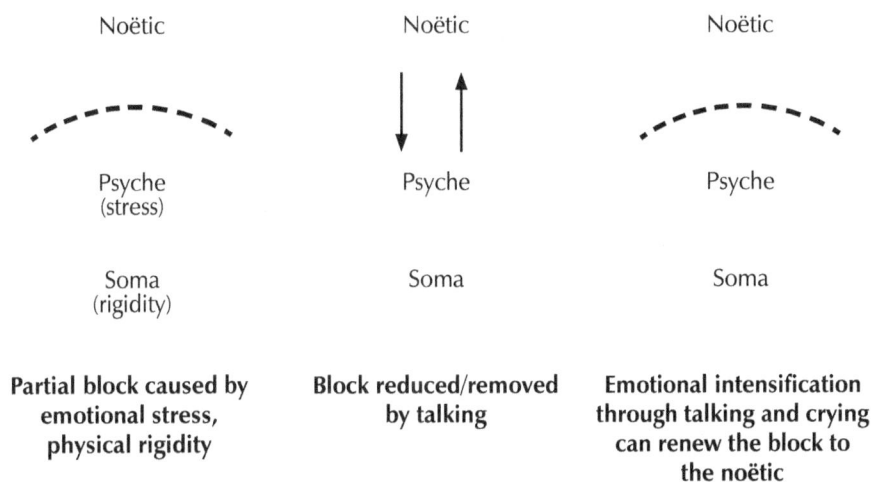

Noëtic	Noëtic	Noëtic
	$\downarrow \uparrow$	
Psyche (stress)	Psyche	Psyche
Soma (rigidity)	Soma	Soma
Partial block caused by emotional stress, physical rigidity	**Block reduced/removed by talking**	**Emotional intensification through talking and crying can renew the block to the noëtic**

To be sure, the logotherapist does not take the easy way out and forbid patients from speaking about negative matters. However, being aware of the danger of affective aggravation, methods have been developed to keep a "good cry" within healthy limits and gently educate patients to look out for positive things.[23]

This does not in any way mean that all clients must be trained as optimists. But in order to help them become tolerable realists, many positive countermeasures against an unrealistic, negative distortion are needed. It is notable how wrong individuals can be regarding the sum total of negative and positive events in their lives if they are prejudiced by their troubles, that is, by fixating attention on negative matters.

Once I attended an interesting experiment with children in our clinic. Strawberries were in season and we had provided a large amount of ripe fruit, of which approximately one-sixth was spoiled. When the children came for therapy, the therapist divided them into two groups and gave half of the fruit to each group. One group of children was asked to sort out the good strawberries, the other to pick out the bad ones. Then the fruits were placed out of sight and each child was asked independently to estimate the proportion of good strawberries had been in relation to the total. The result was startling. The group dealing with the good strawberries agreed among themselves and fairly accurately estimated the actual proportions. However, the individuals who picked the bad ones far underestimated the proportion of good fruit; it was determined that these group members were unduly pessimistic.

From this, is it possible to conclude that, by analogy, the concentration on psychological problems obstructs our view of the true wealth of the soul, of the incorruptible values of the human existence, and of meaning structures that are interwoven even with inescapable suffering? Let our patients look at the good fruits of their lives and they will, from the positive things they see, draw strength for reconciliation with the negative!

No science can explain the meaning of illness, guilt, and pain in this world. Neither can psychology. But the assertion of the logotherapist is that human beings are fundamentally equipped to find meaning even in illness, guilt, and pain by lifting themselves spiritually beyond them and perhaps even finding their own destiny in the process. The sign of the cross which has for centuries been the symbol of suffering in the Christian world is, in another sense, also the symbol for a plus. Shouldn't this give us food for thought?

$$\dagger \approx +$$

BIBLIOGRAPHY

[1] Matthew 10:39

[2] See case number 19 in Elisabeth Lukas, *Meaning in Suffering*. Purpose Research, Charlottesville, VA, 2nd ed. 2014

[3] Viktor E. Frankl, *Die Psychotherapie in der Praxis*. Piper, München, 5th ed. 1986

[4] Viktor E. Frankl, *Theorie und Therapie der Neurosen*. UTB 451, Reinhardt, München, 6th ed. 1987

[5] Viktor E. Frankl, *Der Wille zuin Sinn*. Piper, München, new ed. 1991

[6] Viktor E. Frankl, *Die Sinnfrage in der Psychotherapie*. Piper, München, 3rd ed. 1988

[7] Viktor E. Frankl, *Das Leiden an sinnlosen Leben*. Herder, Freiburg, 11th ed. 1989

[8] Viktor E. Frankl, *Psychotherapie für den Laien*. Herder, Freiburg, 13th ed. 1989

[9] Viktor E. Frankl, *Ärztliche Seelsorge*. Fischer TB, Frankfurt/M., 4th ed. 1987

[10] Viktor E. Frankl, *Der leidende Mensch*. Piper, München, new ed. 1990

[11] Elisabeth Lukas, *Meaning in Suffering*. Purpose Research, 2nd ed. 2014

[12] Viktor E. Frankl, *Zur geistigen Problematik der Psychotherapie*. Zentralblatt für Psychotherapie 1983 and Elisabeth Lukas, *Von der Tiefen-zur Höhenpsychologie*. Herder, Freiburg, 2nd ed. 1988

[13] Viktor E. Frankl, *Der Wille zum Sinn*. Piper, München, 1991

[14] Viktor E. Frankl, *Der leidende Mensch*. Piper, München, new ed. 1990

[15] Viktor E. Frankl, *Man's Search for Meaning*. Simon & Schuster, New York (Quotation: "The role played by a logotherapist is rather that of an eye specialist than that of a painter. A painter tries to convey to us a picture of the world as he sees it; an ophthalmologist tries to enable us to see the world as it really is.")

[16] Viktor E. Frankl, *Der leidende Mensch*. Piper, München, new ed. 1990

[17] Viktor E. Frankl, *Der unbewußte Gott*. Kösel, München, 7th ed. 1988

[18] Viktor E. Frankl, *Der unbewußte Gott*. Kösel, München, 7th ed. 1988

[19] Viktor E. Frankl, "Argumente für einen tragischen Optimismus" in: *Sinn-voll heilen*. Herder, Freiburg, 1983

[20] Viktor E. Frankl, "…trotzdem Ja zum Leben sagen," dtv 10023, München, 9th ed. 1990

[21] Bumke, Münchner medizinische Wochenschrift, Nov. 1931, p. 2003-2004

[22] Bela Horanyi, Journal *Psychotherapie* 9. Jg.

[23] Elisabeth Lukas, *Von der Tiefen-zur Höhenpsychologie*. Herder, Freiburg, 2nd ed. 1988 (Part II, chapter 9 & 10)

B

BEING FOR SOMETHING
OR
FOR SOMEONE

1. Three Fundamental Rules for the Family

Dubold-start uring the last few decades much has been said about the family, good and bad. However, most experts agree on one point: The family faces a crisis. There definitely was a reason for the appearance of family therapy, which tends to depart from the practice of seeing and treating a person as a single individual and, instead, examines the individual's network of intimate interactions. The old hypothesis that a psychologically disturbed person is also handicapped in social contacts has been changed into a new one: A person with disturbed social contacts is also psychologically handicapped.

Would you believe it? The new hypothesis is as useful or useless as the old one. Both offer sufficient cause for declaring a crisis, but only insignificant assistance for overcoming it. Each explanatory model has the drawback that relationships, which to some extent can no longer be changed, are uncovered, thus leaving a certain feeling of helplessness. Knowing why so much went wrong does not necessarily imply that the process of putting it right has started.

It is not my intention to talk about family crises that produce shock waves throughout the country; certainly we have heard and read enough pessimistic comments as it is. What I would like to advance are reasons for a kind of *tragic optimism*, as Frankl called it, for nevertheless saying "Yes" to life, to the future, and to the family. In order to do this, we must depart from the psychosocial theoretical models and the inevitable helplessness in their wake. We must look for a different type of reasoning, one that does not merely document a plethora of causes of crises but rather one that endeavors to reach those sources of strength that can master them. Looking in this direction, however, we find the choice of theories and methods shockingly limited. Indeed, in my opinion, there remains only logotherapy with its declared aim of not only collecting "arguments for a tragic optimism"[1] but of revising and renewing the concept of the human being in medicine and psychology.

That there is indeed a connection between a functioning family and the concept of the human being in medicine was discussed by Hans Schaefer, Professor at the University of Heidelberg, in his booklet *Im Blickpunkt: der Mensch* (*Focus on Man*), in which he declared:

> Man today has fallen from the security of his family, the reliability of a social order, and the foundation of a religious system into a bottomless pit. This man poses new challenges for medicine because in this changed environment he develops new afflictions. Medicine is no longer regarded in terms of medical authority nor merely as a help for physical distress. Medicine becomes more inclusive and its social task encompasses more.[2]

Among the new afflictions of which Schaefer spoke, the *suffering from a meaningless life*[3] comes first. I noted that it markedly impacts the person of today and causes psychological and biological illness because it erodes the foundation of spiritual existence. Whoever suffers from an apparently meaningless life also suffers from a meaningless career, a meaningless family life, and so on. Such a person essentially falls into a bottomlessness which disturbs psychological well-being as much as do social contacts or physical health. They all belong together in one single unit and entity.

Therefore, if we want to think about overcoming crises without wasting time on reconstructing their origin, we can use a simple formula: *Where meaning is perceived, life becomes bearable; where no meaning is perceived, life becomes unbearable.* And this is independent of all other life circumstances. The formula can be illustrated with an example, which is not without a certain comical element. I read once what professional psychologists at a seminar in Hennef/Sieg had to say about the problem of psychological crises in the case of unemployment. They maintained that only idlers and layabouts survive this life crisis happily and healthily because these individuals "voluntarily" seek unemployment; in some exceptional cases, supported by an unemployment check, they build a new life under the southern sun. What does this imply? Whoever becomes intentionally unemployed sees some meaning in being unemployed. Even if this meaning is somewhat questionable for the person concerned, it is a sustaining motive for accepting the disadvantages of unemployment in exchange for some imagined personal gain. This meaning content of unemployment protects the individual from psychological distress.

Conversely, the person who loses employment against his or her wishes is in danger of finding no meaning in unemployment and, as a consequence, the meaninglessness of such a condition can affect psychological health, even if it is possible to rely on governmental aid. The individual does not live by welfare alone, as Viktor Frankl put it.

If one were to search for a brand-name pharmaceutical drug to cure—or even to prevent—the critical consequences of undesired unemployment, such as self-doubt, discouragement, and apathy, one would have to search for meaning potentials that exist even if there is no place of employment. This would not be, as with idlers, *because of* the unemployment but rather, with people eager to work, *in spite of* unemployment; for example, some honorary service or voluntary social engagement.

From my experience I can report on a relevant case that simultaneously will lead us into the subject "family," as it concerns an unemployed father who was brought by his wife to our counseling center because living with him at home had become intolerable. He moaned continuously about boredom and hopelessness that, understandably, was depressing for his family.

As we sat together I asked him how high he estimated his chances of being successful with any one of his applications. He laughed and answered sarcastically "one quarter of a percent probability but no more!"

"All right," I said, "then you will have to send 400 letters of application in order to succeed."

The man was startled and looked at me, but the calculation was obviously correct. "400 applications...." he grumbled, "That is a lot of work...."

"Oh," I interrupted, "that is not only a lot of work, it is also a testimony to your perseverance, to your capacity for coping and to your ability to face fate. Furthermore, you just complained bitterly about your boredom and 400 letters would be an excellent antidote for that!"

Several months later, a postcard from the man reached my desk. The message on it was: "I was wrong; 93 were enough."

As demonstrated, the idea that the large number of unsuccessful applications had a meaning because it increased the chance for eventual success was enough to lead him out of his depressive phase into an active state, and soon he had the situation under control.

Perhaps the reader might think that the man indeed had some chances for finding work, even if they were few. But what happens if one has no chance at all? Is there still the chance for a meaningful search for meaning? Is there still hope of finding—and fulfilling—meaning?

At this point I would like to mention what I once said to a man with a family who had to go into early retirement after a difficult surgery and felt utterly useless because of it. He had two adolescent sons who attended school with only moderate success and were hanging out on the streets as soon as school was out. Referring to them, I explained to the father that, although he had not much chance for his own occupational advancement, he had the rare opportunity to demonstrate to his sons with his own way of life that leisure time can be spent meaningfully; not only with smoking, reading newspapers, and visiting pubs, but with personal interests such as hobbies and volunteer work. His good example might be more important than his being able to work. His conduct in this critical phase of occupational disengagement might one day serve as an example to his sons when they might have to face a crisis. Then the decisive factor won't be how much money the father had earned in the past but rather how courageously and uncomplainingly he endured his suffering and what he did under those circumstances.

This father understood my advice; since then, he has started a painting and wallpapering service among his neighborhood acquaintances and helps them to beautify their homes for a modest sum. The most gratifying result, however, is that one of his sons liked helping his father so much that he decided to train for professional wallpapering after finishing school.

Logotherapy holds that there is no situation that does not contain at least one meaning potential and, in an individual who succeeds in perceiving it, i a Copernican transformation may result in a person's condition in the noëtic, psychological, or physical dimension. To be human starts with the search for meaning and finds its perfection in fulfilling this meaning. As long as the switches are not shifted to this destination, the locomotive of our existence comes to a halt: The signals are on "stop." Only when the meaning potentials in living for something or someone are perceived are the brakes released and we can surmount obstacles that may appear enormous but shrink when compared with the size of a greater goal. Even the past, which according to almost all psychological interpretations represents the most insurmountable obstacle to personal development, loses its significance when confronted with a meaningful present.

During consultations I have confirmed repeatedly and without exception that sad childhood memories, bad experiences, and humiliations suffered will be reactivated as psychological factors of interference if the present is unsatisfactory and the future empty. If one then attends to this emerged past by therapeutically "working it through" (as it is so neatly called) by X-raying and dissecting it, the past gains increasing importance, the present becomes less satisfactory, and the future appears to be more empty. This is a dangerous development.

If, however, the unhappy past is ignored in order to search the present for meaning and to fill the future with purpose, then the bitter memories will soon fade and they will mix with positive contents of the past, which also exist, to constitute a fairly neutral life history.

This reminds me of a young man I met some time ago. He came from a disastrous family background and his childhood was one protracted tragedy. His father brutally tormented and mistreated him, and the hysterical scenes of his mother were even worse. She produced one nervous breakdown after another. I can express this opinion as I know the parents personally.

This young man has developed remarkably well considering his past. He successfully completed his schooling and did his substitute national service in a social institution without any problems. However, it happened that he fell into a dangerous psychological low after a heated argument with his girlfriend that triggered a gnawing insecurity about what to do with his future life after completing his national service. In this crisis, massive anxieties and feelings of self-hate suddenly arose. Toying with the idea of suicide, he reacted nearly as hysterically as his mother had. It is apparent that dissatisfaction with the present and a meaningless future allowed the unrestrained takeover by the shadows from the past. Nevertheless, I refrained from recalling the cruelties perpetrated by his parents in order to explain his condition. These cannot be eradicated and would only have burdened his self-concept because, as the alleged victim of his upbringing, he would have felt unable to lead a healthy and normal life and this feeling would indeed have disabled him. Instead, I asked him if he often wished that his parents were kind and thoughtful towards one another and could understand love as being-for-one-another rather than this continuous power struggle?

Without hesitation, he answered my question affirmatively. There now remained only one thing for me to point out to him: That, although he is not responsible for what his parents did, he is very much co-responsible for what happens between him and his girlfriend here today, and that in this present love relationship he has a decisive influence for making it better and more harmonious than that of his parents. Suddenly, the past suffering in his family assumed some meaning for him; it became a warning to protect him from imitation. Then and there he understood that he is by no means merely the product of his childhood but the architect of his present destiny, and as such he is responsible. This realization served to extinguish any hysterical outbreak from the start.

The most interesting aspect of the case is that the young man was able decisively to cut the ties to his unhappy past when, after completing his national service, he fully committed to studies in social work. If I were asked today what prognosis I would dare to give concerning his career, I would say that he will give his best to his profession, especially because the suffering in his own childhood made him more sensitive to the suffering of his fellow men and women.

Let us refuse to believe what traditional psychologists keep on telling us, that all negative events in our personal past will remain a constant burden throughout life. The textbook of reality tells a very different story. There are many people who enjoyed a happy and protected childhood and yet floundered in their lives. The converse is also true, namely, that much goodness and wisdom has its source in painful experiences.

Of course, there can be no doubt but that the first years in life are important. These years also leave their imprint on the adolescent years, but during maturity every person carries the energy for further development within and can supplement any upbringing by *self-discipline*.

If, however, it is suggested by professionals that one's childhood is to blame for all the mistakes of the present, then the impulse for self-discipline is extinguished, since it is so much easier to pass all the guilt onto the parents rather than undertake the effort of self-improvement. Thus depth psychology has unintentionally contributed a great deal towards making parents into scapegoats. It has provided excuses for the inconsistencies of unstable persons; the resulting fruits have been poor.

These results were presented in a humorous article by Elisabeth Hielscher in the *Sueddeutche Zeitung* for Mothers' Day, 1984. I would like to express my special thanks to her.

Mother is the Best... Excuse

Again and again, especially in May, it is claimed that our society does not pay enough attention to mothers. If one listens carefully, one can't agree with this opinion. Whenever and wherever people in our society begin to talk about their lives, they sooner or later talk about their mothers. Up to now, however, the public has not yet recognized the full significance of this fact. For example, a casual laborer, Helmut, aged 22, relates: "Actually I wanted to become a test pilot but I detested school. Moreover, I couldn't stand it at home. My mother only had me, so she was at me all day, washing, cleaning, cooking, and so on… Somehow I always felt guilty. When I turned 18 of course I ran away!" And he adds: "If she had been different, I would surely have completed school and I would be better off now!"

The psychology student Ilsebill, aged 30, has longed for some time for a lasting relationship. "But all my partnerships break up" she says. Even a journey to Baghwan in Oregon couldn't change anything. She has been in psychoanalysis for two years. "And now I understand that an unresolved conflict with my mother was the reason for my conflict with men. Basically I hate her terribly because she always favored my younger brother." Since Ilsebill was finally able to talk to her mother about it, she feels much better. "Unfortunately my mother still does not show any insight. A fortnight ago she even knitted a pullover for my brother's 18th birthday! This has thrown me back emotionally so badly that I had to break up with my boyfriend!"

After completing his training as a communication designer, Michael, aged 24, worked for three months in an advertising agency. A year ago he had to break off his career abruptly. "That was when my girlfriend had her baby," he tells us. "At first everything went beautifully. While Gabi was at school, her mother looked after the baby. But after Gabi had completed her commercial examinations, her mother wanted to go back to her job at the bank and expected Gabi to stay at home herself." Even the memory of it arouses Michael's indignation. "But that was out of the question! Gabi had the admission to a college of remedial teaching virtually in her pocket! So we genuinely agreed that I will look after the baby and so on." Meanwhile Michael quite enjoys his role as "father-at-home." "I can be a father—partner for my son and observe his development in every phase!" The relationship to Gabi's mother however is not yet back to normal, he says. "She only wants to pay the bare minimum rent, pocket-money and that's it! Not withstanding the fact that she was the one who manipulated us into direct dependency !"

So much for Helmut, Ilsebill and Michael. But surely many newspaper readers know numerous similar cases from their own experience, which demonstrate the importance of the mother in our society.

Elisabeth Hielscher

From developmental psychology we know that maturation in its natural sequence has two phases during which the adolescent is extremely critical of his parents. One is at the onset of puberty when the childlike faith in the infallibility and omniscience of the parents vanishes with the discovery that parents are, after all, only human with human weaknesses. The other is in the early 20s, on becoming an adult when in the struggle for identity an adolescent discovers his or her own weakness. Especially in the second phase of disillusionment about one's own imperfections, which gradually becomes evident after the period of storm and stress and which should flow into constructive self-discipline, there is a strong tendency to blame the parents, political systems, etc. Furthermore, if the hypotheses of an easily misunderstood depth psychology reason along the same lines, then the branch of responsibility for oneself, on which future life was supposed to grow, is easily cut off. Actual infantilism is the denial of constructive self-education and the passing of responsibility off onto others.

I began with an abbreviated formula, that the endurability of human life depends on the perception of meaning. Furthermore, I tried to indicate that such a perception of meaning is not related to favorable external conditions nor to a harmonious life history. Indeed, meaning can be experienced or discovered at any moment, even in distressing situations, such as in being unemployed or recalling unhappy childhood memories. What does this imply for the family as the smallest unit of people of different ages and sexes who are close to one another? Do the same rules apply?

THREE FUNDAMENTAL LOGOTHERAPEUTIC RULES

Rule 1: The endurability of life is related to the perception of meaning.

Rule 2: The perception of meaning is not related to favorable external living conditions.

Rule 3: The perception of meaning is not related to a harmonious life history.

At times, I think that the quintessence of my 18 years of experience in educational and family counseling is simply the realization that the same rules that apply to the individual also apply to the entire family. This begins with the fact that the family, too, is only endurable if it has a certain meaning for its members. It continues with the observation that happiness in a family is surprisingly unrelated to the quality of external conditions, although very often the opposite is asserted. Finally, the family history—and every family has its own history—cannot conclusively predetermine any further development of the family. Likewise, within the family there are self-discipline and self-responsibility that are capable of defying diverse corrupting influences. Let us look at these fundamental rules one by one.

First, there is the *endurability of the family* that in every case determines whether the family will remain united. We need not discuss the average quality of family cohesion in the present. Besides the divorce statistics, the number of aging adults placed outside the family is staggering and the number of youngsters leaving the family prematurely competes with that of the older ones.

All things considered, it is not only the extended family that is breaking down; the nuclear family is also crumbling. If, however, family life today has become intolerable for many, it indicates that for them it has lost its meaning. This lost meaning must have affected something of mutual concern, something which otherwise would have opposed a breakdown. I believe it is the dimension of *needing one another* and *being needed by one another*.

Today, we have fought for a certain self-assurance and are proud of it. We don't easily listen to anyone, be it "father state" or "mother church," a teacher at school or the supervisor at work. We have emancipated ourselves, we know our rights and dues and we know how to obtain them. Nobody needs to suppress any needs; economy and trade provide all kinds of articles for consumption; the law provides equal rights; the social safety net will catch us; everyone is free to actualize him- or herself. There only remains the question: Where is this happiness that should have entered our heart and minds together with all these many advances and privileges?

Approximately four years ago, a young mother came with her husband to our consulting rooms. They could not agree whether the woman should take up her career as a dental assistant again or not. Their two children were then aged two and three and the father wanted his wife to stay at home with the children. The young mother, however, wanted to go to work. She found it too monotonous at home and she was of the opinion that the children could go to a kindergarten during the day. I suggested that she should wait at least another year before starting work and proposed some ideas for small adjustments and upgrades to her existence as a housewife. But the young woman decided against my suggestion and started to work. Nine months later, she returned to our counseling clinic because she had difficulties with the children. When she got home in the evening and was tired, they horsed around, didn't listen or go to bed, and really got on her nerves. I tried to explain that the children had to do without their mother all day and at least in the evening needed her concentrated attention and devotion, and they used every trick to get it. I suggested at least half-time work for the mother; again, my advice fell on deaf ears.

Six months later, the father came to our consulting rooms; he was worried about his wife's health. She had become nervous and irritable and cried over every trifle, so that he didn't know what to do any more. I suggested a recovery holiday in a spa for the mother, which was duly arranged by our medical doctor; I also arranged for family care during the mother's absence. However, with all the best intentions it proved to be the wrong thing to do. During the holiday, the young woman met a man and left her family suddenly. The father had no option but to place the toddlers in an institution where he visited them regularly every fortnight. In the meantime, a divorce was granted. I did not see the young woman again but, by chance, I talked recently to one of her acquaintances. She told me that the liaison between the mother and her holiday friend was only transitory. Afterwards, in her loneliness, she started drinking and lost her job as a result of it. Now she lives in a single sublet room and is supported by social welfare.

This tragedy deeply touched me and my colleagues and we asked ourselves whether we could somehow have prevented it. After much discussion, we concluded that neither the work nor the holiday of the mother were the basic cause of the breakup of the family. Rather, the woman's inner attitude towards her family was not oriented towards the meaning of the situation but towards her ego and its momentary wishes. Today, individuals are adept at making their demands on life and getting what they want, carelessly overlooking their human kinship and the bond that ties them together in needing one another and being needed. They slide from self-confidence via self-actualization into self-love, and with all this self-concern they lose sight of human fellowship and its meaning. Their self-assurance whispers in their ear that they must not need anybody so as not to depend on anybody, which is, after all, the highest aim of any emancipation. Self-love supplements this motto by adding that it is incomprehensible why other people should need one, if one does not need them. In the end, what is left are loneliness and emptiness, the existential vacuum. A person who needs nobody and is needed by nobody is unfit for family life, perhaps not even capable of living itself.

We must therefore retract a bit from our self-assurance and make the concession that people need one another and depend on one another, but we can add with a clear conscience that, in it, one of the most beautiful and sustaining potentialities for meaning is hidden. In the love for a "You," the "I" unfolds more purely and much more naturally than in any hectic chase after an illusionary self-actualization.

If the woman in the above example could have seen the meaning of her situation as being needed daily by her loving partner and helpless children, as well as seeing that she needed her family as a place of home and safety, the terrible suffering that she and her family members endured would never have occurred. That perhaps she sometimes longed for self-confirmation through her career or some small adventure may well be true. But the meaning of her life and work, interwoven with the welfare of her family, should have made her family at least appear tolerable. It might even have added the gift of a little serene happiness.

When we speak in logotherapy of the endurability of events that give a meaning connection, then we speak about the most basic foundation of our existence, sheer survival, so to speak. In addition to that, we believe, in our optimism, that the experience of meaning provides incomparably more spiritual benefit than a mere tolerance of existence, namely the ultimate, highest fulfillment of being, a feeling of delight—to have lived not in vain.

This leads us to the second rule, which states that *happiness in the family is independent of the quality of external living conditions.*

We asked ourselves earlier where, amidst all the "liberation" and prosperity of the last decades, contentment had its place? The question arises from an error in psychological reasoning that implies that positive external conditions also produce a positive inner echo and vice versa, applying, so to speak, the motto: He who lives well is satisfied. That this is not the case we have learned in the meantime from a bitter lesson, for one searches in vain for contentment in our affluent society. Logotherapy recognized this error in psychological reasoning long ago and confronted it with a much more realistic model. According to the latter, inner contentment is not the automatic consequence of external comfort; rather, *the inner attitude towards external conditions, whether positive or negative, becomes the deciding criterion for the inner contentment of the human being.*

Let us look at another example from life: A married couple came to our consulting rooms with a medical inquiry. They wanted to know the risk of a baby inheriting the blindness with which the husband had been born and how one could handle this risk responsibly. While our medical doctor referred to the appropriate specialists and explained their opinion of the situation, I had a few general talks with the couple in order to find out how they coped with the husband's blindness. I was in for a succession of surprises, as I had rarely encountered such a successful partnership. I was deeply touched when they told me how they spend their evenings together. Their shared leisure time could easily have caused friction and breakups if one considers that activities like dancing, TV, hobbies and others were inaccessible to the blind man. But the couple made a virtue out of necessity by reading aloud in the evenings, which was a pleasure for both of them. The woman read the latest news or special chapters from books and enjoyed closeness and fellowship with her husband while doing it. He frequently and affectionately placed his head in her lap to listen to her voice. He, in turn, enjoyed these "evening celebrations," as he called them, because his wife opened the gate to the world for him and brought light into his inner world. Neither wanted to skip these nightly readings and were quite content with their lot although the external conditions of the man's blindness undoubtedly represented a heavy burden. If one compares them to other couples who use the strength of their undiminished health for torturing each other with senseless bickering, then one understands what Viktor Frankl meant with his emphasis on attitudinal values: There are values that can only be actualized on another, higher level than that of needs and their satisfaction: a courageous adjustment to negative external conditions that cannot be changed, such as this man's attitude to his disability, or the similarly exemplary adjustment to positive external conditions placed in the service of a meaningful task, such as the attitude of the wife who uses her sight for reading aloud and, through it, creates joy. These are values whose measure cannot be assessed with the usual yardsticks of drive satisfaction. They are light beacons of the human spirit.

Attitudinal values are always related to the willingness to compromise, that is, a readiness to balance a personal sacrifice against a personal gain for the sake of a higher value that is beyond renunciation or gain. Therefore, a meaningful compromise is more than a fifty-fifty concession in the achievement of one's own intentions; it is also the intervention of a *superseding will* which sets a goal beyond self-interests.

If, for instance, two members of a family, one of whom wants to go for a long walk and the other wants to stay at home, come to an agreement to go for a short walk together, then each of them has partly succeeded and partly given in. One could say that each had half a loss and half a gain. In total, however, both have gained by the compromise, because they did not separate or fight but found a common activity which was acceptable to each of them, notwithstanding different wishes. The wish for fellowship and for meeting halfway was given a higher value than the individual wish for hiking or staying at home. But, regarding the former, both have won, so that the overall gain is greater than the loss.

In world politics, it is not very different. For instance, a compromise concerning the issue of disarmament presupposes some concessions by both superpowers, but is, at the same time, a document for an overriding will to peace. This brings a considerably higher benefit for both sides than the loss of power and prestige due to their yielding.

In logotherapy, this superordinate will to mutuality and peace is equated with the *will to meaning*: It is that will in the person which stands above personal, individual wishes; it can reach a compromise with them that includes even personal renunciations. However, these never exceed a tolerable amount, simply because they can become acceptable in a context of meaning.

For the family, this implies that, with external conditions as hard and difficult as they may be, compromises can be reached if the inner attitude of the family members is oriented to a meaning beyond the situation. Alternately, the best external conditions don't help if they don't meet with a positive, meaning-oriented inner attitude.

Let us finally look at the third rule, which is similar to the second one, yet has to be discussed separately because of the widespread recognition of the fixed idea that the life histories of the individual and the family are overpowering and predetermine present and future events. Almost every counseling and psychotherapeutic method today overwhelmingly consists of illuminating and retracing past events, from which conclusions for the present are drawn. This would not even be so very wrong if it were brought into relationship with the potentials of the future, but frequently exactly the opposite happens. Thus future potentials are undermined because the impression is created that the future, as a result of the past, offers no choices at all—that is, everything is fixed already. However, this is a precarious and terribly wrong conclusion that paralyzes any effort to improve the present situation.

It happened that I accidentally overheard a talk between a teacher with a background in psychology and a foster mother of a four-year-old. The teacher explained at great length that the young child had suffered through hospitalization due to early repeated changes of parental figures, and had very little chance for normal development in the future. Because of the child's disabilities, the mother would have serious trouble with him once he went to school; when he turned 14 she would be very sorry that she had taken him into foster care because during puberty his disturbed social behavior would fully break through. When, after the talk, the foster mother lovingly took the little fellow's hand and with tearful eyes left the room, I ran after her. I couldn't help it, although I had been a bystander. I told her that science is by no means equipped to make prognoses for such a long period. The mother should not be afraid because children are much more flexible and adaptable than we adults often think. They can blossom in a favorable milieu even if their former upbringing was less than ideal.

Naturally, there can be damage in the past that may continue to have effects in the biological as well as the psychological sphere. But this should never lead to a fatalistic attitude that present efforts are meaningless since nothing can be restored. *Something can always be redressed until the last breath.* It is always meaningful to work towards restoration, whether by overcoming hurts of the past, repaying an old debt, getting over a heavy loss, or filling a squandered life in retrospect with meaning. As long as a person can think, as long as one has a spiritual capacity, as long as that which is good can be known, it is possible to restore and make amends. It is not only possible but necessary and meaningful. This is another argument of our logotherapeutic optimism. It would be wrong to think that logotherapy neglects the life history. By no means. The early life history has its place, but it has no exclusive power over anyone's life. This is the difference in approach that is made by the logotherapist.

Unfortunately, however, focusing on the past has become common, due to a profusion of psychological information in popular literature. Often clients come to me, sit down, and spontaneously begin talking about their childhood without mentioning their actual problems in any way. They apparently expect that, for a psychologist, they have to start at zero, if possible with their feelings in the womb, so that any present failure can be interpreted from their memories. I never join in this game. I always demand that we start with an inventory of the present situation; in other words, by conferring about the present position in which all thinkable improvements and goals for the future that give meaning to present efforts are roughly indicated. After this, possible obstacles on the way to the goal can be viewed from a certain distance. Of course, it happens that past events are mentioned in our discussions, but within the perspective of their optimal handling and not as compulsory constraints in life.

I shall not deny that, in the past, people tended to swallow their problems and to leave their sufferings untold or, one could say, to suppress them. Back then, encouraging patients to talk about their problems in order to make them more understandable and comprehensible was a healing adjustment. But since then, times have changed. With increased self-confidence and psychological enlightenment, the suppression of problems has turned into its opposite—into *hyperreflection* of problems, just as authoritarian education has changed into anti-authoritarian education.

Today people tend to treat their past experiences as excessively important and they feel sorry for themselves to their heart's content, or else they ascribe every present discomfort to their upbringing and to environmental influences in the past. Therefore, today the healing adjustment is to encourage people to become responsible for their own lives and to point out to them that their actions here and now determine their future more than the tears shed yesterday. Suppression and hyperreflection are both unhealthy extremes of one and the same continuum. Between them lies a healthy reconciliation with fate and with the past, and from this reconciliation alone can a human being become free for a life with dignity.

Relating this to family life, one could therefore say: As important as it is to perceive and accept needing and being needed, and as important as it is within limits to compromise with one another and the existing unchangeable realities, it is just as important to let the past be and to muster a daily willingness for a new beginning. A person who keeps recalling the past (and that usually happens in sessions characterized by casting blame) gradually destroys the family, because that activity leaves no choice for the future. However, a person who can put an end to something is also able to open new doors.

In connection with this, I would like to mention a counseling conversation I had with a married couple. At the beginning of their married life they had stayed with the wife's in-laws. This had caused serious conflicts. They later built their own house and moved into it. During the strenuous building phase, the couple were very close. However, as soon as the house was completed and they should have been able to enjoy their comfortable home, both started with reproaches and recriminations and it invariably ended with hashing over the old trouble with the in-laws. In the end, the woman was convinced that the husband had only exploited her labor, while the husband complained that he should have listened to his parents and never married. This example again shows the lack of correlation between comfortable external conditions such as home ownership and inner happiness.

It seemed as if the couple's problem was in the unresolved past, but this is a deceptive hypothesis for, as mentioned before, the shadows of the past sneak into a present devoid of meaning. Where the sun does not shine, darkness takes over. Thus my aim was not to lift the shadows into consciousness but rather to let the sun shine again. For this, the present relationship between the partners had to be filled with meaning. In the marriage guidance sessions we searched together for something that both partners liked to experience together; we discovered that, many years ago, shortly after the wedding, a trip to Canada had been planned as they had both wanted to visit a school friend of the wife. Naturally, at that time there was not enough money and later everything had been invested in the house. Now, however, both felt rather unsure of starting such a long journey with their long-forgotten knowledge of English. Consequently I made the following suggestions:

1. That they enroll together for an English course at a language school.

2. That they get informative material about Canada and study it together at night.

3. That they come to an agreement that whenever one starts to talk about the unhappy times with the in-laws, the other one quietly gets a map of Canada and holds it in front of his or her face as if to say: "Think of the future and not of the past!"

Both agreed to the proposals. One year later, they actually went on their overseas trip. They even visited me once more to show the incredible, beautiful photos the husband had taken. While scores of photos were spread all over my table and they were busy commenting on every tourist attraction on their different stops, the woman let slip a comment which made me smile secretly. She said in passing that the in-laws were very enthusiastic when they saw the photos. I was careful not to pursue the subject, but I was glad that the old enmity within the family had somewhat abated.

In summary, we could thus extend and complement the basic rules of logotherapy for the family:

Rule 1. The endurability of life is related to the perception of meaning.
Validity for the family: The perception of meaning within the family is the acknowledgement of needing one another and being needed by one another. Without this knowledge, the family becomes meaningless and thus unbearable.

Rule 2. The perception of meaning is not related to favorable external living conditions.
Validity for the family: Happiness within the family is independent of favorable living conditions. Only the meaning orientation of an inner attitude towards external living conditions determines contentment within the family.

Rule 3. The perception of meaning is not related to a harmonious life history.
Validity for the family: The development of a family is not predetermined by its history. The meaning orientation of the family members' present actions alone decides the future of the family.

Every family has at any time a great number of potentials for meaning realization if only it is conscious of them. In past years, sexuality within the family has been far too overvalued; it was a reaction to a time when sexuality was taboo. Sexuality is an important part of marriage, but it is neither a necessary nor a sufficient condition. It is simply the expression of a love relationship. Meaning orientation, on the other hand, is a necessary and sufficient condition for a happy family life, because it incorporates—and elevates—the love relationship and makes it into something special, something more than sexuality.

One can't express something that doesn't exist. In other words, sex without a love relationship is nothing. A true love relationship, however, can be expressed in hundreds of ways, and it does not necessarily require an active sex life.

> The fascinations of the senses
> die with their satiation.

This is not some new psychological wisdom. It was said long ago by Friedrich von Schiller.

> The potentials of a meaning
> are alive in their realization.

This quote, on the other hand, is valid in terms of logotherapy. Every meaning potential has its "once and for all" character; once realized, it remains for always, and once missed, it is missed forever.[4] For example, the young mother who left her family thereby lost the meaning potential for bringing up her two children. Perhaps one day she may have other children and bring them up, but this *one* meaning potential was lost to her and she will have to live with this loss until the end of her days. In contrast, the couple mentioned last secured their trip to Canada together as one meaning potential of their present life. Even if difficulties should again arise, indeed, even if the marriage should break down, this one meaning potential was realized and anchored in the past as a beautiful and uniting experience, and it will remain so for both of them until the end of their days.

Concerning the example of the family in crisis, I would like to state in conclusion: There is no family that does not still have its positive potentials. However, to paraphrase Hermann Hesse, in order to achieve the possible one has to attempt the impossible again and again. Or, to formulate it in logotherapeutic terms, for the "I" to become itself, it must submerge in a "Thou."

2. Saying "Yes!" to Problem Children

In the Old Testament, one of the Ten Commandments deals with the relationship between parents and children. For readers who are not familiar with it, I will quote it: "Honor thy father and thy mother, that thy days may be long upon the land which the Lord thy God giveth thee" (Exodus 20:12, *KJV*). Now, by no means do I want to enter a subject for which I am not qualified, such as that of religion. I want to consider this commandment, or we could also say this ancient wisdom, solely from the perspective of psychology, and I am amazed that general psychology hasn't done so up to now. As it is, the commandment contains a statement about a peculiar correlation between two facts that apparently have nothing to do with one another. The respect and honor that individuals have for their parents is very different from the quality of life choices and the length of life; these are not easily connected by rational thinking.*

However, we can't deny the fact that the respect children have for their parents has hardly ever been as low as it is today; it is a time in which Western culture has seemingly given up the concept of authority, and in which our youth have also hardly ever felt so little well-being or life worth as in our time of material prosperity and spiritual decay. Is the ancient saying perhaps more than just a moral admonition? Does it contain a grain of truth that today demands its bitter tribute?

But even if this were so, could we ever return to a parent-child relationship in which concepts such as reverence and respect by the young towards their elders still play a role, so that the young may live well on the land? Most of us will silently shake our heads. There is no turning back; the wheel

---

* We commonly think of it as being the opposite, namely, that it will go well with the children if they are loved and respected by their parents!

of development turns faster and faster; the chasm between the generations gets wider and wider and understanding one another becomes increasingly more difficult. Teachers no longer get a chance to change the world but rather try breathlessly to chase after a world that has already changed. What then? Must we also surrender the well-being of our descendants?

Actually, we may have to do this. We will have to give up the idea that we, as parents and teachers, are solely responsible for the destiny of our protégés, that we have to see to their welfare at any price and if, in spite of all this, they should fail to develop and thrive then it can be no one else's fault but ours. Because of our bad consciences we would have to care even more diligently for their well-being.

From the ancient commandment we should learn something that is timelessly valid: Well-being, in so far as it is not dependent on circumstances of fate, is always a consequence of one's *own* behavior and not the product of parental care. On the contrary, the more protective an upbringing, the more it can inhibit a child's ability to make decisions, just as the other extreme, neglect, can have negative consequences in its wake.

What upbringing actually has to offer is the *living example*, and this example should in the strictest sense be "honorable" and nothing more. Whether it is actually followed by the up-and-coming generation is not the teachers' concern. It has to be one of the decisions of youth and, therefore, is one of their responsibilities for their own lives. It isn't the teacher's responsibility to create well-being, but only to set an example worthy of imitation. This means one could exhort today's teachers with the debatable but well-meaning advice to "behave in such a manner that you will earn the respect of your children, if they can still have respect for you!" This advice can never be wrong.

I mentioned that overprotective spoiling, as well as a negligent style of upbringing, have inherent dangers. The best combination appears to be a pedagogic maxim that should be well known: "love coupled with steadfastness." Less known, however, is the fact that children and adolescents coming from homes with generally good upbringings have psychological disturbances, too. If one were to search with a magnifying glass, one could find faults with every father, mother, and teacher. Nevertheless, a certain minimal number of mistakes in upbringing by no means justifies every maladaptive behavior in the one being reared. Every human effort is by its very nature imperfect; parents would lose their "humanness" at the very moment they became perfect. There isn't anything more tragic than pedagogues who try to be perfect. They lose not only their humanness but also their naturalness, and that is a heavy loss, which we shall discuss later.

Parents thus are permitted to have their weaknesses, as long as they remain within tolerable limits, without having to fear damage to their children. But how is it possible that the number of children with psychologically disturbed development is at present so high, even though for years adults have become increasingly concerned about the question of upbringing and in every adult education program, in every consulting room, useful suggestions for raising children are offered? How can this happen when bookstores are overflowing with a vast amount of pedagogic literature and even the media do not avoid the subject? *How is it possible that, with increasing pedagogic sophistication, the number of children with problems is increasing?*

Sketch by Barbara and Jim Dale, USA, 1984

The question is not difficult to answer because the educational background contributes only in part to a person's total development. Besides, there are other decisive influences of a spiritual nature, such as the pressure of the *zeitgeist* ("spirit of the times") and especially the individual character of the person. Let us take a short look at these two powerful influences which are totally outside the teachers' control in order to understand that defective psychological development of adolescents is possible in families or other communities that provide all the requirements for an exemplary upbringing with love and steadfastness.

In order to characterise the *pressure of the zeitgeist*, I would like to take one of its many aspects which was discussed in a presentation on German television in 1984. It concerned brutality among school children. One-third of school injuries are caused by pupils attacking one another, by beating, scratching, biting or "finishing off" someone with a bicycle chain. About 400,000 such regrettable incidents are registered per year in Germany. The commentary on television was, "Violence is rampant in the schools and the parents are worried. The teachers, often just as shocked as they are helpless, raise the alarm. One accuses the other. Parents argue that teachers should know their trade and put a stop to these explosions of violence. Teachers pass the buck, saying that the children should learn proper behavior at home. However, some parents are virtually an example of aggression!"

Interviews with those involved indicated fairly clearly that it was not a question of responsibility. Teachers generally do their best and parents are on average far less aggressive than their children. However, two experts consulted during the program identified the problem by pointing to the circumstances of our time. The chairman of the Union for Education and Science, Dieter Wunder, said, "In recent years freedom has increased. This is welcomed by everybody. But with freedom, the insolence of children has increased as well." The chairman of the Society for Education and Development and former president of the World Teachers Association, Wilhelm Ebert, added, "It only seems to be easier for the children of today compared to previous generations. They don't have to worry about basic needs such as food, clothing, and accommodation. However, many adults are no longer able to transmit a sense of meaning to their children. Thus boredom and emptiness take over. These can suddenly turn into aggression."

With this statement, Wilhelm Ebert echoed a hypothesis which was formulated by Viktor Frankl at a time when pupils were still obediently sitting on their benches. It was in the 1920s and 1930s when Frankl saw the dawning of a new zeitgeist as a universal feeling of pathological meaninglessness. To counter this trend, he developed logotherapy; he saw that this feeling of meaninglessness had developed into a veritable crisis of the human being. Again, it would be unfair to blame parents for not transmitting enough meaning, for it is precisely this experience of meaning that cannot be *transmitted* but can only be *demonstrated*. It can be demonstrated by example and here we are again with the pedagogic example, the only means we have in the education process that benefits personality development.

Meaningful living can only be lived, but when the parents themselves doubt the meaning of their lives, and many of them suffer from just that (even more so if they have trouble with their children), then they are incapable of setting an example of meaningful living; with that, the vicious circle closes. Whether, however, a meaning crisis has to turn into aggression devoid of any meaning, or perhaps can be channeled into a constructive frustration that motivates a search for meaningful pursuits, depends on the uniqueness of each person. Of course, it is obvious that a child does not have the same opportunities as an adult, but even children don't have a confirmed right to abreaction of their annoyances or boredom. Even they have different ways of dealing with it and therefore they must be responsible for themselves to a certain degree, depending on age and insight.

We now come to a second great spiritual influence that is not in the teachers' hands and which gains importance for the adolescent with increasing age. It becomes even more important than the pressure of the zeitgeist, and that is *individuality*, or as Frankl put it, the singular uniqueness of each person, which begins to crystallize during youth and continues to be formed according to the individual's will and in a continuous working out of his unique character. The human being is not a dough whose ingredients of inherited factors are mixed and molded into the desired form by the hand of the educator and finally baked in the oven until done. Becoming a person is not that easy!

There is another totally unique and incalculable element, something that can't be deduced from genetic research or psychology or sociology, and that is the spiritual element in the person. Frankl referred to this in his book *Die Anthropologischen Grundlagen der Psychotherapie* (*The Anthropological Foundations of Psychotherapy*) with the noteworthy sentence: "The parents contribute their chromosomes in the act of procreation of a child but they do not breathe in the spirit."

This expression can be extended to the process of upbringing. The educator trains, praises, punishes, and sets an example, but even here, the spirit cannot be instilled. The *uncreatable* in the individual determines in the final instance what is to become with what was given to the human being in his or her creation. The *unmeasurable* in each person determines that which is psychologically measurable. This thought is simultaneously comforting and frightening; it shows that, with the creation of each human being, we must face a risk for which there are no guarantees, not even in the best homes or in wonderful times. However, it is comforting to know that the responsibility for a young life does not depend solely on pedagogic efforts. We are responsible for the example we set—but not for its effectiveness.

The reader might ask why I should begin recounting aspects beyond the reach of education if I want to talk about the handling of problem children. The reason for this is easily explained. The person who does not know about his pedagogic chance will not take it. But the person who is not aware of his pedagogic limitations will not be able to say *nevertheless "Yes" to the child* when the chances taken did not bring the result hoped for. The truth is not just that psychologically unstable parents cause disturbances in their children. It is also true that psychologically unbalanced children can easily cause disturbances in their parents. These parents experience themselves as unsuccessful in bringing up children, suffer from fear of failure, fight and blame each other, or otherwise react with acute inadequacy. Therefore, in order to stabilize a child, the persons involved in bringing it up must be stabilized first. This will not succeed by way of criticism or by pointing out mistakes, but only by way of encouragement, by helping them to accept the child *as he or she is* with love, without continuously searching within themselves for the causes of the child's failings and trying to repair them. Only when the nevertheless "Yes!" to the child is said on the foundation of admitting specific individuality, strengths and weaknesses, hereditary and acquired tendencies and disturbances, the entire spectrum of incipient personality under the influence of the spirit of the times, only then is it possible to deliberate together calmly on the best didactic approach to minimize the prevailing problems.

At present, unfortunately, we have a concept of the human being that is far too mechanical. It is a computer model, in which the person occasionally appears to just have a "screw loose" that has to be tightened up by the expert in order to get the "human entity" functional again. However, just as the teacher does not produce growth, the doctor does not produce physical health nor the psychologist mental health. The individual grows—and recovers—independently. The "screws" are, so to speak, self-threading. From the outside we can only contribute with either inhibiting or advancing impulses, hoping that they reach their goal. This is the situation with a psychologically disturbed child. At the time this disturbance began, the self was somehow involved; when the disturbance is removed, then it removes itself, too. The parent/educator can only add a small part and the best contribution, beyond all pedagogic, psychological skills, is a fundamental "Yes!" to the child, that kind of love which always includes a "nevertheless" whatever happens.

If, therefore, I mention a few guidelines that could make it easier for parents to live together with children or adolescents who manifest maladaptive behavior, then I don't do it believing I have a panacea for all possible difficulties, but rather with the conviction that somewhere in every difficulty there dwells a hidden meaning potential which, by fostering the growth of a love that has been tested in suffering and misery, was not found wanting.

The first guideline I would like to discuss has already been implied. It is to *maintain naturalness* in pedagogic behavior. In this respect, we can learn a great deal from Frankl's logotherapy. Not even in the application

of psychotherapy does it relinquish naturalness, although its methods
are applied in a very goal-oriented manner. Naturalness in psychology
and pedagogics does not imply thoughtless spontaneity, but rather tying
methodological approaches to the natural environment. This means that
therapeutic efficiency is maximized while the therapeutic situation is natural
and authentic. A beautiful example of such a "method-oriented naturalness"
in the medical field was reported in the *Medical Tribune* of March 23, 1984.
It concerned the idea of a pediatrician, Edgar Rey, of the San Juan de Dios
hospital in Bogota, Columbia. It read:

> Neonates with a weight of less than 1000 grams don't often
> survive in developing countries simply because there is a lack
> of incubators and other intensive-care facilities. The idea of this
> South American pediatrician is to wrap the premature baby
> tightly and warmly to the mother's breast. In this way, one
> of the main postpartum problems of insufficiently developed
> babies, namely, temperature regulation, solves itself. The natural
> nutrition of mother's milk furthermore eliminates a number of
> immunological and nutritional problems. Thus these children
> suffer far less often from diarrhea or constipation. This is
> in addition to the positive psychological effect of intensive
> mother-child bonding. The United Nations branch for child
> care, UNICEF, has declared the results of this type of caring as
> "dramatic"—in a positive sense. Three out of four babies with a
> birth weight of about 1200 grams survive with this new method.
> Until now, about 20 million underweight neonates have died
> every year throughout the world. The survival rate of children
> with a birth weight of between 1200 and 1800 grams has
> increased from 30% to 90%.

Although the problem of premature births is only indirectly related
to our subject, we can learn a very important lesson from it. On the
one hand, there is the *method* which is supposed to ensure temperature
regulation, feeding, protection against infection, etc. for the premature
babies. Certainly this is done efficiently in the incubator, but at the price
of sterility, artificiality, and loss of contact with the mother. On the other
hand, there is the natural behavior of every healthy woman. She loves to

cradle the baby to her breasts and give body contact, affection, and a sort of psychological closeness. But this instinctive maternal behavior by itself would not be sufficient for premature babies. However, the *combination of both* a methodological approach and a natural background provides optimal results. Let us learn from this example that method itself is not everything, not in psychology nor in psychotherapy and definitely not in everyday educational practice.

Whatever method we use with our children, whether careful distribution of praise and punishment, whether iron discipline or a coming together as partners, whether encouraging creativeness or balanced training, there should never be anything artificial, unnatural, or fake involved. Therefore methods should not be applied with extreme determination or stubbornness but must be handled effortlessly and flexibly, otherwise the entire milieu of education is under a shadow of darkness. Normal parents can't possibly hand out praise and punishment conscientiously without interruption. They must be able to say an unearned encouraging word—or scold "by mistake." They cannot be absolutely consistent either, because yielding, being persuaded, forgiving, and making peace are natural behaviors which somehow belong. Neither can they always be partners because there are situations in which parents and children simply are not partners. Neither should parents always design programs for the encouragement of their children's creativity or their balanced training because this would inhibit the natural development of their children's fantasy, which only emerges if the children have to think for themselves occasionally. Conversely, in dealing with children a teacher can't abdicate directiveness altogether; otherwise, a situation emerges that is similar to that of the Berlin kindergarten teacher who had an extremely antiauthoritarian and nondirective policy, and each day the children moaned: "Must we do what we want again today?"

What I want to say with all these examples is that we should not sacrifice our naturalness in handling children for a certain educational tactic which we read or heard about that promises success. Such a sacrifice would frustrate any success before it even materialized. (This observation can, unfortunately, be frequently made with children of teachers, psychologists, doctors, etc.)

Another important guideline which we should never surrender, besides naturalness, is of course *taking life and hope for granted*. This aspect is even more important, for if this taking for granted of certain basic values is lost once, then it is lost forever. Parents, for instance, who threaten suicide don't realize what they do to their children, for they negate the fact that we take life for granted—as good or bad as it may be—and they virtually germinate the idea that one can escape into death. Likewise, parents who repeatedly tell their difficult children that one day they will be sent to an institution gradually destroy the feeling that they unquestionably belong at home; this stance undermines the ability to take *home* for granted. There is no question that, under certain family circumstances, an institution or boarding school may be a better alternative. But, if this should be the case, then it should be presented as a meaningful, temporary solution for all parties involved and not as an imposed punishment implying banishment from home. One's home, just as life itself, is a fundamental value per se that should never be in question. The psychologically unstable person is especially very much at risk regarding experiences of this type: If nothing is safe for a person, neither the continuation of his or her existence, nor its meaning, nor its security, then hope is extinguished and so is the will to live.

We discussed the present high level of aggression among school children today, but we did not mention that there is also a silent aggression, of which educators are almost more afraid than the active one. This is found in children who tune out by taking the attitude, "I don't like it—leave me alone—nothing interests me—I won't do it." No reward or punishment has any effect, no promise entices, no threat scares them. No prospect of any kind can get them to move. They have lost hope. One could say they have lost the ability to take hope for granted, and that is a tragedy.

There is a tendency today, among adults as well, to talk things virtually into the ground. For instance, we talk about peace until we can't take it for granted any more. When peace is not taken for granted any longer, the possibility for war is born. There is also much talk in families about separating and leaving one another, and, with it, the peace in the family is undermined and cannot be taken for granted any longer. There are problems that become problems only through the attention given to them. Once they have been given a name, they become insurmountable obstacles in our way. May nobody accuse me of suppressing or hushing up real problems! For nearly two decades, I have dealt daily with the problems of strangers. However, it was precisely this work which taught me that *difficulties and worries actually belong in a completely normal life*. They represent a challenge to the human spirit rather than a danger to psychological health. However, magnifying problems prevents finding their solution. This even applies to the handling of children with maladaptive behavior. The more one talks with them about their misbehavior, the worse it becomes.

In any case, talking too much is not recommended. Gottfried Keller knew about this when he wrote: "I have observed that many persons who always have something to say never understand those persons who, because of them, can't get in a word edgewise."[5] These words of wisdom should be kept in mind considering our present trend to talk openly with children about everything. Here again, the rule applies that a method should not be pursued to its extreme if it contradicts simple naturalness.

Without words, we can let young persons entrusted to our care feel that, as a matter of course, "we are there for them"—by patient listening, by sharing with them, by trying to understand, by respecting their individuality. When confronted with their aggressiveness, we might hold on to the saying, "kindness disarms." However, this does not imply that the educator should give in all the time. A distance or boundary must be established from serious misbehavior, but even this distancing does not imply abandonment. One can step back but remain kind; one can say "No" to the child's actions but nevertheless say "Yes" to the child.

Until now, we have focused on maintaining naturalness and taking things for granted. We also turned to talking and discovered that, besides too little speaking, which is certainly detrimental from a pedagogic point of view, there is also too much, which not infrequently pushes children into resistance. I would like to discuss a second aspect to the subject "talking" that is found in Frankl's logotherapy and seems relevant here This no longer concerns the quantity but the quality of what is said. What and how is the best way to talk with problem children? In short, in my opinion one can say anything to them directly, as the words come to mind. However, there is one thing that must not happen and that is *iatrogenic damage*.

I have to explain what is meant in logotherapy by the word "iatrogenic" as I will return to this topic later to show that something very similar also happens in the field of pedagogics.

The word *iatrogenic* has its origin in the Greek word *iatros* which means "medical doctor" and the suffix "gen" always has to do with origin and genesis. "Iatrogenic" therefore means "caused by the doctor." Indeed, we know about neuroses and depressions in psychotherapy which are, as has been demonstrated by Viktor Frankl, caused by nothing other than thoughtless comments by a doctor or psychotherapist who unintentionally and unknowingly hurts the patient.

The worst I ever heard in this respect was the report by a totally insecure woman about something her psychoanalyst had said. He had treated her for four years without improvement. The doctor explained this to her in his own way. He said "Swallows born early enough have time for growing. They develop strong wings by autumn. Therefore it is easy for them to cross the Alps when winter approaches. Those swallows, however, who are born later in spring are not developed and strong enough when it gets cold. They also try to cross the Alps but in the icy high altitudes their strength is soon exhausted and they perish." Then the doctor added in a very friendly manner: "You see, you are like the swallows born late. You came too late for psychoanalysis and now I have not enough time to make you strong enough for the demands of life. You will never get well again."

One can imagine the effect of the doctor's words on this sensitive and already very depressed woman. She locked herself in her apartment and left the blinds down day and night because she could no longer stand the chirping of the swallows outside her window. She would have withered away in her apartment if a resolute friend hadn't got her out and brought her to me for counseling. It was difficult and took a lot of trouble to repair the iatrogenic damage.

Of course, this was an extreme case, but in psychology and pedagogics one has to be very careful, for such damage is sometimes generated in a very subtle manner. For instance, a mother seeking counseling told me casually that she was the second born of her parents. The first born had been born a year before but died soon after. She related that previously she had always felt positively about this because she thought that, after the loss her parents suffered, she was even more wanted. But when she told the story of the sibling who died before her own birth to her family doctor, he, with a stern expression, voiced the suspicion that, this being the case, she might only have been a "replacement" for her parents and that the parents' love was probably not meant for her but for her deceased sibling. This thought troubled the woman for many years, and the previously easygoing relationship with her parents was never the same. It must be admitted that, in both of these cases, totally senseless iatrogenic damage was caused which brought nothing but suffering.

As a last warning example, I would like to relate a dialogue that I listened to during doctors' rounds in a neurology clinic. The senior medical officer asked an alcoholic who had been in the clinic for several weeks how he was feeling. The patient replied that he was feeling comparatively well, except that on the previous weekend, on awakening in the large ward, he had experienced an anxiety attack. All his fellow patients on the ward had been up and about already; he had felt alone and abandoned and had become frightened of the future. The senior medical officer turned to the physician in charge, who stood next to him, and asked whether this anxiety attack could be regarded as an aftermath of his alcohol abuse, "No," she responded, "the patient has been dry too long for that. He is just a very unstable type of person…" "Aha!" said the senior medical officer and proceeded to the next bed. I don't know whether the reader can sense the drama in these few words. A person has been labelled as an "unstable type" by an expert and the supervisor's "Aha!" finalized the statement. How can such a patient ever regain self-confidence? How can the fight against addictive tendencies be taken up courageously? How can the future be faced, of which there is much fear, if such a negative self-evaluation results?

At this point we can cross over to the field of pedagogics which teaches that, for young people, anticipatory attitudes and identity-finding processes are crucial for their whole future. Concerning these anticipatory attitudes we must, however, distinguish between *external* expectations (that is, what others expect of a person) and *self*-expectations (that is, what a person expects of him- or herself). Generally, the greatest danger of external expectations is that they are too high and too positive. This places the person concerned under considerable stress and pressure and causes fear, because of the seeming impossibility or the extreme effort required to fulfill these expectations. But there is also a danger of too little and negative external expectations: They also inhibit development because they deprive the person of the trust and expectations of others who are loved or respected.

The greatest danger of self-expectations is that they are too low to begin with; the person concerned thinks too little or only negatively of self. At least since Seligman, we know about learned helplessness, which starts in childhood with low external expectations and is integrated into adult life with extremely low and negative self-expectations. Beginning with the attitude that one can't do something anyway prevents the person from accepting a task. The result is that, if one has to do the task, the individual is unable to accomplish it, for whatever reason. There is yet another extreme in self-expectations, namely those that are too high and unrealistic and cause a breakdown.

As noted, the human being is not a dough that is kneaded passively by events and the environment. One can't choose external expectations, especially as a child. However, self-expectations are controlled by the individual; even children have some chance to share control. Thus, low external expectations can be balanced with high self-expectations. This was demonstrated by an actor who became famous as a spectacularly muscled bodybuilder under the name "Conan." Due to the fact that my father-in-law was a teacher at his school, I know that the actor as a child was the frailest in his class. Nobody expected any physical achievement from him, nobody that is, except himself. He was not discouraged and exercised hard until he was able to show his amazing successes. In cases like this Frankl spoke of the *defiant power of the human spirit*, which is able to overcome miserable conditions and negative external expectations.*

Let us return to the problem of iatrogenic injury or "pedagogic damage," which we can now assign to the group of inadequately negative or low external expectations. For example, parents who say "you won't understand it anyway" or "you will never amount to anything" can lower self-expectations considerably if their children can't muster enough defiant power to withstand these damaging predictions. It is especially the psychologically disturbed child and the psychologically unstable adult who are most vulnerable to this kind of diminished external expectation.

Therefore, in working with children let us beware of exposing them to external expectations that are either too high or too low, but especially *too negative*. In case of doubt I would even suggest that we should expect a little too much rather than too little. Let us trust that even children who exhibit neurotic symptoms with bizarre behavior can still develop into happy and healthy adults. This trust would be our greatest service of love for them, the best package that we can offer them for the road to independence.

I once happened to witness a group activity in a children's home. Cards were played, and after each game places were changed. Suddenly one of the chairs was declared a magic chair, and whoever managed to sit on it would win the game. Indeed, the next few rounds were won by the players in the magic chair. Then it was the turn of a pale little girl and, as she climbed onto the chair, she whispered softly: "I am unlucky; for me it won't work!" And she lost.

It was a game of chance and I won't draw any conclusions from it, but today we know that the attitude of expectation has an enormous, mysterious power to attract precisely what is expected. We should keep this in mind when dealing with children who have all types of problems. As long as they consider themselves "unlucky," they *are* unlucky. Let us help them to abandon the role of being unlucky and their run of luck will begin. Let us

---

* [American readers best know the actor who played the title role in Conan the Barbarian as Arnold Schwarzenegger. —Editor]

not psychologize them but rather normalize them by addressing them as partners with a potential for developing, whose every option is still open, however hopeless the present situation may appear. The human spirit certainly has more in reserve than pedagogics can imagine!

This should conclude the subject of "talking." Let us now turn to our last subject for discussion, which may seem surprising. It is *thinking*. It concerns thoughts that parents have about the difficulties faced by children as well as the parents' own need to cope with these challenges. As is well known, everything in life can be viewed from a different perspective and correspondingly assumes a different significance. This significance in turn determines the so-called "organic resonance" that is the biological reaction of the body which is closely related to the psychological condition. For children, the different perspectives start in the womb. One can be very happy about the expected child or one can have serious reservations. No pregnant woman can be blamed if she has valid reasons for tending towards reservations, but undoubtedly the pregnancy will be more of a biological strain for her in this case.

Should children have a disability or show unusual traits in their psychological development, most parents would be concerned about it. Regardless, few parents remain indifferent or disown these children, and those who do we will disregard because they are beyond this narrative. Those who are alarmed, however, adopt some form of mental attitude to the problem confronting them and I am concerned with this *inner attitude* because it determines both the well-being and the suffering of a family.

Frankl's logotherapy repeatedly outlines the danger of *hyperreflection*, which occurs whenever someone keeps brooding over some worries and thoughts keep circling around the problems; a total fixation eventuates. The consequences are catastrophic. Everything else that is not related to the topic and is perhaps perfectly intact loses importance, while the hyper-reflected worry is blown up to a gigantic dimension and usurps the person's total life perspective. Furthermore, the person's organic immune system is weakened; as a result, vulnerability to disease greatly increases.

From American long-term studies in cancer research, we learn that, in the first years after the loss of a partner, whether by divorce or death, the cancer risk increases five- to tenfold. This is only the case when the loss is hyperreflected, that is, the remaining partner can't come to terms with the loss and thoughts are focused on blaming fate and brooding over the causes of the loss.

Parents who can't come to terms with the physical or psychological disability of a child and keep on fighting it or are despondent about it are in the same danger. Obviously, parents will try everything possible to help their child. But there is a time when one has to come to terms with the situation, even if it is only the realization that time and patience are needed. Now, it is essential not to hyperreflect on the problem so as not to endanger one's own health as well, but rather to remain composed and focus one's thoughts on existing positive elements to make the best of a given situation. That is sheer artistry, a remarkable human achievement that can be consciously and deliberately intended and accomplished! To bring out the best in whatever exists, it must not only be perceived in all its fullness, but the totality of all its latent meaning potentials must also be recognized. The best can only be chosen from a selection of what is good. Therefore, in order to find the best, one must recognize what is good.

I would, therefore, urgently appeal to parents and educators of so-called "problem children" not to be misled into continuous worrying about these disturbances. This would draw them into the whirlpool of hyperreflection. They would only hurt themselves, their health would suffer and they would not help their children either. Rather, they should muster an inner readiness for focusing on the meaning potential of the given situation. There is no other way of doing this than to be satisfied and work with what choices exist and to focus on what is "good."

This brings us back to our initial considerations, in which we established that many circumstances are not in the hands of the educator. Thus, there is today no longer a childhood in the true sense of the word, nor even a stage of puberty. Childhood has been violated by the media, which carry by way of television all the processes of adulthood into the nurseries where they cause a relentless "enlightenment" of a general nature so that the children grow up at a rapid rate. Puberty has to a large extent been robbed of its functions by the "emancipation of youth." As there are scarcely any ties to the home left, the process of detachment from home becomes a farce which retards the process of maturing. Growing up too fast and maturing too slowly; lost childhood and premature adulthood; the fascination of technology and claims in the name of freedom as provocation; all this burdens the process of bringing up children today. There are many other factors, but enumerating them would not help to improve the situation. Let us make the best of what we have and accept it. Let us be an example, but let us hand over responsibility step by step; the next generation needs its tasks too. We cannot protect them, nor can we do their tasks for them!

If we maintain the naturalness of behavior and are able to take life and hope for granted, if we keep verbal communication with our children to a healthy average and don't expose them to any external expectations that are too negative, and finally if we face our problems seriously but quietly and keep our eyes open for nonproblematic matters that also still exist and provide strength for coping with the rest, that is utterly sufficient and then we have done our duty.

The science of psychology has dedicated itself to the uncovering of faults in education with the most careful precision. It can't be denied that a number of psychological inhibitions in children can be traced back to shortcomings in their upbringing. But, coming to the end of my exposition, please permit me to comment: In divorce proceedings, the principle of guilt has now been abolished and likewise the principle of guilt in educational problems should gradually be reviewed. If 13-year-olds are old enough for sexual intimacies, which was indicated as the "lower limit" by the Institute for Sexual Research in Frankfurt, and if 18-year-olds want to be socially accepted with full majority in our complex world, then the age groups in between must already take some of the responsibility for what they do or don't do and can't blame their parents for every failure.

For example, taking at random one mistake in upbringing, spoiled toddlers naturally can't be blamed for their outrageous behavior since it is frequently the result of pampering. Spoiled adolescents, however, have an increasing choice whether they want to exploit the pampering situation or not. There are quite gratifying examples of young people who voluntarily renounce excessiveness. The fact that it is easy to extract money or presents from parents by no means justifies doing it. A thief who intrudes into an unlocked house is still a thief.

We see that it would be a cheap shot for young people to squeeze their parents dry, then turn around and insist it was the parents' own fault for spoiling them. It isn't that simple. Adolescents can, concurrently with their spiritual maturation, reject positive influences from their educators. We have to accept that. But they can just as well brush off negative influences from educators and free themselves from the confines of faulty upbringing. Simply put, there is no psychological disturbance of adolescents which is outside their power of self-control except if it has an organic basis.

Therefore, let us confidently take up the task of rearing children. Let us not be afraid of making mistakes, but rather endeavor to be an "honorable" model and trustingly leave the future to the coming generation as its responsibility. Above everything, however, let us never stop saying "Yes!" to our children—perhaps one day they may again say "Yes!" to us parents.

3. The Career Woman:
Between Stress and Fulfillment

Recently I found an item in a newspaper, one of many of its kind:

> More and more women between the ages of 30 and 50
> tend towards depression. According to observations by
> psychologists, the women are usually married, they live in
> comfortable financial circumstances, and they themselves don't
> know why they should feel so wretched. The women feel there
> are too many demands on them. They therefore tend to worry
> and blame themselves for burdening husband and children
> with their condition. Frequently, their marriages suffer.

I would like to examine this passage, for it contains much that, in my opinion, is unacceptable. What is stated here? Many women feel wretched, they are "depressed." "Depressed" certainly not in the sense of a clinical diagnosis but rather in terms of the modern trend which labels any kind of dark mood with this designation.

Furthermore, this excerpt sounds an alarm signal: *More and more* women are depressed; more and more women are psychologically troubled. What kind of women are they? Like the women in developing countries whose children die in their arms of starvation? Or like the women in the Eastern World who have to labor for many hours each day until they are exhausted? No, neither of these. Most of them are comfortably married, have healthy children; some work, some don't; most are in secure financial circumstances and don't know why they should feel wretched. Strange, isn't it? One might subtly comment that the human being obviously can't cope with good times.

This was observed by psychologists, who are trained to be skillful observers. What becomes apparent here are actually the shadows of a widespread discomfort that has been observed for a few decades, which has been particularly noticeable since the economic boom in our countries. To be sure, there is a great chasm between observing a phenomenon and interpreting it; psychologists have never been as good at interpreting as they are at observing. There were frequent misinterpretations in the particular newspaper item in which the increasing tendency of women toward depression is explained with the statement: "The women feel there are too many demands on them and therefore they tend to worry and to blame themselves." This statement is far from the truth and can only be understood in terms of an outdated psychology that is no longer relevant.

To really understand this outmoded way of thinking we must remember that psychology began at a time of much misery, oppression, unemployment and, last but not least, two World Wars in Europe. Naturally, this had its effect on the new science. Psychologists naturally started from the premise that the individual must be happy provided no deprivations are experienced. Since psychologists did not feel responsible for external living conditions such as unemployment or war, they concentrated on somehow removing people's inner troubles in order to lead them to happiness. The intention was pure, but unfortunately things went wrong. For happiness is ultimately not "being free *from*" something but rather "being free *for*" something.

In any case, for 50 years psychology made an honest effort to eliminate the individual's inner needs. The first step was to free the human being from any torment due to drive pressures. In particular, each person should be able to release sexual and aggressive drives without complications. That the relief of one person can only take place at someone else's expense was accepted as an inevitable side effect. The psychological maxim being voiced was "don't suppress anything, don't displace anything." Regarding others, it was whispered, "That is *their* problem." This creates a curious contradiction: In previous centuries, those in Western culture had to cope without the help of psychology, while today families are shattered despite the presence of the abundant knowledge of a psychology that "wants to offer happiness" available for support.

But the intended liberation from inner trouble was pursued. Following the deinhibition of drives came the liberation from authority. "Don't put up with anything" was the new motto handed out to both parents and children. "Resist, be assertive, be able to say 'No'" were the new prescriptions for happiness. Pedagogics, a sister field of psychology, took up the maxims and dared to advance to the brink of chaos, as we discussed above. In the meantime, liberation from all social restrictions had progressed. "Do your own thing" was psychology's headline for all its efforts, encouraging ego strengthening with every word of its literary deluge. Doubts? There is a very effective antidote against them: "Others are to blame for your misery !"

"The insults of your mother, your father, and the environment are all to blame for your misbehavior!" How wonderful! Even liberation from a bad conscience seemed to work. What obstacle was left on the way to happiness? Nothing at all. Inner inhibitions had become "removable" by psychologists. Even external conditions started changing. By the end of the 1950s, prosperity had arrived. In the meantime, individuals had learned to demand satisfaction for their drives. Suddenly free from authority and norms and with well-strengthened egos, they could satisfy all their desires without problems, whether for consumer goods, sex partners, demonstrations of power, or a rejection of any excessive demands. Everything was oriented purely to satisfy desires. In terms of psychological dogmatics, they had to be deliriously joyful, infinitely happy. Yet, at this very moment, the house of cards collapsed—never before had the people of our progressive "first world" been so unhappy and psychologically ill as in our present culture of narcissism.[6]

With great difficulty, psychologists are learning to revise their thinking. In many areas, it has to start from scratch. Today it is still in this process of renewal; the guidelines provided by Viktor Frankl are most helpful. It was Frankl who warned that the human being's priority is not to be free *from* something but rather to be free *for* something. Put simply, it is not sufficient for an individual to throw out obligations, connections, and claims and to foreclose on a vacuum with every need satisfied. Rather, it is of primary importance for the person to make something meaningful of life, to be there for something, to be good for something, simply to be free to choose from the opportunities life offers.

How is this related to the situation of the working woman? It is relevant to the extent that it affects the self-perception of each individual, including that of the working woman. As long as the idea persists that the unhappy woman *has* to be unhappy because she can't satisfy enough of her demands and desires, every unhappiness will be decoded in terms of those factors that could prevent happiness, so-called stress factors that confine a woman and put her under pressure. It is too easy to forget that, in the absence of stress, happiness is not ensured either, as is often demonstrated in times of prosperity. Indeed, sometimes this idea is so forcefully defended that, even in situations where positive living conditions prevail, some obscure stress factors are presumed to have caused the unhappiness. The newspaper excerpt at the beginning of the chapter makes this point: Depressed women in comfortable circumstances must feel that they are under "excessive demands."

It can be assumed that exactly the opposite is true. Something like the overexertion of strength is possible, but it rarely has its source in prosperous financial conditions and even less often does it lead to depression. It usually is a certain basic dissatisfaction with life that grows out of conditions of prosperity and overshadows the emotions. One could say this is more often the effect of a lack of *spiritual challenge*, "having without knowing for what," a "being without knowing why"; it is experiencing one's existence detached from higher goals or deeper values.

Why do the women in the article worry so much? Why do they blame themselves? They are searching for something; this search applies not only to them but to all of humankind. They are searching for something but not for marketable commodities or for need satisfaction. They have all these. They seek a spiritual horizon to restore a sense of orientation and meaning. For thousands of years, the evolving human being was still partly animal; instincts dictated behavior. More recently, for thousands of years the person was a being who created culture and the prevailing traditions dictated what to do. Today, the human being is in turmoil and change. Neither instincts nor traditions serve as strict guides. Human beings must now decide on their goals, objectives, and destinations. Each person must travel through life being self-responsible.[7] Many people who are depressed without apparent reason fail in this arena. They are not depressed by the stress factors in their living conditions but rather by the fact that the meaning of their life is in question.

Let us turn to the specific situation of the *career woman*. This situation is something entirely new in the development of the human being, at least in our society. This does not, however, imply that women of former ages did not work. On the contrary, we can assume that women never had any time off. Because of this, they never had any opportunity to apply themselves to works of art or to the sciences. Women were engaged around the clock at home (if we disregard those of "high society"). It was the woman's task to bring up an often large number of children under poor and primitive conditions that we can't even imagine today. On the farm or in trade, the women diligently helped their partners to supplement the family income. They worked hard virtually all day and never talked about stress, but, of course, the word "stress" did not exist then. By no means is it my intention to glamorize those times and declare all the women of the past happy. Some of them surely suffered terribly. But they had one advantage: They did not ask about the meaning of their activities; it was quite obvious. The meaning concerned their and their children's survival, the overcoming of the forces of nature, and the struggle for provisions. Being or not Being. And being able to Be was meaning enough.

In our time, on the other hand, being able to Be has become a matter of course. It is nothing special any longer, not a blessing or a gift. In fact, sometimes it is perceived as an unpleasant burden to have to Be. Today's women who don't want to do the housework can use machines and buy precooked meals. Women who do not want to go to work can remain at home, supported by the men and relatives or, if need be, by welfare. Women who don't want any children take the Pill or if there is an "accident" they give their children up for adoption. Women who don't want to be tied down stay single or get a divorce. They have their own salary without having to share with anybody.

Whatever lifestyle she prefers, her ability to Be is secure in any case. It takes a lot of work for someone's life to be allowed to "go down the drain." In this sphere of "being in any case," the question for a motive for individual actions is on a different level than in the past. Whereas previously action was essentially a means for maintaining one's existence, today existence can be maintained as a means for doing something. The question is no longer "what will I do in order to live?" but rather "I live in order to do what?"

The restructuring of the question has not been as abrupt for men as it has for women. Historically, men have had an aspect of their lives—their chosen career or occupation—that pointed beyond a mere maintenance of being to an objective task. Of course, the shoemaker and the blacksmith were working to support their families, but they certainly wanted to produce good shoes or useful metal implements as well. This indicates that the meaning of their work was manifold; it reached beyond the satisfaction of personal and family needs into the environment which was to be formed and was simultaneously a test of ability. Even today, more often than not, men see more than just a source of income in their occupation. They are interested in it, involved in it, and extend the scope of their work into their personal life sphere.

In contrast, women had to adapt. For centuries they dedicated themselves to serving the family. They hardly knew any work besides that for the family. The meaning of their labor was the family who benefited by it. Suddenly they were tossed about by the waves of a psychologically underpinned emancipation and confronted with occupations that have nothing whatsoever to do with their family if one disregards the money they perhaps contribute to the family coffers. The new aspect in occupational employment of the modern woman is thus not the fact of her being productive, but the fact that it is *externally centered*. It begins with her leaving the home, which is very significant for the children, and it continues as she enters a different sphere of life outside the home, a new sphere whose meaning she had been unaware of from time immemorial.

This is where the weak link in the whole structure appears. Today's women have more or less lost the meaning of their work at home, but the meaning of their career work has only partially become clear. They are placed *between two value blocks,* looking skeptically at both of them. From a historical perspective, compared to men, women have had far less time for learning to integrate these values optimally. Nevertheless, the integration can succeed and can actually be an enrichment for the woman's whole existence. In that event, however, we have to cease all the endless talk about stress and have to associate occupational work with the dawning of some meaning.

This again leads us back to the approach of logotherapy, which focuses exactly on this weak point that characterizes modern life, undiminished in spite of all liberation from psychological inhibitions and all remnants of prosperity. It is the instability of a generation that has no guidelines either from instincts or from traditions, the changed situation of women who have to exchange or replenish an ancient sphere of meaning for a new one if they do not want to waste away in a spiritual vacuum in the midst of their daily hectic life.

If one works in a psychological clinic and frequently counsels unhappy women, as I do, then it is apparent that the question of meaning is a central and fundamental problem; it is far more extensive and pervasive than excessive demands, failure, or other troubles. Women from all walks of life come for consultations, women without a family and without a career, as well as women with the burden of both. There are typical housewives with families and career women who are alone.

Do these different living conditions lead to different attitudes to life? Unfortunately, I have to reply in the negative. Wherever dissatisfaction with life or a feeling that all activity is meaningless arises, they are completely identical. Indeed, sometimes one could foster the suspicion that the patients feel worse the better their living conditions are, just as was implied in the newspaper article.

Women with *neither* family *nor* career complain about the emptiness and uselessness of their lives, about the loneliness that paralyzes them and the monotony of the passing days. On the other hand, women with *both* family *and* career complain about being terribly tied down, about being torn between both obligations and the feeling of not doing justice to either of them. Nevertheless, in spite of all this, they report never finding peace or time for themselves. Women who are busy *only* in the family cultivate their inferiority complexes and feel cut off from the world. They feel financially dependent, their personal development inhibited and exploited by the family, as if they were Cinderellas who may begin to feel they are too dumb to achieve anything better.

Again, women with only a career but no family feel that they have missed the most important part of their lives. They yearn for partnership and motherhood and are afraid the ceiling will cave in on them when they unlock the dark apartment in the evening where nobody is waiting for them. The reader may decide whether it is indeed stress that gets these people down. Is it a case of unfulfilled wishes and drives that can't be lived to the full? Is it worry and self-recrimination that cause depression? Do external conditions darken the joy of life?

Is it not rather the case that in the complaints of these unhappy women a meaning perception for the *other* woman's situation is reflected, but that the willingness to admit meaning potentials in their *own* situation is lacking? How would it be if women without a family or a career did not complain about the meaninglessness and monotony of their days while women with a family and a career were happy about being indispensable in their position and the rich variety of their daily lives? Conversely, how would it be if women with a family and a career did not complain about being tied down and exhausted, while women without a family and a career were happy about their momentary rest and the chance for reorientation and contemplation?

Similar considerations apply, of course, for the other constellations. Instead of women who live for their family only feeling like an inferior Cinderella, women who carry out the duties of only a career could be proud of their independence and capabilities which give them self-confidence and self-confirmation. Instead of women with a career only crying for a nonexistent family, women who are the soul of the family could be thankful for the happiness of partnership and motherhood which is to be guarded and preserved.

We women have all of these meaning potentials open to us depending on our different circumstances and, in addition to this, a colorful range of sidelines that are not entirely without meaning; for example, advanced studies, hobbies, contacts with friends, church work, traveling, artistic or handicraft interests, and sports and games. However, we must be prepared to detect and accept the challenge of each concrete situation. There simply is no situation in human life, even if it is extremely confined and wretched, that does not contain the possibility for some kind of meaning. There is always a spiritual attitude towards it that is psychohygienically optimal because it allows us to perceive the best option in any situation and bring it into focus. My patients taught me a simple truth: *What is positive is in ourselves or it is nowhere.* Our environment does not present us with positive things on a silver platter. It is much more something we have to radiate into our environment from the very place where we happen to be. Then we will rediscover it wherever we look.

In this context, Frankl talks about healthy *noödynamics*, where *noös* indicates meaning and *dynamic* a movement, thus, a movement of the human spirit. In Frankl's view, one must not become static or remain fixed in any condition, not even in a complete inner balance (homeostasis), which can't be achieved anyway. The human being must be in a certain state of tension throughout life—under a well-balanced tension between To Be and Should Be. This tension can be reduced only by doing, thinking, and acting.

For instance, a mother busy mending her children's clothes is intuitively aware of this tension. Being is the torn clothing and Should Be is the tidy dressing of the children. Both can only be reconciled if the mother takes up the work or perhaps buys new clothes. This could perhaps be justified if the time is more urgently needed for something else besides mending, that is for another Should which is in a still higher tension to another To Be. In any case, by mending the clothes she will gain a calm feeling of meaning in her existence, which has to do with fulfilling the demands of the Should.

Someone may object that the continuous subjugation under some Should obligation or other forces people into terrible constraints. He or she forgets that constraints are those environmental demands that are resented by the person concerned. A constraint, for example, would be an obligation handed down from mother to daughter that she should in the future mend her own clothing, while the daughter thinks that there is no hurry about the mending as there are still enough clothes in her closet and dresser.

In noödynamics we do not refer to an external obligation with which one does not identify. We refer to the Should which is open to one's own ego, to the one task for which I am needed here and now, the unique challenge in a specific, never to be repeated, situation. If we perceive this one—noödynamic—task, confirm it and meet it, the reward perhaps may be work, trouble, stress… and yet, it is fulfillment.

What will the consequence be regarding a career? Everyone will say the circumstances of our career efforts are 90% externally determined. Admittedly, this is so. Others, our superiors, tell us what to do, or if we are in a responsible position ourselves, then the circumstances will dictate the directions to be taken. However, I would like to bargain for the remaining 10%. Every career of whatever type harbors some small, undefined free area that is structured by nobody else but the person employed in the job. It is an area full of potentials that do not arise from the duty roster of the employer but exclusively from the noödynamic sensitivity of the employee. Or, if the employer and employee are identical, they don't arise from an objective duty but only from an individual commitment. These are, to put it simply, the practical opportunities for finding meaning in one's career.

That this possibility is unrestrictedly open, even in very simple jobs that leave very little room for creativity, is demonstrated by the story of the custodian related by Bishop Georg Moser[8] to explain the meaning potential of every job. Some years ago, the custodian in our story received the Federal Merit Award because he had untiringly collected broken and discarded toys from trash bins and had restored each of them in the evenings in order to present them to underprivileged children. Let us consider that this person could have made a different choice. He could have spent his evenings sitting gloomily in front of a beer bottle watching television, have lost in thoughts of self-pity, brooding about the unfairness of fate. Here he was, lonely, without a family, and with a dead-end, low-paying job.

And what did he actually do with it? To his daily work, meaningful in any case, he added another dimension of meaning. It was the transformation of worthless junk into something valuable that richly filled his leisure time. The presentation to underprivileged children created an interpersonal bridge for him from his loneliness into the environment. This example illustrates what is expressed in the saying: "What is positive is in ourselves or it is nowhere."

I stated that every job has the opportunity for individual initiative and modification about 10% of the time, even if it is only the attitude one takes towards the work each day. For the custodian, this small area of freedom consisted of choosing whether to save usable materials from the dumpster.

Passivity, however, is not always the alternative with less meaning. There can also be situations where it is more meaningful to neglect something; for instance, total physical exhaustion in the service of some ambitious plan. The friendly word to a colleague that creates fellowship can be more important than the gathering of praise from the boss, which also expedites isolation. A relaxed management team can create a better working climate than strict controls that produce mistrust. A coffee break may be more beneficial than climbing a few more rungs in the corporate ladder, especially for working mothers who have to be fit after work as well. The "one thing that is necessary now"—how difficult to describe it, how complicated to define it in general terms, but how easily it can nevertheless be discovered by the person whose orientation is the meaning of the moment!

It is said about women that we are more emotional than rational, more oriented to persons than to objects in our thinking and attention. This may even contain a grain of truth, although the exception proves the rule. It is certain that a woman's psyche reacts differently from that of a man in certain areas. This implies that, with the emerging career woman, new perspectives have been introduced into the world of work, which had been until recently shaped entirely by men. I don't refer to any feminization of work as such but to a wider amplitude of performance styles at work. At the same time, it presents the opportunity to add a touch of humanity to the calcified routines of each occupation. A mixture of female intuition and motherly dedication can be beneficial in many situations.

It is not without cause that women are so widely employed in pedagogic and caring areas. Being able to care for someone is built in to their genetic code from their biological conception and it is a violation of the female character to fixate this caring exclusively on herself. A woman does not have to become a mother in order to be happy. She does not have to marry to find happiness. But every woman must be allowed *to care for someone.* Somewhere she must be able *to give*, otherwise she cannot receive happiness much less "actualize herself," which incidentally, is by no means the highest goal of human endeavor.

The self is not actualized in a vacuum. The self is only an abstract concept that never concretely exists by itself. What do exist always are meaning potentials in a reality which is the reality of humankind, and this human self is formed by realization or default of these potentials.

A woman must be able to give somewhere and that has nothing to do with any helper syndrome but only with the essence of all human existence, which is characteristically oriented towards a *being for someone or for something*. In man perhaps more a *being for something*, in woman perhaps more a *being for someone*. But fundamentally it is oriented towards a transcendence of self in terms of a task to be accomplished by the self.

"Being for someone" could perhaps even be combined with a career; if not as an intrinsic part of an occupation, then at least within that 10% of personal freedom which can be utilized in every activity. It may also happen that the being for someone finds its focal point outside the career, such as in the family. But if the career offers little opportunity and there is no family then the being for someone must at least move into leisure time. If this does not happen, something worse than depression threatens: emptiness.

Some time ago, a woman came to me for treatment. She had divorced her husband because he was an alcoholic and she had aborted his child. A few weeks after the divorce the husband had died. Thus she was now alone but she had a good career as she worked as a librarian in a large library. There she had good contact with the patrons whom she loved to advise in detail. However, one day a new task was assigned to her. She was asked to recatalog all the books. For this she was given a room separated from the public where she could make the inventory quietly, without disturbance. And this was when she suddenly had a breakdown.

In this case, the existential vacuum can be clearly recognized in the total absence of any being for someone. Being for the classification of waist-high stacks of books does not close that gap. The psychological breakdown of the woman was obviously precipitated by the restructuring of her work; however, *it was precipitated, not caused.* The causes are not located in the sterile surroundings of her new job, but rather in the long, drawn-out process of neglecting meaning potentials in the area of interpersonal relationships. The only bridge to other people in this woman's life was her contact with the readers, and when that was interrupted the entire bridge collapsed.

I am in no position to judge whether the divorce was really inevitable. The partnership with an alcoholic is doubtless a very heavy load to bear. Sometimes it is too heavy for an individual's strength. Nevertheless, even this fate has its meaning potentials, and considering the fact that her husband had died so soon after the divorce, we must assume that he was seriously ill. We cannot reject the notion that the woman was the last vestige of security for her husband or could have been. Neither do I want to condemn the abortion. Doubtless the man would, in any case, not have been able to fulfill his role as father and it is really not easy to raise a child by oneself. Yet this task, too, contains its meaning potentials and if one asks single-parent mothers whether they regret being a mother, one usually hears that they can no longer imagine a life without their child.

However, even if we suppose that both decisions of the woman were right or inescapable, the question arises: With what kind of meaning did she fill her life *instead of* the interpersonal tasks she rejected? Indeed, there was little. She distrusted men, did not know how to deal with women, had developed no hobbies and wasted her weekends with house cleaning. She had preferred an *empty* life to a *difficult* one by making her career her sole daily duty roster. That is dangerous.

To this example, I would like to attach two warnings for the working woman. One we have already discussed. It is *the necessity of being for someone*, of which we should never lose sight, even for those who are totally absorbed in their careers, have very little leisure time, and are always very busy. It is contrary to the character of human beings—and totally against that of a woman—not to have a close relationship with another or a relationship of love in the widest sense, which embraces caring for children, friendships, common interests, and so on.

The second warning links up with the first. It concerns the *one-sidedness* of a career. A career is an important and valuable part of life but it should not become one's *whole* life. A career should not become an idol[9]; otherwise the worker may fall into a vacuum on retirement, if not before. Not only that, but every sickness, every holiday or day off can turn into a catastrophe. Also, any change of career that affects the familiar working conditions, as is often the case today through the advances in computers and technology, could become a catastrophe. It is truly a psychotherapist's nightmare to see the coming generation, every single individual of which one day will sit in a room in front of a computer and there will study, communicate, shop, and work. The psychotherapist would in no way be able to cope with the resulting flood of psychospiritually deformed persons!

Logotherapeutic treatment always has the aim of opening the patient to concrete meaning potentials and increase awareness of the responsibility that goes together with freedom. In the case of the librarian, we joined together. The questions were: How could her private life be made more value intensive? How could her interpersonal skills be improved? In what ways might it be possible to find additional meaning within her career?

It was by no means easy for me to introduce such a spiritual struggle; to begin with, the patient had been drugged with tranquilizers by her doctor to such an extent that she could hardly say her name, much less discuss meaning opportunities in her life. The theory that stress is, without question, at the root of all nervous crises (which can only be relieved by more or less artificially induced tranquility) had triumphed again. Only after in-depth consultations with her physician by telephone, after making sure that no psychosis was present, and after explaining that no situational overexertion was at the root of the problem but rather an existential vacuum, was the road clear for the reduction of the psychopharmaceutics and the beginning of our logotherapeutic talks.

Soon it was a gladdening experience for me to observe how this woman, once she had been set on the right track, brought her own ideas and suggestions to the enrichment of her life and to see her childlike joy in savoring all her different opportunities. After only a short time, she mustered her courage and went to her church's office, where she was granted permission to display a large poster offering a weekly literary circle for lay people. This was the best idea she could have had. This literary circle, which still exists, was exactly the right answer to our questions. It gives her a full private life in that she has to prepare book reviews or selections of texts at home. The circle offers her interpersonal relationships from which, even at this very moment, a harmonious relationship is blossoming and it adds another meaning factor to her career that had been lacking. Her extensive knowledge of the book market enables her to make recommendations to bookworms and to find suitable authors for everyone's taste. It is superfluous to say that as a result of this therapy-initiated idea not only has the woman herself recovered but a number of other people have also benefitted from it.

I mentioned at the beginning that thinking in psychology is gradually beginning to change. Cases like the one above suggest that it is by no means always efficacious to dig up old history. If I had made the woman's marriage traumas and any issues about her pregnancy the center of our consultation she could have "talked it off her chest" in endless hours of talks; however, nothing would have happened to her present situation. Instead, she learned that every phase of life, every career development, indeed, every moment of existence has its positive opportunities and that the sum total of all choices made and experienced makes up the fullness of life.

Therefore, I would like to give this advice to career women: Don't be afraid of stress; rather, fear the feeling of meaninglessness about the things you do or don't do, and—by acting on them—don't let it arise at all!

Never exchange a hard life for an empty one; you will regret it bitterly. Don't make your career into an idol. Your career is no god. Rather, discover and embrace each and every meaning dimension contained in your career. Then your work will offer you infinitely more than just a salary. And, as commonplace as it may sound, besides your career, don't forget love. In addition to being for something, the crowning achievement of human life—and especially a woman's life—is being for someone.

We don't always have favorable conditions. There are also dark hours and lonely hours, hours full of suffering, and yet we are involved in directing and responsibly shaping every hour of our life. Rainer Maria Rilke was so right when he wrote:

> If your daily life seems poor,
> Do not blame it;
> Blame yourself,
> Tell yourself that you
> Are not poet enough
> To call forth its riches.

4. The Career Man:
Between Success and Dedication

I have more women than men in my psychotherapeutic consultations. For this reason, I have paid more attention to the problems of women and mothers up to this point. May men, and especially fathers, not rebuke me for this. Their worries will have their turn too. And today's fathers have serious problems: As shocking as this may seem, they are increasingly deprived of their children.

In the annual records of our clinic, patient data are calculated statistically. It becomes apparent that, on average, only about one-third of the children attending our clinics live with their natural fathers. All other children have either no father, a substitute, or friends of their mother serve as uncle figures. Considering the fact that the children are usually brought to us because of some developmental disturbance, the conclusion seems obvious that the father, and by this I mean the biological father, plays an important role in the process of bringing up children.

It is not as easy to replace the father as divorce and separation procedures seem to suggest. Children need a father and mother. They need the love of both and they need to respect both of them. I have the deep suspicion that fathers in particular get short-changed, both regarding the love to be given and also the respect to be received when a family breaks up. Usually they turn into "Sunday Daddies" who try to compensate for the insidious estrangement from their children with material offerings, while paying alimony for the consequences of actions for which they are no longer permitted to be responsible.

This does not imply that all orphans of divorce would be better off with their fathers than with their mothers. Neither do I have an answer to the question of how best to divide the children of a broken marriage, for the question as such is already a poor answer to a quite different question confronting all parents: How do they together do justice to the self-imposed parental duties? In reality, parents cannot divide their children; they can only lose them, and, as noted, the fathers are generally the losers.

In this connection, the law usually points to the fact that fathers have a career that claims their full attention. Certainly a career is a large part of the father's life. It is part of his identity but it would be wrong to claim that his earnings come first, and only then comes everything else for which the money was earned. It would be just as mistaken as the saying "primum vivere deinde philosophari," which could be translated as "first glut yourself, then moralize." My old teacher commented on this one evening over a dinner in Vienna: "You know, Doctor, it is exactly the opposite: *Without morals one can't overcome hunger.*"

It is somewhat similar with a man's career. Without a meaning or purpose in his daily work load, he would not be able to cope with it. Without a family that he can support, without children for whom he can provide, and without some other goal toward which he can aim, all his income counts for nothing. For that reason, the tragedy of fathers who lose their children has a greater impact in our divorce-happy society than is visible at first sight. Not only do children lose their fathers and with them a significant part of parental example and parental relationship, but the place where the fathers' industriousness is applied loses some of the working capacity of those fathers. When the wherefore at work becomes clouded, the energy investment decreases drastically. Thus broken marriages represent losses in the sphere of work; worries about the family become initiators of career failure.

At this point, I would like to add a few fundamental observations to the idea of *success*, which, as the word implies, must simply follow as a matter of course ("succeed") and can't be forced. Success is an addition, a bonus, for commitment. That is to say, if a person is totally dedicated to his work, carried away by the aims of the objective and convinced of the importance and rightness of his actions, then, in addition to his work, success may be added as a bonus. However, if a success-obsessed man thinks of success as something that must be procured at any price, or conversely lets himself be dragged along by routine while his thoughts are elsewhere, then he is not paying attention to his work and his commitment is lacking; the bonus of success evaporates.

I once experienced a remarkable case of career crisis, in which a lack of commitment prevented any kind of success with a patient who was a young priest. The man had only recently been ordained and had started working in a parish when a series of symptoms afflicted him. Especially when reading Mass, his knees started knocking, his breath was labored, his hand movements became erratic, and he broke into a sweat. Finally, he was hardly able to complete the ceremonies. He was released from his duties and underwent a thorough medical examination. Nothing definite except an indeterminate diagnosis of vegetative dystony. After that, he was sent to me. The interesting part is that he confronted me with an open question. In a few months' time he would have the opportunity of being assigned a new congregation, a small one in the country, but he was not sure *whether he wanted that*. He did not say, "Please help me to be fit for accomplishing this task!" but instead asked: "Do you think I should accept this task?"

That put me on my guard, for why did he follow the vocation of priest if not to fulfill priestly duties? What did his vocation as a priest mean to him?

He could easily explain that to me. He always saw himself as a shepherd in ceremonial garb among his herd, surrounded, recognized, respected, bestowing his benediction. He liked the picture; I did not. Certainly, he described the idyllic picture of a minister, but in simple psychotherapeutic language it meant he always saw only *himself*. When he actually celebrated Mass, he saw *himself* as the one on whom the eyes of the faithful are focused. Those eyes which miss nothing when the minister has the shakes or gets mixed up in his prayers, to whom it is relentlessly obvious how nervous he is and how they would make fun of him without pity if he failed in his revered role. Here, with all its trimmings, we have the fulcrum for all his psychosomatic sweating. Whoever is primarily concerned with becoming a successful priest must tremble with the fear of being unsuccessful, and whoever wants to harvest admiration must fear ridicule.

"Have you ever held a mass to the glory of God?" I asked my patient.

He looked up, perplexed.

"Exclusively to God's glory," I continued, "to serve Him? Regardless of the way you come before Him as a trembling, crying, failing, mocked child, everything will be placed in the sacrificial vessel, to His glory. Have you ever tried that?"

"You as a psychologist say that?" the patient asked surprised.

"Why not?" I replied. "The antidote you need against your affliction you must produce yourself. It is dedication to your vocation. You shouldn't concentrate on observing yourself or whether you are perfectly in control of everything. Rather, you must forget yourself completely and turn your thoughts to the concerns of your position. Then you *will be* in control and able to handle your vocation!"

The young priest followed my advice and with heart and soul took root in his new parish. He even sent me a written invitation to his inaugural mass, and to please him I was among the guests. At the climax of the mass he lifted the consecrated vessel longer than usual and I think I know what went through his mind. He probably brought his fears of this "test of authenticity" as a sacrifice before God who apparently graciously accepted it because, as I later learned, no further symptoms occurred during Mass.

In comparison with this case, I enjoy thinking of another minister I met at the Fourth World Congress for Logotherapy in San Francisco. I will always admire his capacity for commitment. His name is Gordon Hatcher, and I mention his name and that of his son, Merrell, with the purpose of establishing a written monument to them. To the son, for his untimely, inculpable death; to the father for the testimonial of his reaction to this tragedy, which was a testimony to what a person can achieve spiritually even in his darkest hour.

Merrell was killed by an allegedly intoxicated driver shortly after his 21st birthday. The father, who is a preacher in a religious denomination, delivered the most painful sermon of his life several days later. He himself interred his son and delivered the funeral sermon, which was recorded by his friends:

> My friends, here I stand. I am standing here because Merrell would have wanted it. He always made demands on me, demands which he knew I could fulfill. This now is the most difficult demand he ever made of me and I accept it.
>
> In my opinion more should be written and said about the degree to which children influence their parents. For though, of course, parents influence their children, I am under the impression that very little has been said about the reverse. Without doubt, Merrell has influenced me and my lifestyle tremendously—for good. Today, I would like to acknowledge his influence.
>
> My friends, here I stand. I am standing here because I can remember an event that happened when Merrell was still very small. At that stage he was a fidgety and babbling little fellow who sat on his mother's lap every Sunday while his father preached. Nobody knew whether he was aware of any of the goings on around him. But one Sunday morning when someone else delivered the sermon, Merrell registered his father's absence. He climbed onto the church bench and shouted for everyone to hear: "That is not my father!" He expected his father to be here and he wanted no replacement. There will be no replacement here today either.
>
> I am not here to punish myself nor together with my family to undergo an ordeal by fire. I am not here to divert my attention from Merrell's death or to reckon with God. I am here to comply with Merrell's request....

Mr. Hatcher then selected several incidents from the life of his departed son that he regarded as worthy of relating and contemplating and he concluded with the comment that, according to his understanding, Merrell's death had been senseless, *but not his life*.

I am convinced that the reader will be as impressed by this father as I am. Viewing it logically, we could say that the man was a success as a preacher.

Let us consider what was so impressive about his actions. Was it the rhetorical fluency of his speech? Surely not, although his simple words were deeply moving. Was it the positive things he said about his son? Certainly not, for who says anything negative about a deceased person, especially if he is a parent? I think it was the *motive* that enabled the father to step in front of the mourners on that painful day and deliver his speech. He clearly expressed this motive in the above passage: "Here I stand…" Why? "…to comply with Merrell's request." That says that he was standing there *for the love of his son*, filled with a love that cannot be changed by death. He was not concerned with *his* feelings, whether *he* would be equal to the situation, whether *he* would choke on the words. Nothing like that. He saw in his attendance the chance for a last labor of love for his child and he took it.

Years later, when I sat opposite Mr. Hatcher in the congress hall and heard his story, I also saw an opportunity: I asked him for permission to publish the essential parts of this story to encourage all persons who have suffered deeply "to remain standing," wherever they were called, however hard it may be for them. If only one reader could be moved by this example to remain solid as a rock in his pain, unbent and unbroken in his commitment to fulfilling a service, then Merrell has not died in vain and Mr. Hatcher can be comforted by the thought that even the senseless death of his son has sometime, somewhere, found meaning.

Let us return to the subject of *working*, which, as both examples demonstrate, cannot be separated from a higher value which is an abstraction in the concrete performance of the work. Many career men tend to work themselves to exhaustion in the concrete performance of their work. This leads to a typical manager's disease and causes extremely high stress on the heart and circulatory system. This can happen only if the "abstract value," which should be recognizable above and beyond the work as the real spiritual goal, has been lost from sight. Others are bored and dissatisfied with their work, but this can only happen if it is not brought into a context that surrounds the concrete activity abstractly and fills it with meaning. "Man always credits fate double with the things he lacks, contrasted with those which he actually possesses," Gottfried Keller wrote, and this idea is often demonstrated by career men who chase after more and more success regardless of what they already possess: a "something" or "someone" for which or for whom they are obliged to practice their career to the best of their ability.

Success only comes to the home of that person who dedicates his or her activity to a duty that knocks at the door from without. Whoever only wants a home to shine inside for one's own comfort in life overlooks the fact that the doors are locked in this way and such a person becomes his or her own prisoner.

5. About Love and Work

Notwithstanding the existing variety of psychological schools, there are at present only two complete concepts of the human being that have been proposed in the field of psychology. One school was founded by Sigmund Freud and was tacitly taken up by nearly all subsequent schools, including the very differently structured school of behaviorism. The other was founded by Viktor E. Frankl. The future may belong to the latter. That the birthplace for both concepts was the Austrian capital Vienna is a peculiar coincidence. One could, however, also see it as a logical and necessary development. It first started with ingenious discoveries based on trial and error and a continuous process of self-correction which led via the "aha-effect" to a realistic scientific theory. Be that as it may, we can't reconcile both concepts of the human being, the "old" and the "new." To the extent that they appear to be thesis and antithesis, so they are incapable of synthesis. Therefore, for the time being, every practicing psychologist has the prerogative of choosing the preferred concept. But once the choice is made, the healer can act, research, and interpret only in terms of the chosen system in order to remain loyal it.

As the two great aims in life, *work* and *love*, are inevitably interconnected with the fundamental conceptions of human life, I would like to compare and contrast these two concepts to bring out a specific and unmistakable distinguishing characteristic. It can best be circumscribed by the concepts *monad* and *self-transcendence* or simply with *closedness* or *openness* of the each individual to the world.

Traditional psychological theories, whether because they have their source in psychoanalytic thinking or because they are based on considerations of learning theories, all regard the human being as a *monad*. This means for them that the person is a closed system. Within that system, there are a number of movements and processes, forces of drive and will, emotions and cognitions, conditionings and automatisms, creativity and spontaneity, consciousness and unconsciousness, influences from within and without, and reactions to them in a plethora of patterns.

There was much theorizing about the different layers of the "I" and about maturation and its different phases, which either stabilize the system or upset its balance and cause psychological disturbances. Much research was conducted about the strength of needs and the question of their satisfaction, which contributes considerably to maintaining normal functioning of the closed system "the person," while stress, shocks, and frustrations endanger it.

Seen from such a perspective, normality is equal to inner balance (homeostasis), and psychological stability is defined as an intact monad. According to this interpretation, whoever is able to release his drives in an acceptable manner, to realize his needs and desires adequately, to not repress his hurts, to adapt his conditioning mechanisms to demands, and to find his identity, is regarded as "healthy."

But where the monad is disturbed because drives are suppressed and irrational maladaptive behavior is enforced by unconscious complexes, external psychological trauma inhibit the unfolding of the I, or where faulty conditioning curtails self-confidence, the natural desire for happiness, success, and attention can no longer be satisfied; psychological stability falls into neurosis or psychopathology. We see that the closedness of this concept of the person lies in the fundamental egocentricity of the system; reduced to a simple formula, such an individual says: "Good is what is good *for me*," or "I stay healthy if I get what is good *for me*," and "I get sick if I don't get what is good *for me*."

Should we want to talk about the phenomenon of work, we cannot make an exception here, and within this specific psychological approach would have to define "work" as "good work" if it is good *for me*. That would mean it is not boring, is not too stressful, does not impose excessive demands, brings enough rewards and recognition, and leaves ample freedom. Should we want to talk about *love*, we cannot make an exception either. It would also have to be judged positive insofar as it offers advantages for an I, such as human closeness, a partner for talking openly, as well as for security, safety, and the satisfaction of drives and pleasures.

I don't deny that in the concept of the monad interactions with the environment are possible, for something has to be invested in work or in a partnership or there could be no return benefits. But this interrelationship is also governed by the principal doctrine of optimal wish satisfaction of the person concerned, just as every human action and feeling in general, from its deepest motivational roots, is oriented towards the satisfaction of one's own needs and the maintenance of an internal balance. It is a concept of the person that appears very clear and reasonable, yet leaves a certain uneasiness when it tries to answer an age-old question about the essential identity of the human as a "being chasing after happiness"; specifically, "one's own happiness."

The fundamentally different approach, which was developed by Viktor Frankl, starts from the premise that the person is not a monad and not a closed system. According to Frankl, the human being, unlike other creatures we know, has an opening to the world. In his concept, the many different energy potentials found in the monad model are by no means denied, as they demonstrably exist. They are, however, complemented and elevated by a motivational force that cannot be placed on the same level with needs and processes of the psyche, because it reaches beyond the self, "transcending" the self into the environment. It is *the will to meaning*.

Of course, forces of will are already present in the traditional concept of the person in psychology, but what is special in the concept of a "will to meaning" that destroys any idea of a monad, is the repeatedly highlighted fact that this meaning is not centered on the self. It is much rather the *specific meaning of a situation,* which contains an objective component that is to be grasped subjectively. Meaning, therefore, is the link between a person and the world and is never merely "meaning for me" but always simultaneously a part of "meaning as such." The answer to the question about the human being is thus no longer that the individual is a being chasing after happiness, more specifically personal happiness, but that the person is *a being on a search for meaning, specifically for a meaning in the world.*

Let us examine this enlarged concept of the person with the examples of love and work. Taking the human ability for self-transcendence into account, "good work" is then equal to "meaningful work," and "meaningful work," in turn, refers to work that brings something meaningful into the world or that changes something that exists into something better. In short, it brings something good closer to perfection.

Normally this kind of meaningful work is rewarding even more so than work that is merely not overdemanding or performed merely in exchange for money. There may, however, be extreme situations in life in which meaningful work is extremely difficult and very troublesome. Thus the reward it brings is not short-term happiness but is nevertheless valuable and important and therefore endured with fortitude. The criterion of self-interest is valid only within the limits of the monad. Beyond it, the meaning of the moment as such is valid.

It is no different in regard to the phenomenon of love. According to Frankl's thinking, love is much more than the satisfaction of an elementary or sublimated sex drive. It involves an element of meaning belonging to the external world, namely, to the loved one. Just as the value of the object to be created merges with any work that is worthy of human effort, so a love worthy of the human being merges with the worth of the partner to be loved, on whose well-being the attention of the lover is concentrated. And again, committing oneself to another normally reflects into one's own heart, but there may be situations in life when it is difficult either to maintain a close interpersonal relationship or to let go of it, depending on what the meaning of the situation demands. Where this is achieved, it is out of a genuine love; it is a love that enables a person to disregard his or her own self-interests.

A beautiful example of the confrontation of both psychological schools is provided by Berthold Brecht in his drama *The Caucasian Chalk Circle* in which he describes two women who fight for the same child. One of the women is the natural mother of the child who, without doubt, would be entitled to the child. The other woman, however, raised the child under great hardships and loves it as her own. The functioning of a monad can now be explained from the behavior of the natural mother. Her rights are supposedly being curtailed and, as a result, her feeling of self-worth is upset. In order to regain balance she must insist on enforcing her rights. The judge, having placed the child in the center of the chalked circle and the women to the right and left of it, commented that the true mother would be able to draw her child to her. She pulls with all her might. The servant who raised the child on the other hand, mobilizes her ability for self-transcendence and lets go because she reasons: "Before the child in the middle of the circle is torn apart, I'll waive my claim to it!" In the drama the judge then finds it easy to decide which woman has the real claim to the child.

For the psychologically trained observer, it is not difficult to predict which of the two women would have been happier if the judge had decided in terms of his original statement: the natural mother with her triumph over her rival to the detriment of the child, or the servant with her painful sacrifice for the love of the child. We can safely assume that inner contentment would have been found with the latter even if her feeling of self-worth had decreased much more than that of her counterpart.

Although the story is an extreme example, it demonstrates unmistakably what is meant by a person's being open to the world. The biological mother does not open up; she remains closed. She has to work through the trauma of losing her child, she has to abreact her aggression against her rival and has to defend her interests. She is busy re-establishing her own psychological balance and being so busy with herself and her problems she is hardly aware of her environment. She does not really see her child although she fights for it. She does not really fight for the child but much more for her own happiness. She is the prototype for a *being chasing after happiness*.

The maidservant, on the other hand, opens up to the world. She also has a trauma, for she gave up her boyfriend for the child. She also has aggressions inside her about the mother who once indifferently left the child and now comes and demands it back. Indeed, her psychological balance is at least as much disturbed—and her interests to be defended are at least as strong—as those of the biological mother. In spite of her own problems, she is able to take cognizance of her surroundings, and what she sees in them is an innocent child on whom pain is to be inflicted. It is a senseless suffering and this is where her will to meaning revolts and gives her strength to leave her monad and, with it, to leave all her problems. An objective meaning of the situation becomes recognizable: The health of the child must be maintained! And the woman hastens to fulfill this by transcending herself. She acts as is appropriate for a *being in search for meaning*.

If we share the idea that the human being can see into the surroundings by means of spiritual perceptions and find meanings there that are not directly connected to emotional needs, then we have to re-admit two concepts into psychology that had previously been disposed of—the concepts of *freedom* and *responsibility*.

In a closed system, neither can exist, because there the mainly unconscious forces of drives and experiential history determine the actions of the present, and where we have predetermination and predestination we don't have guilt. In an open system, it becomes more complicated. Impulses from the external world with their attributes of "meaningful" or "meaningless" meet with the existential longing of the person for a meaningful life and challenge spiritual forces that are neither open to predetermination nor predestination. They are free forces whose application or lack of application must be correspondingly justified. Let us contemplate this with an example that has less to do with love but more with work.

There was once an impressive film named *The Devil's Reporter*. This film was supposed to have been based on a true story about a laborer on a construction site who was buried alive in a hole and had to be rescued. According to experts, there were two alternatives for rescue. One was relatively quick—direct drilling; the other would take somewhat longer—constructing a tunnel. After estimating the available oxygen and the condition of the person in the hole, it was assumed that he would be able to survive either rescue operation. That is, he would survive the longer lasting rescue operation as well as the shorter. But, naturally, all the estimates were more or less guesses as communication with the victim was difficult.

The accident attracted many curious onlookers, among them a reporter well known for his excellent news coverage. He used all his influence to encourage the construction of the tunnel, the prolonged rescue operation, thus gaining enough time to offer exciting stories to his readers and fill his column for days. Many strangers descended on the place from all over to witness the rescue; because they required board and lodging, they brought additional income to the village. When the victim was finally reached, he was dead.

This story shows us in the person of the reporter someone who does excellent work and is crowned with success. He writes exciting reports and earns publicity and reward. Yet everyone will have to agree that, in this case, he went too far: A human life was at stake, which should have taken precedence over any reporting, however good it may be. In psychological terms, we can again choose from two alternatives. One comes from the monad model and the other allows for self-transcendence. In the monad model there is, as we stated, no guilt. The action of the reporter can be perfectly explained as an expression of his personality. One might perhaps suspect an inferiority complex resulting from his childhood, which demands as compensation his reaching the summit of his career. Or one could plead for a deficiency in social sensitivity, which can be traced back to lack of social training in his development. Some would place at least part of the responsibility on the conditions of the social environment that supports the egotistical plan of the reporter and the considerable pressure that was exerted on him by his readers.

In Frankl's concept of the person, all these arguments are only partially valid; they represent only one side of the scales, namely, the fluctuations of the reporter's psyche. On the other side of the scales rests the meaning of the situation, which entails saving the accident victim. We must distinguish very carefully between an external psychological influence, such as the social pressure of the environment, and the presence of an objective meaning, which has no influence as such but is only discernible by the individual's spiritual perception. The situation of the man buried alive and the meaning of his rescue, which lies encoded in it, are exclusively environmental elements, even if they have a certain intrinsic demand character. They have nothing at all to do with the psychological stability and coping capacity of the reporter.

Until now, there has been agreement in thinking but now we reach the assertion that separates the new concept of the human being from the old one. It is the contention that, because of his ability for self-transcendence, the human is almost so independent of his psychological stability or coping capacity as to give a spiritual response to meanings that he perceives in his environment by fulfilling them or not. This is a person's responsible freedom which has been introduced into psychology by Frankl. *It is a freedom for fulfilling meaningful tasks in spite of diverse (inhibiting?) influencing factors.* Self-transcendence is thus also a "being able to overcome oneself," a "being able to react beyond the limits of the monad" into a world full of meaning, even if that meaning is only vaguely perceived. The conscience, by definition, is the human sense organ for detecting the specific meaning of a situation; and the freedom to respond to this perception is *responsibility*. Guilt can be described as resulting from a "No" to the question of meaning, the "No" that was expressed by the reporter in the film.

The second example also concerned an out-of-the-ordinary event that probably does not belong to everyday life. Yet we will find numerous similar challenges in every ordinary life if we search for them, although most would not have the same serious consequences. What is interesting is that they concern mainly the phenomena of love and work. There are mothers who want to extract top achievements from their children in order to bask in the reflected glory and pride. There are also mothers who want their children to have the best possible education so as to give them a good start in life. The fine distinction is in the self-transcendence of the latter. There are women who complain about frigidity because their men don't manage to help them achieve optimal orgasmic experience, and there are women who can give themselves tenderly to their husbands, even if sexuality does not mean that much to them. Again, self-transcendence makes the fine difference. Whoever really loves another person, whether a child or a partner, can't chase only after his or her own happiness and misuse the other as a means for satisfying selfish desires.

This is analogous to work. There are authors who write books in order to reach the best seller list and there are others who write to bestow a gift on their readers. There are doctors who want to build up a profitable business and others who want to fight disease. There are assembly line workers who do piecework to achieve a higher living standard; there are others who support their large families with their work. The fine difference lies every time in self-transcendence, namely, including objective meanings from the environment in one's own motivation.

For me as a psychologist, these reflections do not hinge on moral considerations but rather on the psychological interpretation of the human being. Can a person incorporate the welfare of others or the meaning of a work to be created into one's personal decision-making process? Sigmund Freud said "No"; Viktor Frankl said "Yes." This "Yes" is not an antithesis, nor a simple negation of the no, but no less than a new definition of the person. As Frankl asserted: "The more he forgets himself in his task and gives himself to his partner, the more he is human and becomes himself."[10]

Thus happiness, which is held by all the other schools to be the highest aim of human striving, was for Frankl no aim at all. For him, happiness is the automatic by-product of a meaning-filled existence, which in Bernanos' words draws its contentment from "the grace to be able to forget self."[11]

Having clarified the positions of both concepts of the human being, I would like to add two short reports from my psychological experience to round off the subject. They are associated with Frankl's perspective of love and work and may give food for thought to the professional and the layman.

The first case is of *diagnostic* interest and relates to spider phobia. A young girl went into all sorts of fits of screaming and unconsciousness when she saw a spider anywhere. The history of her affliction indicated that there had been a number of events in her childhood which could have had a precipitating character, especially the fact that as a young child she had lived in a dilapidated old house. There had been many spiders that often had even crawled into her bed. Another factor was that her parents had often sent her to bed during the day as punishment, which made her very unhappy. Whatever the reason, the parents later moved to a better house. The punishments ceased but the fear of spiders remained and was intensified to such an extent that even the picture of a spider in an illustrated book could start a phobic attack.

Because I not only search for a dominant problem and its genesis while investigating the history of an affliction but on principle look simultaneously for positive attending circumstances, I asked the girl whether she had ever had an experience with spiders that by any chance had been a positive one. To my amazement she answered in the affirmative. Only once in her life had she managed to pick up a small spider from a window sill with her handkerchief and throw it outside without breaking into a panic, storming out of the room or screaming for help. Naturally, I was very interested to hear how about a person who had loathed spiders since childhood but could never touch them, who later developed a full-blown phobia, suddenly managed to throw a spider out of the window without any apparent trouble. What could have happened?

The reader can imagine that some trace of self-transcendence had to be involved, otherwise the monad would not have opened. A dear friend of the girl had been visiting and was not feeling particularly well. She had just been discharged from hospital and was still feeling very weak and had therefore gone to rest in the girl's bedroom. They chatted and then the friend fell asleep. The girl rose and stood at the window and there saw the spider. She was confronted with the choice of either running from the room screaming, and thereby waking and frightening her friend, or removing the spider quietly. She chose the latter course. Her consideration for the friend was stronger than the power of fear.

I think we should learn something about psychological diagnosis from this example: A person can't just be pigeonholed in a set of typical behavior patterns. Anyone can at any time react atypically if he or she has a strong enough reason for it. Therefore, it is risky for a diagnostic inquiry to collect exclusively negative connections that exist between the past and the present of a person because this could create the impression that the present is inescapably dependent on events of the past, which is simply not true.

Sometimes a little bit of love—love in the widest sense— is enough to give new and unexpected impulses to the present.

The second story, which I consider even more remarkable, is interesting from a *therapeutic* perspective. It concerns a case of compulsive snacking and eating, that is, excessive consumption of food. The case has a tragic component because it concerns a man who, due to a handicap in his lower limbs, was confined to a wheelchair and, for that reason, naturally moved very little. This, together with his symptoms and the resulting overweight condition, had consequences that were detrimental to his health. He suffered terrible constipation, stomach cramps, etc., which did not react even to strong laxatives.

His overweight had long since been diagnosed by medical doctors as psychological and soon the hypothesis of satisfaction replacement was held, which of course fits without exception any handicapped person because he always has much to give up. However, every therapy approach based on this theory had failed, and when the man came to me for consultations he had hardly any hope of improvement. To be honest, I also saw little opportunity for reducing his dependency but I had my eye on something else. Although the man already had to bear the heavy burden of his handicap and additionally the unpleasant digestive problems which could not easily be corrected, some part of his life had to be worth living.

Therefore, I did an *existential analysis* with him in the best Frankl tradition to discover where his various interests, talents, and abilities were to be found. Perhaps these could then be emphasized to bring content, engagement, and meaning into his rather uninteresting and inhibited life. During our talks, it became apparent that during the war the man had spent several years in a prisoner-of-war camp, and because of his own bitter experiences had a deep sympathy for the fate of all innocent prisoners throughout the world. He could get very upset over news of torture or inhumane prisons and emphasized again and again how he would like to do something for these poor, tortured people.

I don't even recall who first thought about the organization Amnesty International, but it was inevitable that our talks should get to it at some time and suddenly the man perceived a meaning offering itself to him. An organization like Amnesty International could be supported from the wheelchair. He telephoned, made contacts, established a branch of the local agency in his apartment, catalogued articles, and wrote newsletters to members of the organization. In short, he became a forceful voluntary helper of Amnesty International, and after some time he became the hub of many important links. Several weeks later, I sent him a note but heard nothing from him. Occasionally I invited the man for further therapeutic talks but he did not return. He was too busy. Somehow I considered this positive, for I had the feeling that the meaning which suddenly enriched his life was more important and salubrious than any, even the best, psychotherapy.

Nevertheless, I was surprised when, several months later, the man appeared at my consulting rooms without an appointment. By chance, he had been in our area and wanted to tell me about the many interesting things he was doing. He started telling me about them in detail but I could hardly concentrate on his words. I simply had to stare at him in amazement the whole time. He was slimmer than I had ever seen him.

"How did you lose your excess weight?" I inquired.

He laughed. "I don't know myself" he answered, "but I do know one thing: When Amnesty International needs me, I totally forget eating!"

How can this history of an affliction be interpreted psychologically? Can we, in terms of the monad system, accept without hesitation that the patient only changed his type of satisfaction replacement and that now he finds satisfaction in meaningful tasks in this worldwide organization instead of as before with food? Is this perhaps compensation for what he missed during childhood? I think we would be unfair, not only to the man but also to the value of his new task, if we were to declare his involvement as an expression of a neurosis and his help to political prisoners as a means for working through his psychological complexes. Every human contribution, however small, if it improves or beautifies something in our world, contains an objective meaning, reaching far beyond the subjective level of complexes and compensations.

It is, therefore, no disgrace to admit that meaningful work can make our therapeutic work actually superfluous; whenever a meaning experience becomes concrete, so much self-transcendence is activated that a neurosis no longer has a chance. At any rate, we psychotherapists could be as necessary as before to guide our patients towards a meaning experience. And that is exactly the function that Viktor Frankl formulated for his students, to look beyond every psychologically ill patient for a "being in search of meaning" who not only needs help facing psychological disturbances but also for exclusively human suffering. Love and work may be very strong vehicles for emotions of interpsychological processes and they may have all their sources in drives and motivations, but they are aimed at the environment in which human existence wants to find meaningful fulfillment. And only to the degree to which that is achieved is *Being* really human.

BIBLIOGRAPHY

[1] Viktor E. Frankl, *Sinn-voll heilen*, Herder, Freiburg, 1983

[2] Hans Schäfer, "Das Menschenbild der Medizin" in *Im Blickpunkt: Der Mensch*, Veritas, Wien

[3] Viktor E. Frankl, *Das Leiden am sinnlosen Leben*, Herder, Freiburg, 11th ed. 1989

[4] Viktor E. Frankl, *Der leidende Mensch*, Piper, München, new ed. 1990

[5] Gottfried Keller, *Der grüne Heinrich*, dtv Weltliteratur

[6] Christopher Lasch, *The Culture of Narcissism*, W.W. Norton, New York, 1979

[7] Viktor E. Frankl, *Der Mensch vor der Frage nach dem Sinn*, Piper, München, 7th ed. 1989

[8] Georg Moser, *Wie finde ich zuni Sinn des Lebens?*, Herder, Freiburg, 1981

[9] Viktor E. Frankl, *Psychotherapie für den Laien*, Herder, Freiburg, 13th ed. 1989

[10] Viktor E. Frankl, *Der Mensch vor der Frage nach dem Sinn*, Piper, München, 7th ed. 1989

[11] Georges Bernanos, *Tagebuch eines Landpfarrers*, Arche, 1975

C.

PSYCHOLOGICAL MINISTRY

1. Fear as a Challenge to the Human Spirit

Most people associate the concept of *fear* with something negative and unpleasant, but actually the feeling of fear helps us to survive. We would be lost without fear. We would go swimming among sharks, amble across an intersection when the traffic lights are red, scramble up precipitous mountain peaks in loose sandals, eat poisonous fruits or berries, or face the hardest exams without preparation. The respective consequences can be imagined in rich imagery. It is fear that protects us against this type of carelessness, and in the human sphere it has to do with the imagination, with being able to visualize a picture.

Naturally, fear has this safety function in the animal kingdom as well. Just imagine what would happen if the song birds of the woods tamely perched on every hiker's shoulder. They would be plucked, cooked, fried, put in cages, or pressed as toys into children's hands! For animals, it is an *instinctive* safeguard, guaranteed by their inborn fear. No bird would be able to anticipate what the more or less well-inclined wanderer has in mind. For us, the feeling of fear is usually associated with an *inner anticipation* of imagined threatening events that could happen and therefore must be avoided. It is similar to the warning siren that has a specific function and protects only the person who understands its meaning. A fire alarm protects the person who quickly flees to safety, but not the person who stays in his seat and complains at great length about the noise.

Originally, fear was positive and lifesaving; for us humans it is also a prognostic activity with a prophylactic character which can and ought to lead to the prevention of mishaps. Unfortunately, the opposite is also true. Fear can lead to misfortune. This happens every time fear loses its essential meaning and becomes autonomous. Then, so to speak, the fire alarm goes off every few seconds and confuses the residents in the house totally although there is no fire.

To take this example even further, suppose that the fire alarm starts by mistake because of some harmless cigarette smoke, but perhaps it causes someone who is busy ironing to leave the apartment in such a rush that the clothes catch fire, and thus a real fire is started. In the psychological realm this is exactly what happens with *anxiety neuroses*. These have their source in an exaggerated, unrealistic fear but often they lead to very real discomfort which appears to justify the original fear, although that is erroneous.

Suppose a swimmer in safe waters, fearing there could be a shark after all, becomes agitated into a state of paralytic panic and swallows water. Such fear would not be justified even if drowning were the result. Or suppose a pedestrian correctly crosses the street at an intersection but, because of the fear of walking into a car, jumps back and forth and is consequently knocked down. Again, such fears would not be justified even if what is feared became reality. Justified fear, and that means sensible fear, is one that warns of an accident but does not cause an accident.

From these few examples it becomes quite apparent that it is not always easy to differentiate between justified and unjustified fear. However, it is important to know how to distinguish between the two because they have to be handled very differently. We should respect justified fear but disregard its unjustified counterpart; we should take one seriously and make the other ridiculous by minimizing its importance. Indeed, while justified fear, beyond its emotional quality, is a useful, preventive act of reason, the other is, in addition to its pathologizing effects, a challenge to the human spirit.

Before concentrating on the best way of dealing with justified and unjustified fear, I would like to say a few more words about the differentiation between the two in order to clarify contingent misunderstandings. In particular, I want to focus on misperceptions that arise in the wake of an unbalanced egocentric psychology that has the theoretical goal of getting rid of fear altogether while actually creating much unnecessary fear. It is obvious that such an undertaking is utter nonsense because eliminating sensible fear would be as irresponsible as creating senseless fear.

It is similar to the much-propagated psychological goal of conveniently teaching inhibited people to learn to say "No." It is presupposed that these people are polite, pleasant, and friendly with everyone because they are actually afraid and unable to look after their own interests. There is no doubt that not much good can come of it if, because of some inner inhibition, someone always says "Yes" but means "No." However being able to say "No" by itself is not enough. And the reason is that it is part of a fulfilled life to be able to say "Yes" to tasks that are given and to say it with all one's heart. How can one decide when a "Yes" is required and when a "No" would be appropriate? I repeatedly point to the optimal criterion for differentiation, the only one worthy of human existence, as noted by Frankl: *the meaning of the moment*, which is available in each situation.

I want to explain this with an example. Suppose that, 10 minutes before closing time, a patient arrives at the consulting rooms without an appointment and begs me for help. Let us further suppose that it is especially inconvenient for me because I have to attend to an urgent matter at home. According to conventional psychological thinking it would be the sign of a stable and self-confident personality if I said "No" and turned the patient away. Conversely, my inhibitions and lack of assertiveness would be expressed if I said "Yes" and attended to the patient. But is that really the case? Can I simply decide in my own interests and do what suits me? And moreover, is *that* really inner strength?

My mentor, Viktor Frankl, would say there is no other way than to test the meaning of the situation. Concretely, this means spending the remaining 10 minutes in establishing how urgently, how necessary, and therefore how meaningfully my immediate help is required by the individual; that is, whether our consultation could be deferred till the next day or the day after. Only when it is established whether overtime on my part is meaningful can I give a wise "Yes" or "No." Only then does my inner strength or weakness become apparent. If the person seeking help is, for instance, in a very bad psychological condition—or even suicidal—then my "Yes" would be anything but a mere inability to look after my own interests. It would be an act of charity and, moreover, the ethical duty of my profession. Relinquishing my free evening would then be the reflection of inner strength, while insisting on retaining it would reveal nothing but inner weakness. Conversely, it could also happen that the patient simply wants to jump the queue of waiting patients by confronting me with an accomplished fact, although the problem is of minor importance. In that case my "Yes" would really mean a "No," given out of inner weakness when a refusal would have been required.

This example shows that fear itself is always important on the individual level of feeling; furthermore, the subject of fear and the reasons for surmounting it are also worthy of attention. These considerations facilitate an answer to the question: When is fear realistic and therefore protective, and when is fear unrealistic and instead pathogenic?

In the case where anything meaningful can arise from fear (whether it serves as a warning, a lesson, or a challenge to change one's lifestyle or simply an admonishment to be careful), the objective is not to conquer fear but more to understand its significance as a corrector of behavior. But where nothing meaningful grows from fear (and it only gives rise to a burdened life, an encroachment on freedom of movement and decision, troubled interpersonal relationships, or even a neurosis), fear represents a true challenge to the human spirit, which does not have to put up with everything from fear but is quite capable of opposing it.

Let us now inspect the first possibility in greater detail and later turn to the second, which is of more concern.

As demonstrated, realistic fear has a protective quality. Whoever is afraid of reaching too far out of the window while cleaning it is well advised to listen to his inner voice. Whoever is afraid to fail a test is also well advised to master the material. So far everything is clear. But what if it concerns a realistic fear of something outside of one's own control? One is afraid of a surgical procedure, surely with reason, for every surgery carries a risk. But one can't avoid the procedure if it is needed. Or one is afraid on behalf of a relative who chooses to take the wrong path in life, and yet one can't hold that person back. The inner anticipation of imaginable events makes it possible for the individual, as a being privileged with a spirit, to look into the future, even if it is only a *possible* future and not the one that eventuates. Occasionally the imagined, though negative, outcome does occur as a result of fate, independent of any action taken.

Here the question of meaning presents itself in a different light. But in these cases as well, fear, properly understood, still has a protective function. It does at least protect an individual from a sudden shock through a surprise attack by fate. In the example of realistic fear, the individual has more or less dealt with it already, has considered the serious consequences, and in a way has integrated it. Such a person has already partially accepted some things that have not yet happened. When they do actually happen, that person is already familiar with them in spirit, although it is natural to fight them emotionally.

To summarize: A realistic fear—appropriate to the prevailing situation—always has a protective function, whether it is possible to do anything about that which is feared. If something can be done about it, then it is most expedient to do so. If nothing can be done, at the least an inner preparation can be made. If the feared event occurs, the person is forearmed. If it does not happen, the individual will receive the gift of joy and relief gratefully. When realistic fear can no longer influence behavior, it can at least be an attitude modifier, and that has its meaning in life, too. Therefore, let us not be afraid of fear, for—as peculiar as it may sound—with it, nature means well for us.

However, in the area of unrealistic, irrational, exaggerated, and neurotic fears the situation is different; unfortunately, in our culture we are all vulnerable. From the spider crossing our path to the Armageddon that threatens at the end of the age, from the fear of tomorrow to the existential anxieties which pervade an entire life, we know all shades of unhealthy fears. Most of them still have a touch of relevance to reality but are nevertheless inappropriate to the individual's life situation. Such anxieties, devoid of meaning, are marked by three aspects: *expectation*, which is the permanent anticipation of something terrible, *blackmail*, which is acting under pressure against one's will, and *humiliation*, which robs human beings of our most precious possession: freedom. Let us look at these aspects individually.

We have already indicated that inner anticipations of future events in the form of premonitions are anxieties which always accompany human fears. A dangerous exaggeration of this is the direct *expectation* of negative events, which leaves hardly any room for thinking about a positive solution to the crisis. While mere apprehensions tend to release energy for preventing the feared event (or for reconciling with it), expectation blocks these strengths because everything seems to be for nothing. For instance, those who are certain that they will lose a contest make no effort to give their best and fail for that reason alone. Or a job seeker who is convinced that there is no chance in a job interview and does not go to the interview misses the minimal chance that might otherwise have been possible.

Expectation anxiety thus blocks; in this manner, it is an impediment to the free unfolding of personality. And the less the personality is able to unfold, the more the person comes to expect further negative responses from within and from the environment, thus reinforcing the blockage.

There are anxiety neuroses that arise solely from the negative expectation of some unpleasant symptom, because the expectation promptly brings on that very symptom. There are even "expectation depressions" which arise only from the firm conviction that one should and will react depressively under certain circumstances. There are a number of negative prophesies that are fulfilled, not because they are realistic, but for the simple reason that they are *believed to be real*. On the basis of these autosuggestions, one behaves in such a way that they *become actualized*. It goes so far that a patient who is told that he suffers from an inflammation of the pelvis and therefore expects to have pain in the area of the kidneys could actually feel such pain, even if later it is discovered that the test results had been mixed up with those of another patient and the diagnosis was only a mild stomach upset.

The Israeli doctor Paul Schuger investigated these dangerous expectation phenomena on a large scale. He reported an event in West Jordan which drew the attention of the World Health Organization in Geneva. It started with two school girls who suddenly fainted. Afterwards somebody spread the false rumor that the drinking water had been poisoned. Within a few days, 946 girls from that school were admitted to the hospital for nausea and stomach aches. However, blood and urine tests showed that they were perfectly healthy. The expectation of the illness alone was sufficient to produce the concomitant symptoms, although the drinking water was perfectly clean.

One is not immune to a wrong diagnosis or mass suggestion, but one can fight against one's own expectation anxiety wherever it may be directed and so prevent the attraction of that which is feared. By means of letters written by two readers (reprinted with permission), I would like to point out how best to do this and thereby underline the effectiveness of a special method of fighting fear, designed by Frankl and frequently described by me:

Excerpt from reader's letter no. 1:

It was a family party. I climbed down the steep stairs from the kitchen with a large tray full of glasses. Suddenly I had the thought: "What if you fall with it now?" Stop on the next step. Then: "Okay, fall nicely!" In my mind I could hear the fall, the crashing, saw the mess which was somehow funny. A small shock went through me; smiling, feeling secure and easy, I stepped on down the steep stairs....

Excerpt from reader's letter no. 2:

The event happened at a nursing college during my practical course in child nursing. I witnessed the preparation and the course of examinations. Just prior to the arrival of the test panel, I went to the students waiting to be examined and saw that one of the candidates was trembling all over and near to tears. So without stopping to think I took up a position facing her, took her hands and started jumping up and down with her. While doing this I said to her: "Now we shake to our heart's content and afterwards you don't have to tremble anymore! You learned well and everything will be fine!" To my surprise I observed that the pupil's tension dissolved immediately and when she went into the examination room she was calm and knew the answers to her questions. I still remember that her final result was "Excellent."

What is the essence of both these stories? We hear of two exaggerated fears: the fear of falling down the stairs with a tray of glasses and the fear of failing an important exam. Both are indeed possible but in these cases highly improbable, for with such a fragile burden one negotiates stairs exceptionally carefully, and if a student is well prepared, as was this elite student, failure is unlikely. Therefore, let us consider these fears as unrealistic. With this classification, we automatically mark them as dangerous, especially in case they become fixed as a negative expectation attitude. The expectation of falling could cause the feet to become so insecure that it really could come to a fall. Similarly, the expectation of forgetting everything learned as a result of agitation could cause the mind to go blank.

What is this special remedy that was implied in both reports? There is no evasion. No, the crash is even mentally provoked, and there is moreover a trembling contest. One smiles inwardly about oneself and voilà, fear is suddenly reduced to a realistic level at which it can again resume its protective functions by inviting alertness but not upsetting the balance. The method applied here looks relatively simple but is not easily accomplished. Its name is *paradoxical intention* and it is based on the fact that the person is a paradoxical being. Never have I found this more succinctly expressed than in a poem by Wolfgang Hilbig, as follows:

> You built a house for me
> Let me start another one.
> You have set up easy chairs for me
> Put dolls in your easy chairs.
> You have saved money for me,
> I'd much rather steal.
> You have laid out a road for me
> I struggle through the brushwood
> At the side of the road.
> If you said one must go alone,
> I would go with you.

Although I have a suspicion that Hilbig had modern youth in mind when he wrote the lines above, his poem says something fundamental about the person. The human being loves contradictions, so much so that individuals will contradict themselves, and that is also a therapeutic opportunity. If a person is in a state of fear and considers all the reasons not to be afraid, he or she is still afraid! If, however, the tables are turned and whatever is feared so much can be wished to happen instantly, then, in spite of everything, the situation becomes utterly ridiculous. The thought, "Okay, then fall nicely," immediately provokes a sense of opposition in the woman with the tray who found her own fantasy of the "pretty mess" suddenly hilariously funny; because of it, she was able to overcome her exaggerated fears with a smile. The sentence, "Now we shake to our heart's content," had the same effect on the frightened student. The instant she had to tremble, she became calm.

Viktor Frankl, whose method of *paradoxical intention* has become known worldwide, also used this technique with success in cases of most severe anxieties and compulsive neuroses by advising his patients to wish for just as exaggeratedly—indeed, to long for with the same intensity—what they feared so exaggerated. Both exaggerations neutralize each other. This makes a normal life with *meaningful* fear but without *meaningless* anxieties possible. It is immaterial where these fears come from; that is good. Today, we understand that the diverse physical and psychological causes for the world of human feeling and experiences—brought about by disposition, upbringing, and society—are mutually interconnected in a net-like web of effect and countereffect, like an inextricably tangled ball of twine. This net is far more complicated than are our original linear causal ideas of becoming fully human.

It will never be possible to trace an irrational fear to its deepest roots, but with a healthy defiance it is possible to prevent its growing and to cause it to wilt with a distancing laughter. One can hardly credit what healing power there really is in humor. A fear that can be caricatured is no longer a fear, at least not one that can cause damage. Humor is a spiritual potential, *exclusively* at a human being's disposal, for no animal can laugh. As far as neuroses are concerned, humor is really the best response to pain of all kinds such as shyness, excessive worrying, and the tendency to dramatize. Whenever humor comes into play, the challenger "disease" is soon beaten. That this was known to our ancestors is illustrated in the following cartoon:

"And it hurts agonizingly here, and here too, and especially here!"

From the beginnings of psychosomatics
(Schülke & Mayr GmbH, D-2000 Nordewrstedt)

Before relating an impressive case history from my records, I would like to comment on the second aspect that seems to follow in the footsteps of unrealistic fears: *blackmail.* Unrealistic fears not only challenge the human spirit by suggesting a dangerous expectation of negative events, they also enforce behaviors of which a person disapproves very much. For instance, someone who is exceedingly afraid of infection by bacteria washes all day by necessity. Perhaps the hands are washed so often that they are red and wrinkled or a fortune is spent because clothes are dry-cleaned so frequently. Perhaps many places are avoided because of the fear of infection, places that the person actually would like to visit. In short, at some time or other the person becomes encapsulated within four super-clean walls and leads a life not worth living. The tragedy is that such a person becomes deeply annoyed inside; this turn of events is unwanted; there is some understanding that all this is nonsense, but the victim is in the clutches of a blackmailer, fear. In common with every blackmailer, irrational fear is never satisfied. The more one gives in to it, the greedier it gets and enforces the absurdest avoidance behavior on the person concerned.

The madness of it is that the anxious person who is trying frantically to keep every risk to a minimum has to put up with ever greater risks until finally the entire life is at risk. To stay with our example: Fear weakens the immune system of the person, thus increasing the vulnerability to infections. The more security and protection are sought at any price, the more such a person is exposed to individual weaknesses, thus becoming weaker and less protected. There is really only one escape left that one can take at any time without outside help: paradoxical intention.

The inner dialogue with the tendrils of fear should be somewhat like this: "Come here you masses of bacteria! You are my guests and you are cordially invited to sit on me! You can form colonies on my arms and legs. I am not mean. I hope you are happy with me, for all is well!" With this unusual type of approach, fear will shrink like a pricked balloon. No blackmailer likes to hear the means of extortion being praised instead of feared. What must now be used as threats? These threats won't work any longer. Neither will they work against the person filled with anxiety if the courage for a paradoxical wish is mustered. The pathological washing of hands ceases and so does the excessive cleaning of clothes; after all, one can't scare away the darling bacteria with whom one has just made friends. The person leaves the house again, but this time in order to get fresh supplies of bacteria so that the colony does not have to worry about the new generation. Above all, what results is that nothing happens, nothing at all. Quite the contrary, the person feels healthier than has been the case for a long time. This gives courage to face inner fears and rather than running away. Instead, the person no longer takes them seriously or obeys their coercions.

I know of a man who suffered under such an infection phobia for many years and who proudly says today: "As far as I am concerned, bacteria and viruses can infect my entire body from head to foot but they no longer have access to my soul. There peace reigns and I won't let it be taken away by ridiculous obsessive thoughts." Aren't those brave words?

I would now like to relate the example I mentioned earlier. It concerns a woman who mastered her fate at least as bravely. Since childhood, she had suffered diverse fears, especially fearing every new situation with which she might not be able to cope. A journey or a change at work or among her acquaintances was enough to "send her off her rocker." This was indicated by her inability to eat. She was despondent and thought about all sorts of terrible things that might happen. The fantasies she produced had at times an almost absurd character. For instance, after extended drives in her car, she was plagued by the idea that she had run over someone without noticing it. Sometimes the fear actually lured her into retracing her route although, of course, there was no trace of an accident anywhere. It is obvious how the stench of a negative expectation works together with the blackmailing pressure of fear. The patient knew very well that, in actual fact, she would never run over a pedestrian without noticing it. Nevertheless, she returned from time to time to make quite sure—albeit the assurance she hoped to gain was deceptive. For, whoever gives in to unrealistic fear is its slave, body and soul. The more often she foolishly retraced her route in search of possible victims, the more uncertain she became lest she might perhaps have overlooked one of her imagined victims on the second pass and the stronger she felt the pressure of fear to make a third run. It is easy to imagine that a patient who is enmeshed in that kind of irrational thinking will never find peace whether on the streets or at home and tears herself to shreds with needless self-torment.

When this woman came to me for treatment, she told me that she had undergone a number of different therapies. There had been intermittent temporary improvement but with every change in her life situation the fears re-emerged and she did not know what to do about them. At that time, she showed me a picture she had painted that depicted a small figure cowering on the ground with its head pressed on its knees looking like a heap of desolation and helplessness. Behind the figure a huge bird of prey with large black wings came flying towards it, its sharp beak aimed at the neck of the crumpled figure as if to tear it to pieces at the next moment (see below). "That is me," said the patient pointing to the cowering form on the paper, "and the bird is the symbol of my fears. It attacks from behind and I can do nothing against it. It is stronger than I am, and destroys me!"

"There is something in you he can't destroy," I replied. "It is the spirit in every person. The bird of your nightmares can wreak havoc with your feelings. It can humiliate you and drive you to do things you yourself can't accept. But the healthy spiritual powers of your *I* are invincible. With their help you can even place your self *above* the bird and ruffle its feathers so that it doesn't know what is happening! To do this, however, you have to get up, turn around and face it. And not only that, you have to lure it to you with open arms and press it to your bosom. You will then see it transformed into a very sweet and nice little bird that, as it were, will eat out of your hand!" The patient was very surprised at my words, but a first faint smile had already lightened up her face.

Then I explained the method of paradoxical intention to her, and we had a contest to see who could find the funniest description for some frightening situations that might arise. The patient had a lot of excellent ideas. For example, she decided to tell herself when facing a new situation: "I don't even dream of coping with the new situation. I am and want to remain the biggest failure in the whole world. Perhaps one day I shall get into the *Guinness Book of Records*!" Or, concerning the pathological idea that she could have run someone over without realizing it, she sat down comfortably as soon as she got home, saying to herself, "I hope I struck more than one! Then at least for today I have done my part towards solving the problem of overpopulation!"

Of course, the patient was well aware that her humorous talks with herself were not to be taken seriously, but they also helped her to stop taking her senseless fears seriously. What is most important is that they took away all of the power that these fears had over her, because if she wanted to fail or run somebody over, what had she to fear? And if she was not afraid, she would not fail, and of course none of the spurious road accidents, which had only been a nightmare anyway, could occur.

Thus over time the patient learned to manage her fears, and also how to lead a life much more free from needless worry; in the process, she became more self-confident at facing changes in her everyday routine.

One day, when we had almost completed our therapeutic talks, she brought a new picture that she had painted [see back cover of book]. It showed a small hill on which a figure was enthroned—there simply is no other way to describe it. Proudly she sat there on a strong solid base, serenely calm and relaxed. The figure had her head lifted and in her hand she held two paintbrushes and a palette with many colors. Next to her were four brightly colored pots. The most astounding aspect of the new picture was the birds. There were two of them this time. One was again the huge black bird of prey which this time tried to approach the figure from the front with its sharp beak directed at her feet. The other was directly in front of her, a bright, shining, colorfully feathered bird which had just left the figure with widespread wings and its beak lifted towards heaven.

"That is me now," the woman said to me, pointing to the enthroned figure. "I know now how to tame birds of prey. One just has to invite them in a friendly manner for a beauty treatment and paint their fluffed-up black feathers colorfully. Then they look so funny that they are embarrassed and quickly fly away. Lately they don't even dare come near me...."

While saying this she was laughing and crying at the same time. I shared her happiness at having been able to allay the curse of her anxiety-neurosis so heroically. Certainly, from time to time she will have an anxious thought not in keeping with reality but she won't panic immediately; instead, she will pick up her paintbrush of paradoxical intention and paint a few more of the bird's feathers with bright colors, and it will leave her in headlong flight.

Unfounded fears, compulsions, depressions and feelings of despair are challenges to the human spirit that, in the final analysis, can only be answered spiritually by taking a stand *against* and *above* them. If one does that, it is a magnificent achievement of which one can be proud—proud in the finest sense—and this noëtic certainty more than anything else renders the disease impotent. Nobody really has to bow to fear. One only *thinks* one has to. This leads to the third element that accompanies irrational fear: *humiliation*. Fear humiliates a person, although actually it is the person who opens the door to humiliation by denying the freedom that is still there.

Viktor Frankl commented on this: "In the final analysis, human behavior is not dictated by the conditions man finds but by the decisions man makes. Whether man is aware of it or not, he decides whether to defy conditions or give in to them. In other words, whether at all and to what degree he lets himself be determined by such conditions."[1]

The humiliation that comes from inappropriate fear is the consequence of: "Because I am afraid, I can't do this…" or, "I happen to be afraid and therefore am unable to do that…." But that is a neurotic fallacy because ability and competence are not at all influenced by fear. Only believing one is unable makes one unable! There are certainly diseases in the psychological area, especially among delusional-psychotic symptoms and those on an endogenous [biologically caused] basis, which greatly affect the capabilities of a person, but neuroses are *not* among them, and the exaggerated timidity of some sensitive individuals that are still considered "normal" even less so. One can feel claustrophobic in a supermarket and run away, but one can also experience these symptoms and still complete one's shopping, though with clenched teeth and white knuckles. In both cases one pays the price; if one wants to flee from fear, one will always be overtaken by it, for it is swifter than any escapee. But if one opposes it, one has won and emerges from the struggle as victor. Surprising as it may seem, *one can be afraid and yet courageous.* Even the timid have the freedom for courage. Perhaps it requires an even greater courage to do something while feeling afraid, than to do it without fear. Perhaps the fainthearted among us have a greater chance for heroism than the heroes among us will ever have!

That the fainthearted, too, still have the freedom for courage is a very recent acknowledgement in psychology. To be sure, it was virtually unknown before Frankl. For that reason, enormous psychological efforts were made to specify unhealthy fears of patients as accurately as possible. Unfortunately, this discourages patients even more and seems to verify their fatalistic hypothesis that they simply "can't help it." Let us look at the following dialogue between a client and a counselor:

Client: I am afraid of people!

Counselor: What people?

Client: For example, my father.

Counselor: How exactly does he frighten you?

Client: He speaks to me in a loud voice.

Counselor: What happens when he does that?

Client: I can't utter a word from fear.

Counselor: So you are afraid of your father and you transfer this
              fear to other people?

Client: Yes, that's why I avoid contact wherever I can.

Counselor: You probably feel lonely.

Client: [Sobbing] I have nobody in the world.

Let us consider what a client who goes home from such a counseling
dialogue may think. That individual may be angry towards his or her father,
who stands exposed as the author of such misery. Furthermore, I suppose
such a client will have a great deal of self-pity because of the lack of friends
and—because of fear—the inability to make new social contacts. Will
such a client ever know that, in spite of this, there remains the ability to
make satisfying contacts with others? Indeed, would such a person even be
able to talk openly with that stern father, if only there is resistance to the
inner fears? It is a fact demonstrated time and again in emergencies when
inhibited people simply overcome their own inhibitions because the situation suddenly demands it. Therefore, I would suggest that we rearrange
the above dialogue differently:

Client: I am afraid of people!

Counselor: All people, even the aborigines of Australia...?

Client: No, not all people.

Counselor: Which people don't frighten you?

Client: Children, for instance.

Counselor: And why not?

Client: Because they don't shout at me.

Counselor: Can someone's speaking loudly block your own
              willingness to speak?

Client: That is it exactly.

Counselor: But that is a great pity. There could come a time when
              a strong voiced declaration of love is made to you....

Client: [Laughing] In that case, I think I would overcome my
             block!

Let us again consider what a client coming home from that type of
consultation may think. Could we not suppose that, in spite of the inhibitions, there is now more awareness of the available freedom than after the
first dialogue? It might even be that such a client now feels rather silly at
being so upset merely by the loudness of a voice and will struggle to gain a
victory over this weakness. At least this promises more success than passing
the buck to the father and stewing in self-pity.

Once I had a young girl for consultation who opened our discussion with
the statement, "I cannot leave home." Ninety-nine out of 100 counselors
would have responded with the question, "Why not?" or "What holds
you at home?" suspecting parental pressure, sibling jealousy, or something
like that. But I considered this in another light and asked the girl, "If you
could go away, where would you go?" Interestingly, she had no idea where
she would like to go.

So I gave her the task of doing some thinking until the next session as
to where she would actually go if she could leave her parental home for a
long period without restriction. I also predicted that the ability would be
available as soon as a goal-directed intention became apparent. At our next
consultation she knew that she would love to visit her aunt in the country
during the holidays for two weeks. Together we wrote a note to her aunt
and I phoned her parents, and as the holidays approached I prepared to
encourage her for daring to take this small step out of the parental nest, but
she did not appear for her last consultation. She had left two days earlier
because she could no longer wait!

We see that it was not even necessary to decode this girl's fears according
to the traditional rules of psychology. What was primarily needed was to
point out the freedom she had in spite of her timidity—and to connect this
freedom to a meaningful goal. The greatest humiliation a person inflicts
on oneself with unrealistic fears is not only to give up this freedom, but
even more to not feel free to do what is valued as meaningful. The spark of
a meaningful goal can restore the freedom to plunge right into the center

of the objective in spite of all faintheartedness. As I implied earlier, fear is at our service and we should never become its slave. We must remain our own masters and then dedicate our lives to a meaningful task. Only in this way can our lives be fulfilled.

Let us always remember: One can be afraid and yet have courage. This does not refer to the courage of despair but to the courage of a being who understands fear as a challenge to his or her spiritual abilities and accepts the challenge.

2. Guilt as an Opportunity for Rethinking

Only one thing is worse than a pain endured and that is the distress over a pain inflicted. Friedrich von Schiller points to guilt as "the worst of all evils" and it is likely that he did not exaggerate too much, although today many would like to dispose of the guilt concept. But that is not so easy, for a guilt of commission preys persistently on someone's mind, frequently until death. The longing for forgiveness, the hope for a remission of guilt therefore emerges in all myths of deliverance, like a reflection of humanity's primeval longing. In addition to this, personal guilt is regarded in almost every religion as the origin of human misery in whatever way the "expulsion from Paradise" is symbolically represented.

In the field of psychology there is only one way to restore the paradisiacal condition of innocence, and that is with a "Declaration of Dependence" of the person. If an individual scientifically can be declared dependent on the conditions of life, then all behavior can be declared conditioned and all guilt feelings neurotic. Though I doubt whether this is really the way into Paradise; rather, I believe it is a direct way into a neurosis. For only neurotics believe, or want to believe, that environmental circumstances condition people to become who they are, which apparently serves to exonerate them. In contrast, healthy people never believe that; they are deeply aware of their "freedom from conditions"[2] and, with it, their culpability regarding the many decisions needed throughout life.

Every decision, however it is made, is fundamentally one's own, to which the final "Yes" is said by the person concerned. For example, people who are in the process of getting divorced come for advice and claim, "Our marriage just could not go well at all, because right from the beginning it was contracted under parental pressure." There is no doubt that parents can exert pressure even on grown children. Nevertheless, even a situation like that offers choices to those who are mature. Whoever is not convinced that a life together is right does not have to yield to external pressure; generally, those affected are able to oppose parents who attempt to interfere.

However, further investigation often reveals other factors; for example, a home purchase that required two incomes or social rejection if one lived together unmarried. The individuals involved wanted to have everything, a life together, a house, social acceptance, and marriage was the easiest solution. Not for love; no, it was for greed, to grab everything, to go the easiest way and to avoid losing out. There was a "Yes"; but it was not an honest "Yes" to the partner but a dubious "Yes" serving personal gain and benefit. If it didn't work out, it was not because there was no "Yes," but because there was no love for the partner. The failure of the marriage can conveniently be blamed on the parents. Everything is the parents' fault anyway because they exerted pressure.

This is how it is often done. Only one thing is overlooked. With healthy adults there is no such thing as *enforced decisions*. Where decisions are taken, there is freedom, and where pressure is really exerted, decisions are no longer taken. Each decision presupposes a choice, and where these choices prevail, a wrong decision can be taken, mistakes can be made, and guilt can occur. This, then, is one's own decision and one's own fault. Conversely, where no opportunities for choice are given, there is not a personal decision. And if something negative results, it is, therefore, not one's own fault.

Therefore, what we need in psychology are not hypotheses that determine dependency but rather *differentiation criteria for discerning justified and unjustified guilt feelings*. In real life, unfortunately, both are often mixed and very difficult to test for their objectivity by outsiders. Yet it is necessary to separate the two, just as it is important to differentiate realistic and unrealistic fears, as discussed in the previous chapter. Justified feelings of guilt must be addressed differently than those that are unjustified.

There are insecure, despondent individuals and those with little self-confidence who occasionally feel guilty about something for which they are blameless. On the other hand, we all know enough people who have made blatant mistakes in their lives but can't or don't want to admit that they have failed. In our counseling experience, we repeatedly encounter the combination within a single individual of a confession of guilt about something combined with a simultaneous list of reasons why they had no chance to act differently. It would be reasonable to conclude that what is sought from the therapist is an affirmation of innocence.

Why should that be so important? It must be because there is a sense a genuine guilt deep inside, which cannot be admitted, even in the quietest moment. Therefore, the counselor must be careful not to issue blanket "testimonials of innocence" because these can't solve the problem of a real misdeed. It seems to me to be more sensible to weigh the objective facts and, if necessary, to introduce into consideration some "counterweights" to the client's guilt.

If, for instance, a client says, "I was not nice to my mother. I could not know that she would die so suddenly and that I would never see her again," then I don't answer along the lines of, "Sure, you couldn't know that. How could you foretell that it was the last time together with your mother?" This would not remove the *not having been nice*. Rather, I allow the guilt to stand as it is and say simply, "Indeed, it is too bad that your last meeting ended so unfortunately. But surely there were many times in your life when a meeting with your mother went harmoniously?"

Unjustified feelings of guilt are relatively easily treated in therapy. They either have their origin in an error or a sickness. In case of an *error*, it must be pointed out unmistakably that there can be talk of guilt only where free will and a knowledge of the consequences of the action prevail. If, unexpectedly, a child suddenly runs in to a busy road in front of a car and the driver is unable to brake in time, then he is not to blame for the accident, even if it is heart wrenching. These are blows of fate which have to be accepted as inescapable suffering and must be overcome with a courageous inner fortitude. They do not require repentance in terms of a change of thinking. In cases of *sickness,* unjustified guilt feelings must be treated together with the other symptoms depending on the course of the illness.

Compulsive irrational feelings of guilt, for instance, fall into the category of psychological anxieties which can fairly easily be cured with *paradoxical intention*. A depressive irrational feeling of guilt must, on the other hand, be explained as a deceptive feeling and the patient should be encouraged to ignore this type of misperception (through *dereflection*).

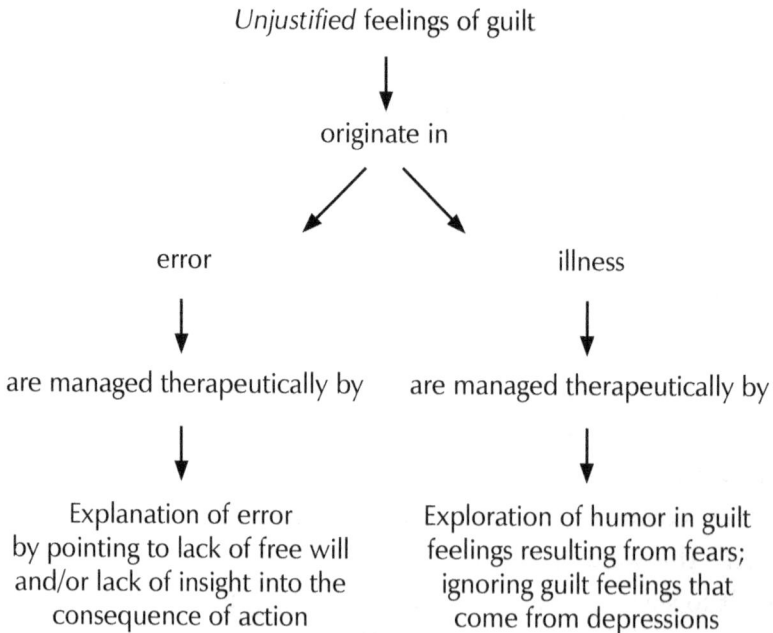

Unjustified feelings of guilt

↓

originate in

↙   ↘

error   illness

↓   ↓

are managed therapeutically by   are managed therapeutically by

↓   ↓

Explanation of error   Exploration of humor in guilt
by pointing to lack of free will   feelings resulting from fears;
and/or lack of insight into the   ignoring guilt feelings that
consequence of action   come from depressions

Now, I would like to deal with the handling of *justified* feelings of guilt, for that is extremely difficult both in counseling strangers and in one's own life, which is not spared from it either. It is that innermost voice of every person that, without fail, starts to speak in the most honest and lonely minutes of contemplation and brings back from the past what should never have been submerged in it. It is the naked truth that comes into view when the solidly constructed dependency hypotheses, which had been erected for protection by externalizing responsibility, start to crumble. There is only one remedy: *reparation*.

Because, as professionals, we can't avoid the subject when we deal with people who want to be counseled, logotherapists have investigated the wide field of potential reparations and found three possibilities of coping with guilt psychologically:

1) By reparation to the original person affected;

2) By reparation to another person;

3) By changing one's thinking, which is a type of reparation on the moral level.

The last possibility is especially uncommon in psychotherapy; it represents a direct step into the area of ministry. But who would put a stop sign on a bridge that spans an abyss?

Let us first consider the reparations to the person affected, especially *reparation to the same person who was harmed*. That is the simplest and most logical way to pay a debt. One has taken something from someone and returns it; one has destroyed something and repairs the damage; one has hurt a friend and apologizes for it. Often, this kind of reparation has an additional price, for it requires a certain humility, the ability to admit having made a mistake and to ask for forgiveness. But it resolves the feeling of guilt completely. No humiliation remains either, for the weakness in which an apology is given is balanced by a later strength.

The *reparation to a different person* is not quite as logical. It is also more bitter, because this solution is only considered if the reparation to the same subject is no longer possible. One has knocked out a person's eye and can never restore it; one has abused a child who is now grown—the childhood trauma can never be annulled. But nobody presents an obstacle to one's being especially considerate and helpful with new tasks and in future situations and to let goodness reign where previously there was hate and viciousness.

I knew a woman who psychologically overcame an abortion by later taking an unwanted child with numerous problems into her care. He thrived in her hands; that was not an easy way to calm a bad conscience but a commendable effort that gave a deeper meaning to the guilt (according to her reports), which resulted from the choices she had made.

Some convicts volunteer for medical research testing to repay something to humanity that they had previously denied by their inhuman behavior.

This type of reparation to other people demands a high degree of strength and self-denial, but there is a satisfying and curative effect: Not only is the feeling of self-worth restored but also the feeling of life worth is increased. In the case of an irrevocable offense which does not allow restitution, this restorative effect is otherwise considerably reduced.

Finally, let us look at the least logical of the three types of reparation, which can only be understood in metaphysical terms—*rethinking*. The guilty one carries a responsibility for something without ever having the freedom to make up for it.[3] The decisive factor is found in the inner attitude, in how the person thinks about it.

An individual might be in an intensive care unit of a hospital and looking back on life without having any time for reparation to anyone. Perhaps the person is in a prison cell and has forfeited most possibilities for choice and activity. One might be so poor or handicapped that the possibilities of doing something good are very limited. Such an individual can repent. Repentance somehow cancels guilt; it permeates the past with the meaning that at least the guilt has led to the *comprehension* of the mistake; and every process of understanding is a process of growth.

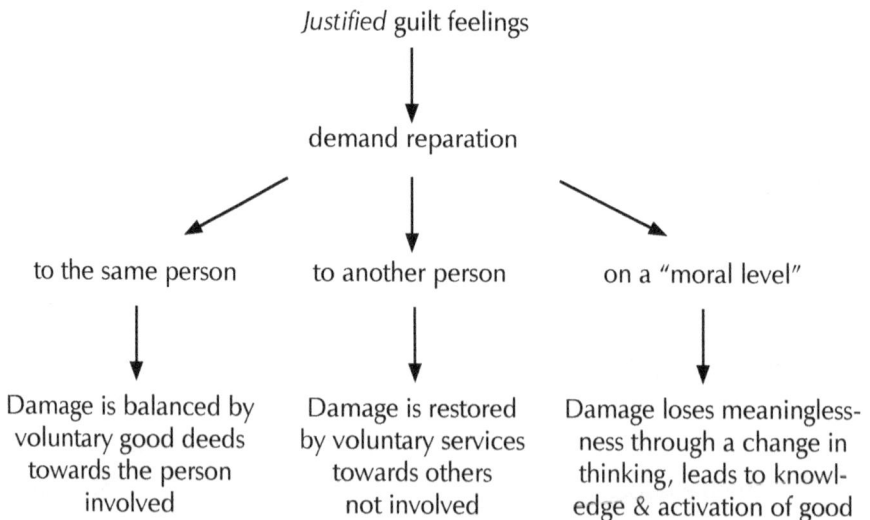

Justified guilt feelings

↓

demand reparation

↓

to the same person	to another person	on a "moral level"
↓	↓	↓
Damage is balanced by voluntary good deeds towards the person involved	Damage is restored by voluntary services towards others not involved	Damage loses meaninglessness through a change in thinking, leads to knowledge & activation of good

Repentance by no means refers to torturing self-recriminations, which in the end assume a masochistic character. It concerns the recognition of a Good that liberates rather than the futility of the no-longer-changeable Bad. A person who has a change in thinking because of guilt somewhat outgrows the previous ego. After the change, this person is no longer the same as before and has become someone else, perhaps even someone better. If this should be achieved, then guilt—and the suffering it brought—were not in vain. In the light of a deeper meaning, guilt brings a metamorphosis.

I would like to relate a dialogue I had with a patient in order to make it clear to the reader that from Frankl's tragic triad of suffering, guilt, and death it is *guilt* that can mar a person for life, longer than any suffering experienced, longer even than an encounter with death. A woman, aged about 60, had been referred to me from a care facility by her doctor because the psychological condition for which she was being treated had not improved. Since then we have had a number of discussions, but our first one had a key element insofar as it helped to motivate her to change her thinking.

In order that the dialogue can be followed not only in terms of content but also from a professional perspective, I will give some comments in between.

Mrs. X: I am so afraid. It is as if something is pressing down on me....

I: Please think about it carefully. What are you afraid of?

Mrs. X: That is just it. I don't know. There is absolutely no reason for it. Perhaps there is something in the past... that I did not cope with everything.

If a patient suffers from fear, it is advisable to investigate the cause. If the individual knows the subject of the fear and the fear does not bear a reasonable relation to it (for instance fear of bacteria, fear of being hurt by sharp objects, etc.) then the suspicion of an anxiety reaction pattern offers itself and the method of paradoxical intention could bring relief. But if the patient does not know the feared object, then something else lies behind it. Surprisingly, it is frequently a problem of the conscience. In any case, more intensive investigation is strongly indicated.

I: Is there something tragic in your past…?

Mrs. X: [Vehemently] It was hell, really hell with my first husband,
             I can tell you! He only boozed and womanized and then
             he was gone, simply gone.

I: How long did your marriage last?

Mrs. X: 14 years.

Now, in the exploration one could work intensively with the history of
the failed marriage which undoubtedly left its mark on the patient. On the
other hand, there would be a danger of placing too much emphasis on the
first marriage, and since there was talk of a first marriage there must have
been a second. Therefore, it is questionable whether it would be good to
stimulate the memories of the first partner too much. I therefore decided
to begin with a brief investigation of the broad general framework of the
woman's life.

I: And before, prior to your marriage, did you have a good
             life?

Mrs. X: I suppose my parents did a lot for me, but I did not know
             love and warmth. Their marriage was very bad too, and I
             had hardly finished school when they said: "You have to
             go to work!" My younger sister was permitted to undergo
             some training but they wanted me out of the house.

I: What was your work?

Mrs. X: In a factory and later with the trams. That was quite
             interesting.

I: So you did not dislike work?

Mrs. X: No, on the contrary. I always loved to work. [She talked
             about her work.]

I: Then perhaps your parents did not make the wrong
             decision when they sent you to work?

Mrs. X: No, not that….

Here we learn that not only the first marriage but also the patient's
childhood were not the best. Again, very much psychological digging would

be possible. However, nobody can undo what has happened. The only thing that can be changed is the patient's attitude to it and I tried to change that. She can now reconcile herself with her parents' behavior.

I: Mrs. X, you started work when you were young. Did you also marry early?

Mrs. X: Yes, much too early. But it was 1942, you know, and nobody knew what would happen. Many men were killed and on parting we never knew whether we would see each other again.

I: I can understand that. So, your husband returned from the war. Could it be that the experiences of war had changed him?

Mrs. X: True, that's it. He was suddenly a totally different person. But our George was born in 1945. [Crying]

I: [After a pause] George is your son?

Mrs. X: He was the eldest.... [Cries]

Up to this point the patient had talked about very painful life situations but nevertheless the impression was that she could live with them. Even a reconciliation with her first husband's behavior seems, in the light of the traumatic war years at that time, possible. But, on mentioning George, we come upon a strong emotional reaction.

I: Mrs. X, I think it is not really the unhappy marriage with your first husband or your somewhat cold childhood which bothers you like that, but something else—?

Mrs. X: [Whispers] My George died at 16.

I: I am sorry Mrs. X, that is a terrible loss for a mother!

Mrs. X: It is more than 20 years ago. I must be able to get over it. Others can do it!

In addition to her other troubles, the patient was also faced with this tragic death, the death of one of her children. But as she correctly noted, that was 20 years ago, not that a mother could ever accept something like this completely; such a wound goes deep. But in the present case, it does not heal, as her tears show. Why not? We still have to talk about this.

I: One does not forget something like this, Mrs. X, even if it was long ago. Tell me something about George. What kind of child was he?

Mrs. X: [Haltingly] That's just it! He was so good, not at all like a child. He never had a childhood! He always looked after the little one for me. He virtually raised him. In the mornings he took him to the crib. I was so very much alone, without any help. At four in the morning I had to start at the post office and in the afternoons as well. At that time letters were delivered twice daily. My mother did not take the little one off my hands. The social welfare did not help. The woman there said with children of married parents the husband has to help, but he had gone. I did not even know where.... I had no money.

I: You had another child then and your husband left you?

Mrs. X: Yes, Markus was born in 1954 and in the same year my first husband moved out of the house and went underground. He had done something dishonest, some flimflams. The police were looking for him. There I was with the two children. If I had not had George, I don't know what would have happened. And he was only nine years old himself.... He never had a real childhood. [Cries]

With reports by patients that are loaded so heavily with emotion, one has to listen for the nuances in order to detect the cause of the symptoms. Suffering as such does not necessarily cause illness. Quite the opposite; it can contribute to a psychological strengthening of the patient. Only if there is something contrary to meaning or against one's conscience in the suffering, can it cause a neurosis.

While looking out for nuances, the sentence "He never had a real child-hood" had come to my attention. This sentence was repeated and appeared to cause more pain than the sentence: "He has died."

I: That was a terrible time of need, dear God! You had to
          earn the money for the family and your nine-year old son
          had to look after the baby. Both of you, you and your
          eldest son, were very brave!

Mrs. X: [Stops crying and talks more coherently and even a little
          proudly] George did everything for the little one, fed him,
          cleaned him, was always patient with him and tolerated
          everything from him. The little one was sometimes a little
          devil. He bit him in his calf from behind, for instance.
          And when I said: "George, hit him," he only laughed and
          said "Mommy, he does not understand yet." He virtually
          brought him up. That was an enormous help for me. My
          mother did not help me, but she died soon afterwards....
          Later I was able to give Markus to a foster mother. Then it
          was a bit better for us. Then I married the second time so
          that the children could have a father, a really good man.
          He also liked George a lot. [Her voice starts breaking]

I: [Quietly] What happened then?

Mrs. X: At 16, George got poliomyelitis. It took only three days.
          Then he died. A year later polio immunizations were
          introduced.

I: Was the little one in danger too?

Mrs. X: Yes. At that stage I had him back home again. He was
          in quarantine but he did not get it. I never had the
          relationship with the little one which I had with the
          eldest.... I missed the years we were separated, while he
          was in foster care....

I: So you lost the one child who was particularly close to
          you. And it happened at a time when the worst troubles
          were behind you and you were hoping that at last a few
          happy years were ahead?

Mrs. X: That is it exactly. One can't do a thing. One can't change
          a thing. Nobody can change anything. There is no relief
          because one can't turn time back. Everything is inexorably
          finished, past!

The transitory nature of time[4] does not take anything away from the meaning of things past. Nor would a meaningless existence become any more meaningful if it were extended into eternity. The value of a life therefore does not depend on its length, just as the quality of a travel film does not depend on its duration. If the film takes two hours to show travel on dusty roads then it is less successful than if it lasts only half an hour but captures the most beautiful vistas of the landscape that was traversed.

Remaining with the comparison of the passage of life with the making of a movie, it is possible to see that, just as in the movie, life is only "completed" with its ending. Every scene is there forever, immovably fixed, projected onto the screen of the past on which nothing can be changed but neither can it be counterfeited. What was evil remains evil and what was good remains good forever.*

I: Mrs. X, you say one can't change anything. On the other hand you have told me so many positive things about your George, how he helped in need, how touchingly he looked after his little brother—would you really like to have all this changed?

Mrs. X: No, not that. He was an angel who came to this world, did good and left again....

I: Do you see, Mrs. X, this remains too, not only the fact of his passing! His entire life and actions remain good forever, as short as they may have been. Do you believe that the length of a life is its most important aspect? Are there not lives which last a long time but bring little meaning, others again which, in the short time given to them, fill it with a plethora of good deeds?

Mrs. X: Yes, that is true. My George gave me a lot of happiness in his short life. He was such a dear, so sensible and intelligent....

---

*   The religious person can, in this example of an "archive" of the past in which all the "films" of completed human lives are kept, visualize the "archivist" as well, that authority who is the only one to know every film in detail, even the smallest episode. The condition of awareness during the life of a human being would then transform into the condition of being known after death.

I: That, too, remains, doesn't it? The joy he brought to you nobody can take away. The encounter with a little angel, as you call him, belongs indelibly in your life. If you think back today to your dead child, you should actually be grateful that he was given to you as a gift.

Mrs. X: If one looks at it like that....

In logotherapy we call this type of discussion *attitude modulation*. It is not correct that nothing can be changed, as the patient believes. There is something that can be changed. One can at least change one's spiritual attitude to something that has happened, which makes a great difference from a psychological perspective.

I: How would your George have wanted you to see this?

Mrs. X: Oh! He wouldn't have wanted me to suffer and worry. His last words in the hospital were: "Help my mother!" He never thought of himself. If he had a few pennies in his pocket he bought something for the little one, never for himself. He never had a carefree childhood, not at all. [Cries]

There is the sentence again that had caught my attention before and suddenly I have an insight into the pathologizing heart of the matter. I see what is behind the trouble of my patient. Not the pain suffered. Not the death of the child. There is a deep feeling of guilt that was never overcome!

I: Mrs. X, I have the impression that there is something very specific that troubles you. It does not even seem to be the tragic death of your son as such that appears so insurmountable. His sudden death must at the time have been a terrible shock for you, especially as it was so unexpected, but in the many years that have passed since then the shock should have abated somewhat. But there is something which you keep repeating. It is the sentence: "He had no carefree childhood." Is it possible that you still brood about whether you could have given him a better childhood, whether you could have given him more happiness, whether there is not perhaps something that

you failed to do for him and now you can never make up
for it?

Mrs. X: [Excitedly grasps my hands] That is it, Doctor. That's
it! For example, the school went on excursions and my
George was the only one who was not allowed to go.
We did not have the money for the train ticket. Perhaps
I could have raised it somehow…? Or the teacher
recommended a book of animal stories to him, I still
remember it today, and I could not buy it. But the book
might have been in the library for lending. I was often so
tired when I got home from work. I had to get up at 4 am
and did not feel like listening to all his little worries and
wishes. [Sobs loudly]

So that was the reason for the incurable psychological affliction of the
patient. Not the heavy blows of fate in her hard life threatening to crush
her. No, it was the minute remnant of freedom in between that tortured
her with the question whether she had used the last remaining freedom
responsibly or not. She thought she had not.

I: [After a pause] Your guilt feelings are the cause of your
fears, Mrs. X. You suffer from a troubled conscience. Your
boy helped you wherever possible and you ask yourself up
to this day whether you helped him, too, wherever you
could, is it not so?

Mrs. X: [Softly] Yes.

The diagnostic phase of the interview was completed; the therapeutic
phase began at this point.

I: Alright, Mrs. X, we have found the source of your
affliction. In my opinion, you are an exceedingly strong
and brave woman. You coped well with a mediocre
childhood. You have worked hard and diligently all your
life. You struggled laboriously through the war and the
postwar years, and what is more, in a desperate situation,
forsaken by your husband and your mother, you mustered
enough strength to provide for both your children. From

all this I would conclude that you would be able to cope with the tragic death of your eldest son bravely and unfalteringly as well. What prevents you from finding peace in your soul is the question of whether you have become guilty of something with respect to your son. Let us work out together what would have happened if your George had lived.

Mrs. X: Oh! I could have offered him quite a few things later.

I: And the guilt feelings?

Mrs. X: I probably wouldn't have had them because I would have told myself I made up for the things he missed in his childhood....

It is indeed a question for the detached observer just how far the guilt feelings of the patient are justified. According to my gut feeling I would say—as I did indeed say to the patient—that the woman was very brave and hardly had a chance to act differently. Yet there is this 20-year-old discomfort in her and she does not seem to be the overscrupulous type. There could be some real experience that might explain it. The tragic part is that any kind of guilt concerning the child cannot be expiated. Even if it should only be a trifle, there are no more trifles which could balance matters for the same person.

I: True. Let us think further. What would have happened if your son George had been an unpleasant child, a rowdy who mainly loitered about the streets instead of helping you?

Mrs. X: Oh! Then...? I would have cried for him too, but probably not such a long time. I mean I would not have suffered in the same way.

I: And the guilt feelings?

Mrs. X: Perhaps they would have been less strong. Yes, indeed, I think so.

I: Do you realize that your troubled conscience is closely associated with the very special character of your son? The

most beautiful thing you ever experienced in your life was
the goodness, the selflessness, and the early maturity of
your son, wasn't it? At the same time, it is also the reason
why you feel guilty. You remained a human when you
faced an "angel," if we use your own comparison. But now,
you look away from yourself. What was it that made your
George into such a special young person? Was it not the
very crisis situation that made him prematurely mature?
Was it not the fact that he was needed by his mother, who
herself could only offer him little, urgently needed as a
helper in time of need? Was not that the fact that brought
out the best in him? If you had been able to offer him a
carefree childhood would he have become the same?

Mrs. X: You mean, the circumstances matured him?

I: Definitely. Also matured in those moments when his
          mother was weak and tired and came home exhausted,
          when he had no money for entertainment, etc. His noble
          character was formed in those bitter hours and his early
          death has prevented any change in it. What one has from
          life is not as important as you think, but more what one
          becomes in life. Being is more important than having! And
          even if your son did not have very much in life, he became
          great, he became a magnificent young man.

Without doubt the patient idealizes her son a bit. He was certainly not
a "pure angel" even if much of what she says about him is truly remarkable. But the idealization does not matter because it is no longer associated
with any expectations from the son. It merely glorifies a value which is and
remains a high value even without glorification. This is why I didn't touch
on the idealizing (which would have been tantamount to devaluing), but
rather utilized it positively for initiating "a healing change in thinking."

Mrs. X: Yes, he was indeed fantastic!

I: Perhaps even a bit more "fantastic" than his mother? Do
          not begrudge him this prestige. Allow him to have been
          the "better part" of the two of you. Your failing made a
          hero of him. Personally I don't believe that you have really

failed in a broad sense. I am convinced that you have done what was humanly possible for both of your children. But the little mistakes you made as well, because you are not an angel, let him appear in contrast in an especially positive light. Or, in other words your deceased son seemed so fantastic mainly because you in some way failed him.

Mrs. X: I understand. I can be proud of him. He was better than his father and better than his mother. I can't say that of my second son without reservations. But his life is not finished yet. You are right, I have made mistakes and both my sons reacted differently to them. George apparently grew because of them.

I: He even grew to his last breath when his thoughts and care were for you. His last wish was for your welfare and that you should not be plagued by worries and doubts.

Mrs. X: Yes, that is true. [Lifts her head.] I will now go to the cemetery and be with him in my thoughts. I will tell him that I am proud of him. And then I will go home and make an effort to live in such a way that he could be proud of me too....

Since this first talk, the patient has been in a good condition, and on the basis of further talks she has developed a good relationship with her other son, who already had his own family but was probably in the shadow of his deceased brother for a long time.

The old saying that one should give flowers to the living because they bloom in vain on graves contains a deep wisdom that was learned in a painful process by this woman. Every one of us should occasionally remember as well.

To be human means that there always remains something that we owe to ourselves and others, and that simply means that we let meaning potentials pass by without seizing them and without making the right choice at the right moment. Unlike any other creature, it is the price we have to pay for receiving a present: the freedom of will.

How did Martin Buber say it so aptly?

> The great guilt of man is
> > not the great sins he commits.
> Temptation is powerful and
> > his strength is small!
> The great guilt of man is
> > that at any moment he can
> > turn around and does not do it!

The "turning around" begins with a change in thinking.

3. Thoughts on Suicide Prevention*

For a suicide to take place, two occurrences have to happen sequentially. These are:

1. The idea of suicide comes to be seen as a viable option.
2. A concrete effort is made to put the thought into action.

If the first does not take place (that is, if one does not even think of suicide), there exists virtually no danger. But if the life-negating action has already been exercised in thought, then a certain basic danger is ever present, which can be more or less pronounced depending on personal circumstances. Of course, there are many more people who occasionally flirt with the idea of voluntary death than who actually proceed with it. Thank heaven that it is so. But even the flirting by itself has a destructive, so to speak "deadening," effect, because it reduces the awareness of the value of life and thus automatically establishes a feeling that all being and doing is meaningless. This feeling, in turn, lets the thought of suicide appear meaningful.

As far as it concerns the question of suicide prevention, scientific attention must not only be on the prevention of actual suicide but must also engage in preventing thoughts of the very idea of suicide. Unfortunately, there is no agreement about this among professionals, so it comes to the

---

* This essay was originally commissioned by the Federal Ministry for Youth, Family and Health and published by the German Society for Suicide Prevention.[5]

paradox that, on the one hand, high protective fences are erected on bridges, towers, and similar buildings to make it more difficult for those wishing to commit suicide to jump, while, on the other hand, the media eagerly report on every death jump. This, in turn, produces new candidates for suicide through disseminating an idea that a desperate reader might take up.

In this context, Viktor Frankl pointed to a remarkable incident in Detroit, which he learned about while on a lecture tour through the United States. At the time, the incidence of suicides and suicide attempts had suddenly and drastically decreased only to increase just as suddenly after six weeks. This was extremely unusual. Investigations established that, at that time, there had been a six-week newspaper strike and no reports about suicides had been given. This type of correlation gives food for thought and also gives support to those professional voices who keep on protesting whenever a film whose youthful hero commits suicide makes the circuit through the theaters. A number of young people caught in this maelstrom actually take their lives, often for insignificant reasons.

Therefore, if we start from the premise that the mere thought of a possible self-killing is dangerous because there are people who are caught up by the idea, have kept a mental note of it as a possible solution for problems in other crises, and bring it out of its cognitive pigeonhole as a more or less serious consideration, then we are forced to apply suicide prevention long before traditional crisis-intervention schemes find it necessary. Undoubtedly, the idea precedes the deed. Therefore the prevention of ideas should come before crisis intervention.

Let us ask ourselves what promotes the idea of suicide. It is not difficult to answer the question. It is *example*—the youthful film hero with whom one identifies, just as with the cornered man, or the unhappy woman about whose suicide the newspapers write, or the figure in the novel about whom one cries, or the sighing about the hopelessness of life in mournful hit songs. The less solid and psychologically stable the person, the greater the search for support and orientation in the environment and the more vulnerable that individual is to negative environmental influences, to taking on the role of dramatic hero, or to adopting end-of-the-world moods.

Besides these social and sociocultural influences, there is another example with a strong precipitating effect: the *family example*. A suicide in the family endangers all other family members, especially the children. Such a terrible and usually shockingly sudden experience will never be forgotten by any member of the family and sometimes, by depressing and sensitizing, its effect persists for generations. As if under a compulsion, children and grandchildren of those who complete suicide sometimes have to fight the recurring thought of a "radical erasure of all their worries," and they have to put up a resistance against it that is much higher compared with persons in whose families this type of "problem solving" was never even discussed.

There are known suicide chains in some family histories that might start with the great grandfather, find their macabre continuation in the mother, and finally have their last victim in the suicide of the youngest child. Certainly, one could speculate that similar character predispositions or hereditary transmissions are the decisive element in such suicide chains, but the idea of suicide is also undeniably passed on from generation to generation and is always available in those times of crisis, that naturally arise in every life.

Logotherapists, who have thoroughly investigated feedback mechanisms and iatrogenic damage, have concentrated on two approaches to prevent such tragic effects of models:

    a) to eliminate the negative example as much as possible, and

    b) to immunize against the negative example.

The family example can, unfortunately, hardly be eliminated; it does happen, again and again, that someone in the family completes suicide. But the social and sociocultural example could be avoided, as was demonstrated in the newspaper strike. A drastic curtailment of press freedom is certainly not demanded for suicide prevention. It would be enough if the media would handle the subject with more circumspection and would not turn it into sensational reporting, and if literature, art, and films would not specially select a suicide as the center of attention and place those who commit suicide on a hero's pedestal. The artistic task, and one that is an essential part of the news media, to present the world as it is, must be counterbalanced by responsibility for influencing the environment and for mass manipulation. Whoever believes that truth is the primary criterion in the processing of all information is wrong. The more "truths" about atrocities, catastrophes, murder, and suicide are disseminated, the more they increase, so that one can never catch up with the truth in the tragic endeavor of iatrogenic (or media-genic) infection of the "still healthy" with material that is already sick.

Concerning the family, it is a thoroughly logotherapeutic argument to make suicidal persons aware of the terrible burden their deed would mean for the family. In this way, many deeply depressed mothers could be persuaded to give up the idea of suicide completely as a heroic renunciation, made consciously and willingly, bravely living a life that appears valueless to her, if by doing so she can save her children from the curse of imitation. (This renunciation often has the effect that life finds meaning again and no longer looks quite so valueless!)

So much for the possible elimination of examples that encourage suicide. However, because those possibilities are limited, it is no less important to immunize against them as a strong preventative measure. According to logotherapeutic thinking, there are noëtic (spiritual) forces in the human being that confront psychological influences, but which themselves cannot be influenced, at least not against the will of the person concerned. Practically speaking, these are the forces that control a person's emotions and determine the power allocated to them. They are an authority not subject to the rule of the pleasure principle, unlike our emotions. Instead, they follow the principle of meaning.

If psychological conditions such as fear, mourning, or insecurity caused by negative examples are spiritually perceived as meaningless, then one can adopt an inner distance. This enables a person "not to have to put up with every nonsense from oneself" as Viktor Frankl expressed it, who in this connection talked about *the defiant power of the human spirit*. It is important to note that the spiritual dimension of an individual must be intact and not handicapped by psychotic interferences, as this would seriously distort the person's perception of a meaningful spiritual attitude to psychological circumstances. Examples of suicide, including their inevitable psychological repercussions, can be spiritually processed in such a way that they are neutralized, provided that a fairly normal contact with reality exists. This can be through a healthy defiance towards them, emphasizing positive aspects of life where negative ones have become visible. Such a *tragic optimism*[6] can, especially if it is philosophically and ideologically undergirded, become the strongest defense against suicidal tendencies and ideas. It is like a bastion that cannot be overrun even in the darkest hours of life. Psychotherapy should and ought to contribute towards building such strongholds in their patients, but for that it needs a positive concept of the human being and of the world, as is the case with logotherapy. It is a concept of the person that allows for freedom and responsibility, and a concept of the world that affirms the existence of a logos in and above everything, even though at times it may elude the grasp of human understanding.

As noted, even the emergence of a suicidal thought must be opposed; on the other hand, there is a long distance between the thought and the deed. Usually, it is assumed that the deed needs an acute trigger, such as an acute despair. That is the case with some suicides. Someone close has left, a business is ruined, a goal has proven unattainable. A person is confronted with an unchangeable fate, which, however, will never completely remove some arena of freedom. Each person can always choose how to answer the test questions of life. Different answers are always possible because there are empty lines between the questions of fate, available to be filled in by the person with no outside influence. (Could it be that in life only those lines to be written are important and not the questions above them, similar to an exam where only the quality of the answers given counts?) In any case, for every acute trigger there are psychologically healthy and unhealthy attitudes, depending on the life principle. If the pleasure principle reigns, then every setback is a displeasure that leads to despair. If the meaning principle reigns, then every defeat is a challenge to seek a deeper meaning in the situation and to respond accordingly—to be *response-able*,[7] *able to respond to life.*

Because of this perspective, which is unique in psychotherapy, it is the central concern of the logotherapist to guide vulnerable people towards meaning-oriented thinking and to rouse in them supportive attitudes which will prove themselves in times of need and crisis. The often observable, cramped attitude "the main thing is I am well" (which potentially leads to a cul-de-sac because being well can't be enforced), is gently transformed into the attitude, "the main thing is that I am good for something." On closer scrutiny, it becomes apparent that everybody can be good for something or someone, independent of the perhaps miserable position in which the person exists. At the very moment when such a "being good for something" (that is, a meaning element of one's own existence) lights up, the question "why live?" or "why go on living?" is already answered. It is a question that is diametrically opposed to any premeditated death. For example, think of those children who, after a suicide attempt, declare that they "wanted someone to cry for them," children who obviously miss the feeling of being good for something or someone and therefore want to prove, at least with someone's tears, that they were good for something after all!

Here we change from acute distress as a trigger for a desperate deed to another component of life which also supports the enticements of suicide: *total indifference*—the inner emptiness, the supposed valuelessness of all being, the feeling of meaninglessness of all life. Precisely that spiritual authority which we mentioned earlier as the powerful factor of defiance against external or internal negative influences is marked by striving and searching for something meaningful. If this search is not rewarded with a minimal measure of "unearthing," then it sinks into an *existential frustration* which was discovered and described by Viktor Frankl. This existential frustration has an even stronger impulse for desperation than any other precipitating factor of fate. The great danger of existential frustration is not even so much that it causes suicide but that from that frame of mind there is nothing to oppose the idea of suicide. In an empty, meaningless life the reason for living is lacking and without an answer to the question "why live?" there is no answer to the question "why not die?" either.

In logotherapy, a diagnosis of *noögenic neurosis*,* is made if a massive existential frustration is present that needs specific therapy to avoid a risk

---

* The word *noögenic* is derived from the Greek *nous* which means spirit, meaning.

of suicide. It is a sad fact that most individuals who exhibit symptoms of a noögenic neurosis come from decidedly uncomplicated circumstances, indeed can often claim material prosperity, career success, good friends, and physical health, but simply don't know what to do with them to make life meaningful. But this fact is congruent with research, which concludes that about 20% of all suicides are completed by individuals with relatively positive life profiles.

While suicide prevention in cases of desperation must offer solutions for problems and conflicts and work towards supportive attitudes where no solutions can be found, suicide prevention for actions of indifference with a noögenic aspect must concentrate on pointing out the ever-present meaning of life under any circumstance. This effort has for decades been the gravitational center of our logotherapeutic work. We may suppose that this latter effort is more important than the former, for while emergency situations can be fairly well managed in a life that is perceived as meaningful, not even periods of prosperity and happiness are sufficient to give justification to a life that is experienced as meaningless. Therefore, the main idea of all suicide prevention culminates in the presence of an answer that is always available concerning the fundamental question "why live?," an answer which simultaneously satisfies the question "and why not die?"

In psychiatry there is still another area within which it is essential to help the individual find a positive answer to this basic question and that is the large field of those symptoms which were formerly called *hysterical*. The question here is "Why become healthy?" which is a counterpart to the question "Why not remain sick?" For remaining sick there is unfortunately a reason, a reward that misguides these patients into maintaining their sickness more or less consciously. Frequently the reason is some addressee in the outer world from whom the enforcement of certain reactions is intended by means of certain symptoms. These symptoms can, as is generally known, be exaggerated into suicide threats and suicide attempts, to demonstrate to the other person concerned what he or she has brought about. This is from the perspective of the patient. That these unfortunate attempts can sometimes be fatal is nothing new.

In cases like this, we are not dealing with a genuine despair nor with an existential frustration, but rather with a shifting of blame of a special type, simply the *refusal to be responsible for oneself*. The question "Why get healthy?" can only be meaningfully answered by regaining full autonomy over the self, human freedom, and responsibility. The individual for whom this answer is not attractive does not desire to become an active "co-creator" of his or her own destiny because the role of a passive victim of fate is preferred, even if this means sacrificing one's own life.

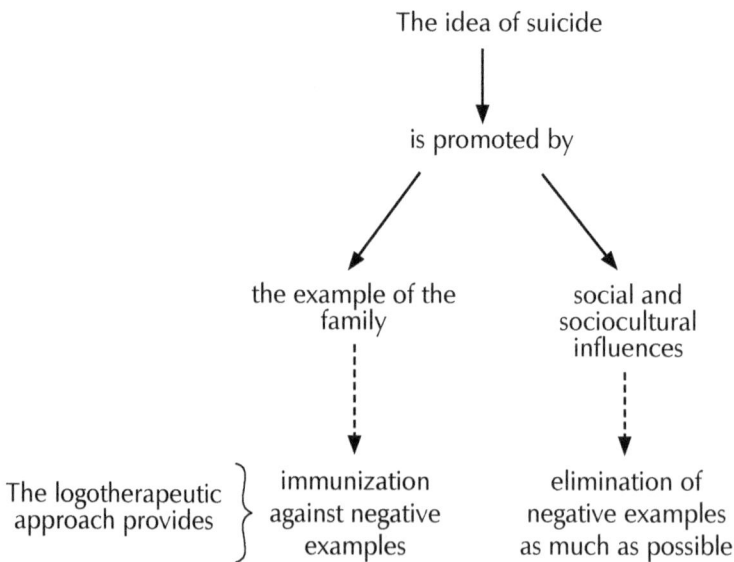

The idea of suicide

is promoted by

the example of the   social and
family   sociocultural
                              influences

The logotherapeutic   immunization   elimination of
approach provides   against negative   negative examples
                      examples   as much as possible

How can such "hysterical" suicide attempts be prevented? There is one way: A continuous appeal to responsibility should be made by every discipline. In this regard, logotherapy is one of the pioneers among the human sciences. On the other hand, a psychology that fosters the patient's blame-shifting by declaring mothers, fathers, siblings, teachers—and even the entire society—guilty of the psychological deformations of the individual can't actually stimulate the will to recovery; the blown-up emotions against the "culprits" that have to be worked through include the disease as a permanent background. Reconciliation with life does not take place on the basis of accusations, or as Søren Kierkegaard says, "Life can only be understood backwards but it must be lived forwards."

The performance of suicide

is risked by   is precipitated by   is prepared by

| hysterical components (tendency to shift blame) | situations of distress and crisis (actual despair) | noögenic components (inner emptiness) |

The logotherapeutic approach provides

| call to self-responsibility | awakening of positive influences | pointing out meaning in life |

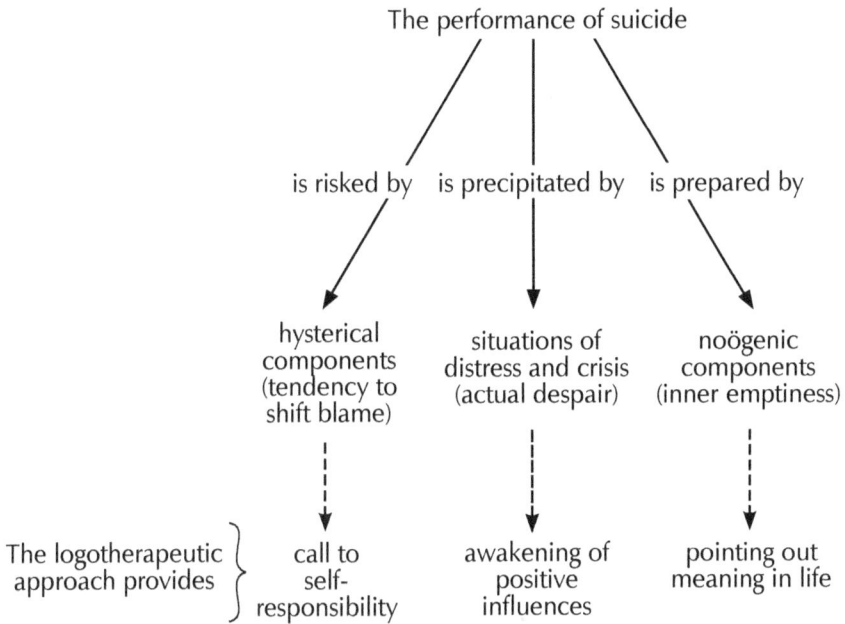

In concluding the subject, I would like to take up another hot button issue: the question of the *right to die*. As usual in such burning issues, every party has its legitimate arguments. As a logotherapist, however, I can offer another argument that until now has rarely been considered, that of *objective meaning*.

Until now all the pros and cons were related to the patient, how much life still has to offer, whether prolonging suffering is not asking too much, and whether there is a right to a humane death. But a human being does not live alone. A person does not live on Robinson Crusoe's island, but is a minute part of the whole. Between each person and the whole pulsates a current of effects and countereffects, radiations, and influences for which that person—as far as they originate from him or her—is co-responsible. Let us examine this aspect with a theoretical example:

Let us imagine a man who is paralyzed from the neck down and who entreats the doctors to "deliver" him. He fights for this, his presumed right, because, as he says, there is not a glimmer of hope that his life will one day be worth living. What radiates from this man?

1. He wants to force a doctor to kill him. Does he realize what this implies? What is he asking the doctor to do? What is he asking from another person who will have to live with this for the rest of his or her life? Do people who lie on train rails to commit suicide know what they do to the driver of the train who runs over them? Did the woman who jumped off the Eiffel Tower and accidentally hit a Canadian tourist who was busy taking photos know what she did? It may be understandable that someone wants to commit suicide, but is it comprehensible that such a person really wants to go with a debt that can never be repaid?

2. The paralyzed man is aware that his battle and his possible victory will be published in the press. Innumerable people will read about it; it can be assumed that a certain percentage among them have likewise little hope of improving their life situations. How many of them will he drag along into death? How many will follow his example? Does he really want to be the leader of a long procession into the land of no return? And what if, for some among them, there was still hope? He fights for his right to die but, in truth, he robs others of the courage to live!

Let us put the question differently: What could radiate from this paralyzed man in spite of his massive handicap?

1. If he could embrace life, he would bear witness to the capabilities of the human spirit. By merely existing, he would already be doing something good! His living "in spite of" would be living proof for others that life is possible even under the most difficult conditions. Therefore, one's own life can also be mastered whatever it brings. Without doing anything at all he could be a catalyst for strength and encouragement, an example and a motivator.

2. There is not only a responsibility for a What but also a responsibility for the How. And in the *how* of enduring his affliction, the paralyzed man would still have a number of possibilities for expressing himself and unfolding his personality, for developing and improving his unique existence. We know of a case where a totally paralyzed

man wrote comforting letters to desperate people in his town with a little stick that he held between his teeth. These letters found a resonance in the recipients that was greater than any notes sent by trained counselors.

Let us, therefore, consider in discussions about help for the dying: Every human life has its unconditional meaning. The hand that ends life also lets this hidden meaning be forever unfulfilled.

4. About Therapeutic Books

In a textbook that is used for German in the Gymnasium there is an excellent analysis of modern novels. It is written by Paul K. Kurz. Here is an excerpt:

> That composition in which the search for meaning no longer ends in the finding of meaning but where even its possibility is opposed and negated must, from its content, be labeled not simply "contemporary" but specifically a "modern novel." Or—and this is the latest trend—the question about overall meaning is no longer asked at all. In his approach, the author of the "classic" or traditional novel fundamentally accepted the world. As a result, his hero also accepted the world, which was reaffirmed somewhere in the novel. The author of modern novels and his characters have renounced this agreement with the world on the basis of previous experiences. In principle, the place of a previous "Yes" is taken by a "No," or at least a fundamental skepticism. Life and acceptance of the world is, if at all, only possible in fragments: Where and to what degree must be established in each case. Every publicly propagated complete system of the meaning of life by society during the past three generations, be it Prussian, Wilhelmic, Imperial-Austrian, Weimaran, Nazistic, or the present prosperous society, is more or less exposed as pretentious by the modern novel. The drudgery of life for the average individual does not take place under the gold-plated dome of an obliging society and a faith in the absolute. Man experiences himself as under pressure from specific, isolated, and often controversial demands. How can he take care of his soul if he never gets done with observing rules of behavior

and traffic laws, serving only the next moment, or with the
swallowing of news fragments relating to moments of the past?
How can he strive for perfect wholeness if his life consists
of countless disconnected associations and drive impulses
flashing on and off, of pills, of momentary contamination
and decontamination, of the smallest liberation—and escape
attempts—from an ever-present and anonymously controlled
encirclement? Therefore the modern novel is mainly a lament
at the loss of the perfect wholeness, criticism and protest
against unacceptable living conditions, abysmal melancholia
about the individual's impotence, and about the inaccessibility
of any ideal, never-ending reflections and chain questions for
the minutest fragments of a liveable truth.

Modern novels naturally reflect modern society but the mirror reflects
back the image it receives. It not only portrays modern society but also
influences it. Everything spiritual continues to vibrate and echo. There simply
is no interpersonal communication without spiritual involvement, and the
book is a powerful instrument of communication. One could even say that,
just as the organism remains alive only through a continuous metabolism,
so it needs a spiritual metabolism, a continuous flow of exchange of ideas
between thinking beings, to maintain the spiritual existence.

This does not mean that an individual's personality is simply the product
of spiritual influences. As implied in the above analysis, there is a strong
tendency to perceive environmental influences as negative and to declare
them the scapegoat for every failure. From environmental pollution and
problems of the arms race to the dawning of the computer age, influences
are registered and transformed into a panicked frenzy to which the individual
is apparently helplessly exposed. These influences are held responsible if
one's life is not successful.

But in this way the human being is given a role that, by nature, he
cannot play. The person is "placed" in front of the wall of fate, just as a knife
thrower in a circus places the partner in front of the wall to unflinchingly
watch the knives fly by, hoping that none of them accidentally pierces the
heart. This is not a role fitting for a creature equipped with spiritual gifts.
We simply do not stand in the midst of multiple impressions impinging on

us from all sides, even if modern authors often present it in this manner. Metabolism is an *exchange*, it is the taking of foreign matter and giving one's own; it is the processing and forming of what is found and a spiritual coming to terms with the world in which we live.

It is not true that nearly all influences around us are exclusively negative. As well as knives, bread is, so to speak, placed in our laps. Nor does it correspond with the fact that we are only "influenced." We each hold a knife in our own hand ready to strike, but we also have the bread to divide and share as well. Spiritual influences have to meet a personal "Yes" to become effective. Only then will the seed germinate for good or for evil.

A book in its essence is not paper and printer's ink, but spiritual substance. Each book transmits ideas that in extreme cases can be a knife or bread insofar as it is capable of undermining or offering spiritual support. It exposes persons of differing degrees of susceptibility to its influence—those who clutch a dagger as well as those who break bread. That makes it worthwhile to ponder the responsibility that rests with the different stages of a publication: on the author as the source of influence; on publishing houses who take up these influences and hand them on; on bookshops as "thought transmission centers"; and, finally, on customers who expose themselves passively to the influence of strange ideas, or face them actively in a spiritual effort. To have an effect, a book travels a long path from the author's pen until it flows into the reader's soul, there to cause either redemption or havoc.

Undoubtedly, there are good and bad books; it is questionable how far the criteria for good and marketability coincide. In the psychological and psychotherapeutic domains, the overlap is certainly very small. This has to do with the fact that everything deviating from the norm, everything perverse, problematic, and sinister, has a great attraction for the consumer, which is not the least reason why producers of crime and horror thrillers make such a profit. For many, it is somehow enjoyable to experience the spine-chilling terror scenes from the security of their own living rooms, knowing full well that they are not involved. I do not intend to dispute the danger, especially for young people, from exposure to movies and video games of sinister quality. The affective arousal through brutality on the screens has long been proved. I want to demonstrate that the intensity of influence is less harmful if the abnormal and conflict-laden subjects of the media, even those of modern novels, has a greater distance from the present life situation of the consumer. Someone who is quite content will be fascinated by a dramatic film or book but no more. He rests in his own haven from which he becomes an interested observer of the world stage.

The medium of psychology, however, caters to a very specific circle of interested persons marked to a frighteningly high degree by a lack of this very feeling of being sheltered. An enormous number of people want to understand themselves by means of psychology because there is something incomprehensible in themselves that they can't handle. It could, for instance, be that they suffer from a personal weakness, insecurities, anxiety, or the feeling of inferiority. Both students who enroll in psychology courses and lay people who read psychological books often do this from ego-related motives. Of course, we must not throw out the baby with the bathwater and must keep in mind that a true, objective, professional interest in the subject also exists that does not have its source in psychological instability. But this is likely the exception.

Naturally, there is no objection in principle for those who purchase a psychological book because they are experiencing problems. That is reasonable and also an expression of a healthy tendency for self-healing. But if the person concerned gets the wrong book, one of the typical modern novels with its lament about the lost meaning of life or one that is like the films mentioned above, oriented to the abnormal, perverse, and morbid, then the necessary inner distance may be lacking to resist its negative radiation and to put it in the right perspective. Then the individual is negatively affected. Every line and every insecurity causes a descent into further turmoil. Such a book is not therapeutic for that type of person but rather an additional pathologizing factor.

In summary, two points are being made: First, spiritual things influence each other and thus books inescapably influence their readers; second, the personality of the reader is of major importance in deciding the appropriateness of a book or film. The more a person is in an inner turmoil (a crisis in the struggle for identity or for the meaning of life), the more eager such an individual may be to listen to someone else's words, the more he or she can be influenced, the more the book is a danger or an opportunity. What determines whether a book infects with despair or immunizes[8] against it, whether it is positively or negatively "contagious," does not depend so much on the topic of the book but on the concept of the human being that it indirectly presents. Many psychological textbooks, for instance, deal exclusively with pathological relationships and traumatizing conditions in the life of the person; however, that is not the worst part. Only when it is unmistakably insinuated that a person under those terrible conditions and circumstances is *constrained* to maldevelopment and so really has a reason for "abysmal melancholia about the individual's impotence and about the inaccessibility of any ideal" (as Kurz expressed it), does the actual danger that clings to these theses begin, because they produce nothing but hopelessness and manipulate the reader into the role of the knife-thrower's partner.

However, I want to speak less about dubious psychological literature and more about those books that have a certain healing power. Let us suppose that persons who are psychologically unstable and vulnerable to neuroses are more susceptible to psychological influences than other readers. Let us further suppose that, because of this, they possess the opportunity, through the appropriate selection of their books, to make a very personal contribution to the recovery and maintenance of their psychological health. But how can they discern which books are most helpful and healing?

I think that, for a solution to this problem, it is enough to place a two-question checklist in readers' hands to use as an approximate measure to assess the basic tenor of a book and get an idea of its aims.

Every age has its problems and today's era has its own, which are undoubtedly acute. A worldwide dissatisfaction has afflicted civilized nations; feelings of emptiness and meaninglessness universally affect the younger generation. An ethical inflation and a continuous loss of values run ahead of economic and financial inflation and affect the stability of entire cultures. How does a book answer these needs; how does it address the pressing questions of the present? This is the first point to be considered when the therapeutic effect of a book is tested. The enumeration of negatives does not diminish the negative. To frighten brings no healing. We must not close our eyes to the fact that it is, to a certain extent, always in our hands to change the bad to something good even if it is only in our inner being. Viktor Frankl expressed it thus: "The world is not healthy, but it can be healed." Therefore I would like to say as a first impulse: *Knowledge about curability is itself part of the cure*. It is at the same time part self-responsibility, part challenge to the human spirit, part understanding the reason why we might be in the world. As long as curability is woven into the pages of a book, the author can talk about trouble without extinguishing hope. If the story does not uplift, it will at least not force readers to their knees in agony.

The healing power of a book is strongest if it forsakes searching for someone to blame for misery, and instead puts the main accent on letting the finding of meaning become thinkable again in our modern world in spite of all modern skepticism. If "pointing out" is the function, then the author should concentrate on orientation charts within the chaos and not on supposed reasons for the chaos.

For instance, I have repeatedly experienced what a terrible influence is exerted by psychological books that trace the psychological disturbances of people entirely to faulty upbringing and to parental mistakes. This type of literature not only reinforces the normally existing tensions among family members to an enormous degree, it also paralyzes any individual initiative of the afflicted person to deal directly with the problem. It is also well known that books about dream interpretation can cause sleep disturbances; books about "finding oneself" usually cause the reader to miss oneself.

In every case it is more humane and therapeutically effective to aim at natural, unreflected family relationships and being oneself whatever may have happened. Simply put, old sores don't heal if one keeps scratching them. Add to this that there are hardly any parents who did not repeatedly make sacrifices for their children even if they failed once in a while, and that the self was often discovered long ago but one keeps explaining it away.

This leads us to the second point in our two-question list, testing whether good and pleasant subjects are still mentioned at all.

I have already mentioned that we are well trained to perceive everything negative; indeed, negative, perverse, and tragic subjects have a peculiar attraction. The idols of our time can't go through enough adventures in bed, today's gangsters can't leave enough dead behind, the best sellers about catastrophes can't expose enough horror. One root of this modern trend goes back to an excessive concern of professionals and writers of our century to never represent a perfect world that does not correspond with reality. Any suggestion of a perfect world has been categorically banned from school books so that nothing might be glossed over by mistake which could later be exposed as less than pretty.

We must recognize, of course, that foremost behind this campaign against the so-called perfect world was a sincere desire for honesty. Perhaps sometimes there was even hope that, through this condemnation of prevailing grievances, humanity might be shaken into realization and reorientation. Unfortunately, this notion does not work out on a large or small scale. A child who is given only broken toys will not start out to repair them. On the contrary, from the perspective of such a child, everything is worthless and damaged anyway and therefore it is of no use taking care of them; the result is a destructive frenzy.

Again, we have to thank Viktor Frankl and logotherapy for our present understanding of the importance of preserving the idea of a perfect world in our hearts and minds. Frankl described human existence as one that must uninterruptedly swing in the tension between Being and Ought, and which becomes totally unworthy of humanness if this arc of tension collapses.

This implies that a being truly worthy of being human presupposes that both a realistic and an idealistic view are spiritually present and that adequate forces are mobilized to transform one into the other if possible. We return here to the noödynamic principle that we encountered in the discussion of nearly every subject in this book, and which time and again has demonstrated that being human is more than being ourselves; what is required is something *for which* to live and not only *from which* to live. The *for* is the Ought before us as the goal which gives meaning to our striving. The *from* relates to the Being, the starting point at the time from which our striving grows and on which our strengths rely.

In connection with the subject of a perfect world, the following parallel can be drawn. The perfect world dreamed of is simply an imagined state of how things ought to be. The world—as it actually is—is a state of Being. But to make the world as it really is better, if only more perfect by a hair's breadth, it is essential that *both* conditions still exist in the imagination, for a person can never strive for a goal that is no longer known within. The individual must be in the eternal arc of tension between Being and Ought in order to experience life and actions as bearing meaning and to unfold the best within. In the same way, humanity on a large scale must rediscover the arc of tension between Being and Ought, to turn the rudder towards a meaningful Ought when the vessel founders unsteadily in the waves of the present existence.

The perfect world is the bedrock of all our longings, humankind's very dream of deliverance. Whoever wants to eliminate this longing, to destroy this dream, takes what is meaningful out of the world and robs human existence of its essential task. Hermann Hesse wrote in this connection: "There is no lack of authors whose despair with our time and whose fear of its chaos is genuine. But there is a lack of those whose faith and love are sufficient to keep themselves above the chaos."

Let us return to the question of the curative power of books and particularly of psychological books. Point one in the two-question model which I would like to recommend was to ask whether a book emphasizes the *curability* of diverse troubles and problems or whether it limits itself to describing troubles and problems. The second point would be to determine whether a *perfect world* above and beyond our reality is admitted as conceivable or scornfully denied. It is my opinion that a book can only be therapeutically effective if it addresses the conditions of Being as well as the conditions of Ought in human life. If it concentrates exclusively on Being, then it produces resignation. If it concentrates entirely on a desirable Ought, then it creates illusions. Only the combination of both Being and Ought traces the reality that may well be queried in many aspects but which is nevertheless worth living and worthy of spiritually vital interaction… and, finally, to say "Yes" to it.

Incidentally, the good and the perfect are often not such a far-off objective that can only be traced to the horizon of our longings. The good and the perfect are found in many different shapes everywhere we look. Today, there are still families who hold together, couples who are faithful to each other, parents who have a harmonious relationship with their children. There is neighborhood assistance, goodness, and selflessness. There is even peace among people without a word being said about it. There are heroes in our time who do their deeds in secrecy. Never, not even in the worst times, was the perfect world completely lost; even in counseling talks with very disturbed patients, traces of some intact living area can always be found. *Something perfect is everywhere and thus can be found in every individual as well.* This knowledge alone is very comforting! There should be no psychological textbook that could not belong under this heading.

These, then, are some criteria suitable for initiating the curative power of reading: reconciliation with the past, curability of the present, and a perfect world as the anticipation of a future to be striven for. These are the main pillars of every bibliotherapeutic volume as much as they are the content of a meaning-centered psychotherapy. Perhaps one could generalize: If the modern novel is to be understood as a reflection of the crisis of modern times, then a book with curative powers is one that helps the people of today to overcome crises—that means pushing forward towards a meaning of life again. In this context I would like to again quote Hermann Hesse: "Even the unspiritual, superficial person who does not like to think still has that ancient need to know about a meaning in his life. And if he no longer finds one, his individual life is marked by wildly exaggerated selfishness and exaggerated fear of death." Indeed, there is no lack of selfishness and deadly fear in modern times.

An observation may be added concerning the *preventive radiation* of books which positively accompanies the reader in his search for meaning.

This type of book could, in the case of an incipient crisis, prevent more human misery than we professionals are able to cure once the psychological affliction has set in. Let us not forget one thing: Numerous people in our society are insecure only because they observe themselves too intensely, because they are weakened by their prosperity, because they don't know what to do with their leisure, and because they are permanently fed by the media with problem awareness. All of them would truly become ill if traditional therapeutic measures were applied because the intensity of traditional therapy is too high for them. As soon as they are diagnosed as "patients," they are made into patients. For these clients, the right book at the right time could bring about miracles by bringing "common sense," stimulating self-help, strengthening the joy of life and, through this, making the introduction of the psychological machine superfluous.

However, where regular treatment is medically or psychologically indicated, it cannot be replaced by a book. At most, it can be complemented. Unfortunately, it must be admitted that professional opinions about indications for therapy diverge considerably. Even so, the best among them agree that necessary therapy must take place, but that too much therapy is no less dangerous than too little. Just as we have become increasingly critical regarding the uncontrolled use of pharmaceutical products, so skepticism is growing about the indiscriminate use of therapeutic resources, especially among humanistic psychologists. Logotherapy in particular is generally included in humanistic psychology* and its practitioners have for a long

---

* Logotherapy is different from other humanistic psychological schools insofar as it does not recognize "self-actualization" as a person's highest achievement in life. Rather, in logotherapy, the highest possible level of development is seen as "self-transcendence," the person's commitment to a meaningful task or to a love-relationship in the widest sense.

From my university seminars came an example that the striving for self-transcendence does not exclude self-actualization; quite the contrary, self-actualization accompanies self-transcendence automatically. One of my students was painfully shy of speaking up in the lecture halls. I had the custom of letting students write voluntary lecture notes and thus earn certain credits for them in the final exams so that they needed to answer one question less in order to gain their passing mark. One day, however, I forgot to ask at the start of the lecture who wanted to write the protocol for the lesson. Noticing this, the particular student overcame her shyness and pointed out my omission. I immediately asked her whether she would like to accept the task and she consented, although she normally would never have

time warned about the damage caused by "overtherapy"; in the process, they have always emphasized the significance of a good book as "anticipatory therapy." The distance to the bottomless pit of human despair is sometimes only one step, and if there is at least a railing to guard the pit (such as a helpful, uplifting book), this can be more beneficial than a whole team of therapists eventually having to lift the person concerned out of the pit.

Books worthy of being read have always been poetically called "friends." And that is what good books are, no matter what the subject or background is. They are *friends of the soul.* But just as it is the mark of a good friend that he or she does not leave a friend in the lurch, so it is the unique mark of a good book that it has a healing power in times of need. Bibliotherapeutic books with a psychological background are perhaps specialized, being not only "friends" but also "helpers" of the soul. However, if needed, every friend is a helper and every good book a true boon. Whoever reaches for a good book in a troubled hour will be enriched by it.

---

volunteered. Months later it so transpired that she could not answer a question in the exam. However, because she had done the notes, she passed.

The self-transcendence that she had once achieved for my sake, to spare me an omission, gained her the credits that undoubtedly represented a step on her way towards self-actualization.

5. Human Dignity and Psychotherapy: From Fate to Freedom*

Human dignity and psychotherapy have been separated from each other for a painfully long time. Through logotherapy, human dignity has again found its way home in psychotherapy. Let me illustrate what this separation means by referring to two cases of criminal offenses.

The first case concerns an incident which took place in one of the public swimming areas in Munich last summer. A young man, fully dressed and wearing street shoes, sauntered over to a teenager who was lying on the grass in the sunning area surrounding the pools and kicked him in the face as hard as he could. He did not know the boy. The boy suffered serious injuries, including a broken cheekbone, for which he had to undergo immediate surgery. The cheekbone healed so badly that it later had to be broken again and reset. He suffered for months from the pain resulting from this brutal attack, and he still bears scars from it.

What could have motivated such a senseless and cruel act? The young man was questioned by the examining judge, who made the attacker undergo a psychological examination. That is how this young man arrived at our counseling center. The explanation: He had just had an argument with his girlfriend, during which she told him that the relationship was not going to last much longer. As a result, he felt an intense rage boiling up in him, which he knew he was going to have to let out somewhere. That's all there was to it, he said.

---

* This chapter is based on the keynote address given at the Fourth World Congress of Logotherapy in San Francisco in June, 1984 as well as on a revised version printed in the Fall/Winter, 1984 issue of the *International Forum for Logotherapy*, pp. 67-84.

The second case comes from a report in the German newspapers. A man had picked up a girl hitchhiker and had tried to assault her sexually. But she resisted, and when the car stopped at a red light she opened the door to jump out. Her foot got caught in a loop of the seat belt and she fell out onto the street. Onlookers tried to help her, but the driver slammed the door shut and stepped on the gas although the girl was still caught in the loop. He accelerated for several kilometers, and the girl was dragged to her death before police finally succeeded in catching up with the vehicle.

In this case, too, faced with a senseless and incomprehensible crime, the question of motive arose. Again, the answer left a feeling of uneasiness. The man explained that he had not "had" a woman for some time and therefore had to find release. When it went wrong, he was gripped by a great fear which caused him to drive away. He didn't notice the girl hanging from his car.

What do these two stories tell us when we analyze them psychologically? Here we have two men ruled by intense feelings, by their basic needs driving toward satisfaction: aggression and libido. And both are in no way inhibited about looking for, and forcibly gaining, satisfaction.

A PSYCHOLOGY OF THE WRONGDOER

Psychology textbooks tell us about those drives and needs that have to be discharged, abreacted. These are needs which supposedly should never be repressed because they would then cause neurotic disturbances! Our psychology textbooks tell us about the therapeutic goal of reducing inhibitions, those very inhibitions which could hinder them in gratifying their needs.

The catchwords of living out our feelings to the fullest, of asserting ourselves, of strengthening our ego ring in our ears. According to these theories, both of these men would just about be all right, but what about their victims?

We have developed a psychology of the wrongdoer; though it seemingly reveals the motives, it simultaneously excuses them. But we have not developed a psychology of the victim, or of how to deal with undeserved suffering, not to mention its prevention. There is none, except logotherapy.

The whole dilemma goes back to a mistake the founders of psychology made a long time ago. That mistake was the *separation of the spiritual dimension from the psychological dimension in the conception of the human being.* Simultaneously, this involved *uncoupling human dignity from psychotherapy.* The psychological human dimension was thoroughly investigated, examined, and analyzed. Out of this came the view that we are primarily regulated by unconscious psychodynamic mechanisms; our most important reason for living is the fulfillment of our needs. Our nature was lowered to the level of our feelings.

From this viewpoint, then, it is not surprising when a person changes the feeling of "rage" into the act of kicking someone. Or when the feeling of "lust" is degenerated into indiscriminate sexual molestation. Or when the feeling of "anxiety" misleads someone into the most irresponsible kind of panic reaction. After all, we have to do something with our feelings.

Yet, what about the necessity of learning to control our feelings, to keep them in check, to exert some measure of self-discipline? Today we are willing to admit that, while feelings are acceptable, we should not allow them to dominate us. Ultimately, something is going to have to control our feelings without us having to repress them. Something has to watch over and guide our emotions, to impose ethical limits upon these basic drives. And that is our *spiritual nature.*

We are faced today with the difficult task of reintegrating the spiritual dimension into our psychological concept of the human being. And we also have to make sure that the spiritual dimension gets that superior value which it deserves—and must have—if our human society is to continue. As difficult as this task may be, it would certainly be an enrichment for psychotherapy. Psychotherapy has its foundation in the concept of human nature prevailing at the time. Unfortunately, psychotherapy is in many ways still based on a psychology "devoid of spirit" and running the risk of degenerating into a mechanical treatment "devoid of dignity."

TWO APPROACHES

An example will illustrate this difference: a comparison between treatments of identical problems in traditional group therapy versus in individual logotherapy. The problem in this case was a patient's anger at her father who, according to her, had treated her badly as a child. This problem of hatred toward fathers is not unusual for psychotherapists in Germany because many of the older generation of parents had considered it normal and appropriate to use corporal punishment in raising their children. Usually, fathers have been the parent who "wielded the heavy hand" on the children. What happened in traditional group therapy was told to me by a woman who was herself present in the session.

After the patient began to talk critically and reproachfully about her father, the therapist explained to her that the extensive repression of her feelings for many years was the cause of her psychological problems; the patient would be able to get rid of them only by reactivating her inner anger before the group. The therapist then rolled up a blanket into the shape of a person and laid it down on the couch as a symbolic substitute for her father. Then the therapist placed a stick in the patient's hands, requesting her to beat the blanket with all her strength and to shout at the same time, "I hate you! I hate you!" In this way all the pent-up feelings could be released and the psychological trauma would be "worked through" once and for all. The woman did as she was told, but in the course of the display of temper she worked herself into a hysterical fit of crying. This could not be stopped and the services of an emergency doctor were required. He gave her an injection and referred her to a nerve clinic for a few days.

Let me contrast the above report with what I once advised a middle-aged woman to do. She had come to talk to me and mentioned the anger she had felt for her father her whole life. As a logotherapist, I never look at the person solely in terms of feelings. Rather, I always include the spiritual aspects of her existence in my considerations. Therefore I saw the problem from a different perspective than the above-mentioned group therapist. I am not disputing that hatred of a parent can poison a person. But the reason this happens is not, in my opinion, because a repressed feeling is permanently striving for discharge; rather that one simply does not live well with hate in one's heart. One dies even less well with such hatred. Hate is contrary to the spiritual striving for meaning because this striving seeks reconciliation and can never be "worked through" except through a forgiving love.

So I asked the client whether she had ever thought of reconciliation. But she replied sadly that it was impossible for her even to carry on a serious conversation with her father. Whenever she went to visit him, he was almost always sitting in front of the television set. And when she broached the subject of what had happened in the past or what had come between them, he would impatiently tell her to be quiet so he would not miss the show. But even after the show there was always something which came up to prevent a real talk between the two. So she had given up on her father a long time ago.

I said to the woman: "Your father is old, and he is not going to change any more. The only thing that can change is your attitude about him. So the issue here is not really a dialogue between you and your father, especially since it would hardly be productive. Rather, it is a matter of a dialogue within yourself—a dialogue between your feelings and your conscience. Your feelings reject your father, and maybe that is justified. But your conscience pleads for forgiveness, because it also is dependent on being forgiven by other people when you make your own mistakes. Until now your feelings have dominated you. How would it be if you let your conscience suddenly get the upper hand?"

"Yes, that is what I want to do," the woman sobbed. "But how do I do it?"

"It's very simple," I said. "When you go to see your father again, and he is sitting in front of the television, just go right over to him and give him a kiss on the cheek without saying a word. Regardless of what he says or does, that kiss can be a symbol of the reconciliation of your feelings with your conscience, a sign of forgiveness toward an old man. Through this gesture you relieve your father of his guilt, and at the same time you relieve yourself of your hate."

The woman followed my advice, and she not only found her inner peace; she was also surprised by the reaction of her father, who, without saying a word, took his grown daughter in his arms and embraced her.

I confess that I used to be more timid about asking people to relinquish various things. I have found the courage to ask my patients to sacrifice something when it is necessary, but only since I have understood two things: First, I have understood that, from the point of view of our spiritual dimension, it is always a matter of values rather than satisfaction; secondly, I have understood that values are often concerned with setting aside one's wishes, whereas satisfaction always has to do with satisfying a wish. Viktor Frankl made this remarkable statement in his book *Homo patiens*:

> What I keep
> does not keep its value.
> But what I give
> gains value.[9]

RESISTANCE TO SACRIFICE

In the same text, Frankl wrote about "giving meaning" (*Sinn geben*) as a form of "sacrificing something" (*preisgeben*), which must be done for the sake of the meaning to be actualized. Nevertheless, it is extremely difficult for a person spoiled by the affluence of the present Western culture to make a sacrifice, even when it would be meaningful and the value gained would be great. Modern people just cannot stand any pain at all, which is good for psychotherapists; people come running at the slightest problem. But actually this endangers the society as a whole because a single real catastrophe would suffice to start the breakdown of society.

This reminds me of an observation of my dentist who told me that, 40 years ago, he could pull teeth without administering any anesthesia. Thirty years ago, he only brushed the gum around the tooth with a mild anesthetic. Twenty years ago, he injected local anesthesia when pulling a tooth. For the last 10 years he has been injecting very strong anesthesia and, he says, people today say "Ow!" as soon as they hear him testing the drill in the air. He said he has not yet found an effective treatment for this last problem.

We logotherapists are not for self-castigation and against enjoying life. On the contrary, we consider senseless distress just as pathological as the senseless suppression of the joy of life. Whenever pain can be reduced, it should be done. And whenever suffering can be avoided, this has priority over all else.

But the concept of "sacrifice" is always related to a "what for," which alone determines the meaningfulness of every sacrifice. *The greater the value of a "what for," the greater the meaning of the sacrifice to be made.*

In addition, mainstream psychology teaches us that there is a reciprocal relationship between the short-term and long-term aspects of personal gains and losses. Doing without something for a short time—we could also speak of "sacrificing"—often makes possible long-term gains in value, which could not otherwise be reached. For example, the long-term goal of the deep satisfaction of having raised a child who is happy and capable demands a great many short-term sacrifices made over the years for the sake of the well-being of the child. Similarly, the long-term and proud completion of an education demands that one relinquish short-term wants for years for the sake of continually studying and learning. Conversely, it can also be shown that the constant search for short-term advantages and gratifications often makes long-term gains impossible, and even gives rise to long-term unsolvable problems.

Parents who neglect their children again and again, in order to find short-term pleasures for themselves, get themselves into trouble in the long run with their children, causing for themselves a great deal of grief and sadness later on. The same thing is true for young people who interrupt their education for the sake of short-term excitement. They will later be punished by unemployment or an undesirable job.

For many psychotherapy clients, their willingness to forego some things for a short time indicates whether or not they will improve. Alcoholics cannot be helped if they are not willing to make a short-term sacrifice and do without that next drink. Compulsive neurotics are completely at the mercy of their compulsions if they are not able to stop that short-lasting but insidious avoidance behavior that only makes their anxiety worse.

It is therefore not at all an erroneous therapy goal to strengthen a person's ability to do without, so long as this is still meaningful. In any case, this is a goal with more human dignity than that of a psychology devoid of spirit, which emphasizes having to abreact and to act out. This idea has already done much damage.

When the therapy goal includes sacrifice, *the threshold of spiritual freedom has already been crossed.* The old psychological determinism was overcome at the very moment when the concept of sacrifice found its way into psychology, and this happened with logotherapy. A sacrifice presupposes not only a what for, but also the freedom to choose. We can also choose not to sacrifice. Whenever this is not the case, whenever people are under compulsion and really have only one choice of responding (which means they do not really have any choice at all) we cannot speak of sacrifice. We can speak of an urge, of suffering, but not of that inner relinquishing which is done for the sake of a meaning.

Thus, sacrifice presupposes freedom. But the reverse is also true. It is a fact that people do make sacrifices, and on a completely voluntary basis, for a cause or for some other person who is worthy of this sacrifice. And this fact proves that the will is free and that we human beings are not the slaves of our feelings or the puppets of a system of hydraulic drives (as noted by Peter Hofstaetter). This talk of having to react and this excuse of having to abreact have shown themselves to be untenable. The same goes for the many theories that deal with the analyzability of our psychological dimension and are alleged to have grasped the very soul of humankind.

FATE AND FREEDOM

For thousands of years, we have been aware of the many aspects of our existence, and for just as long we have speculated about that mystery called the soul. The greatest philosophers were unable to solve the "body-soul problem." They could only describe it, and their most frequent distinctions were that the body is visible and the soul invisible; the body is material, the soul immaterial. The various religions added that the body is mortal, the soul immortal. At the beginning of the 20th century when psychology developed into a social science, it simply transformed the concept of soul into a psychological concept that was the base of all emotions and the reservoir of all learning experiences. In this way, it became the foundation of all our vital impulses. A distorted picture arose of a completely determined homunculus ruled like a puppet by childhood experiences and inner drives.

This inadequate transformation of the soul into something emotional was corrected by Viktor Frankl. He complemented the psychological concept with human dignity and the freedom of the will; in other words, by integrating the human spirit. In this way, the old distinction between body and soul, which had hinged more or less on concretion and abstraction, gave way to a new distinguishing criterion, *the criterion of fate and freedom*.

Perhaps another example from clinical experience can illustrate what a revolution in psychotherapy is effected by this new criterion for differentiation. A few months ago, a physician at the Munich Dermatological Clinic consulted me about a 20-year-old female patient who suffered from a chronic, disfiguring rash. The young woman kept on repeating the sentence: "I am repulsive." The physician was afraid that the worst might happen, especially since the woman had no family to offer support. Because she felt so repulsive, she was also negligent in applying her medicine. There was no hope for improvement if she did not apply the medicine on a regular basis.

One psychologist had tried to trace the young woman's feeling of repulsion back to "playing doctor" when she was a child. A young boy in the neighborhood had once shown her his penis. But the patient indignantly rejected this interpretation, and, in any case, it had no positive effect on her. From the very beginning the question for me was not where the repulsion came from. Something ugly can be repulsive to a sensitive person, and her skin was really anything but nice.

For me, the question was rather how a 20-year-old woman was able to live with such a fate, and what strength she might have to resist it. Now we come to the concept of "fate." What exactly was fate in all of this? Was there any leeway, any area of freedom, within which she could make her own decision? Her physical (*somatic*) dimension was burdened by disease, and this disease was her fate. Her emotional, psychological *(psychic)* dimension was burdened with her feeling of repulsion, and this repulsion was also fate.

But her spiritual (*noëtic*) dimension was completely unencumbered; it was called upon to take a position on her disease and repulsion. The young woman was fully able to adopt any attitude, have any opinion she wanted. There was nothing in the world which could force her to any particular spiritual attitude. Here we found some room for change, an area of freedom. We had to show her this space into which she could move, this area of freedom.

The first thing she learned was that her statement, "I am repulsive," was false. It was false because there was a spiritual part of her that in no way deserved repulsion. The statement had to be rephrased: "My broken-out skin is repulsive," and this she was able to accept. The second thing she learned was to take her broken-out skin and her repulsion together as a psychophysical challenge of fate to her. A sentence by Viktor Frankl helped her meet this challenge, a sentence which I often quote to those looking for advice when they have to have a dialog with their own fears and weaknesses. It goes like this:

> There is something
> you cannot take from me:
> my freedom to choose
> how I respond
> to what you do to me!

Whenever she was overcome with feelings of hopelessness, feelings of hating herself, and feelings of being repulsive, she answered them with the words I quoted, and right there her negative feelings lost their power over her.

The last thing left to do was to strengthen her will to become healthy. Whether the will can be taught or trained is an old, controversial question. It cannot be adequately answered unless the spiritual or, in logotherapeutic terms, noëtic aspects of human existence are distinguished from the "subnoëtic" (physical, emotional, psychological) aspects. At the subnoëtic level it is entirely possible to prepare the way for the will, as we know from educational theory and from work with those with mental disabilities or addictions. On the other hand, it is neither possible nor necessary to train one's willpower at the noëtic level. Here we can confidently trust in our will if we only know what we want.

The will is one of those phenomena that in themselves cannot be wanted. But when something else is desired, one has as much willpower as needed. For this reason, the client could not be led to want to become well. But we both speculated about what she could do meaningfully with her life. And here she overflowed with future plans, which would be a reward for the dismal time spent in the clinic and for bravely going through the necessary treatment procedures. This was a future worthy of overcoming repulsion and strictly following the doctor's orders. The "what for" demanded a voluntary sacrifice, the sacrifice of overcoming the repulsion. The young woman agreed to do this without any additional pressure from outside. From that day on her condition improved, as if her spiritual affirmation of wanting to get well had itself been binding for both body and psyche.

The psychologist at the group therapy clinic, according to his training, asked why the patient necessarily had to feel repulsive, and he made a trauma in her childhood responsible for it. I, according to my training as a logotherapist, asked to what degree the patient was free to resist her repulsion, and I made her personally responsible for her behavior within the limits of her freedom. Her *having to feel repulsive* removed her guilt for her lack of cooperation with the doctors, but it also made her into a person who was not yet able to decide for herself, a person who was at the mercy of her feelings. The *being free to resist repulsion* saddled her with responsibility and made her ready to sacrifice something, but it also made her into a person who could respond for herself.

The lesson to be drawn from this example is this: Pointing out to a person that he or she still has a certain amount of freedom, even if that is all that is left, is more than a psychotherapeutic technique; it is also an act of human dignity.

RECOUPLING SPIRITUAL AND PSYCHOLOGICAL DIMENSIONS

With this in mind, let us go back to the recoupling of the spiritual and the psychological dimensions in the logotherapeutic concept of the human being, and consequently to the new distinguishing criterion of the age-old body-soul problem. This problem is now seen as a dialectic between the psychophysical and the spiritual. We are unaccustomed to think in accordance with this new criterion, and it has had little influence on our usual way of seeing things.

I notice this again and again in conversations with group participants and with students, when I have them write down everything they would ascribe to fate and then everything they would classify as human freedom. Under the concept of "fate" they list bodily determinants such as state of health, age, or sex, accidents of a positive or a negative kind, good or bad luck, and social and environmental factors that the person does not have completely under control, such as war or peace, prosperity or unemployment, friendly or unfriendly relatives, and so on. Under the concept of "freedom" they mostly show how much leeway they have within the limits of their situation, their everyday activity or passivity.

When I then ask them where they put feelings, they usually agree that feelings belong to fate, because we obviously do not freely choose them. It is impossible to order someone to be joyful or angry. This proves that feelings are conscious or unconscious automatic side-effects of the events causing them, events which are not immediately subject to the will. Thus, feelings are part of the circumstances of fate. This does not mean that there are no reasons for them or that we do not have a part in causing them. Rather, it means that at the time when a certain feeling comes up, there was no free inner choice about whether that feeling should come up or not.

Then I ask further: "Where do you place attitudes? Are attitudes determined beforehand by models, experiences, or other influences?" My students usually give a negative answer. Of course, attitudes can simply be taken over from the past or from the social environment, but they do not have to be taken over. There is still a personal choice to be made; it is still a decision of our conscience. Even when we are easily influenced by the opinions of others, we still have the choice of how we stand toward outside influences.[10] Therefore, attitudes are free.

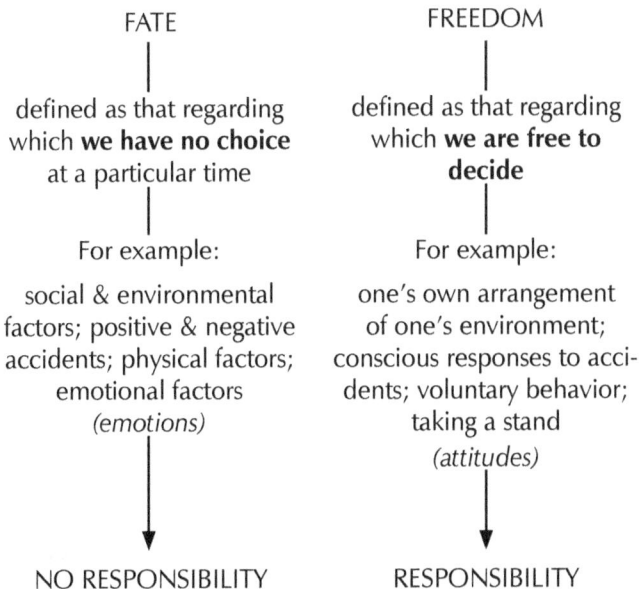

FATE	FREEDOM
defined as that regarding which **we have no choice** at a particular time	defined as that regarding which **we are free to decide**
For example:	For example:
social & environmental factors; positive & negative accidents; physical factors; emotional factors *(emotions)*	one's own arrangement of one's environment; conscious responses to accidents; voluntary behavior; taking a stand *(attitudes)*
NO RESPONSIBILITY	RESPONSIBILITY

I then pose another question, which at first seems easy to answer: "Which do you like better—the fateful aspect of human life, or the area of freedom we have?" Most students immediately say: "The freedom, of course, because we have a say, we can help decide, take our lives in our own hands, and guide ourselves wherever we want to go."

Yes, that is true. Human beings have always been magnetically attracted by freedom. It has been our dream since Adam and Eve. Yet there is one thing which balances out the negative side of fate with a positive, whereas this same thing is inherent in human freedom and cannot be put aside. And that is the aspect of responsibility. Fate entails that the circumstances themselves cannot be changed. But we are not responsible for what we cannot change and have not chosen, nor can we be at fault in such circumstances. However, what we have chosen freely, done freely, decided freely to be a part of our own lives, to this we have committed ourselves with all its consequences. It is undeniably our own feat or our own fault.

When we look at it this way, we may hesitate to choose the area of freedom. *For freedom may well be a gift, but it is also a sentence to responsibility. And fate may well force us to do something, but it is also a pardon from responsibility.*

Thus, the recoupling of the spiritual and the psychological dimensions by logotherapy has had several consequences. One of them is that we are no longer the puppet-like homunculi of an outmoded psychology; now the area of freedom, which everyone has regardless of the situation, is taken into consideration. Another consequence is that the distorted relationship between ethics and psychology has been corrected because the consideration of one's personal freedom necessarily entails a consideration of one's own personal responsibility. Here the reintroduction of human dignity into psychotherapy becomes obvious. If you take responsibility away from people, you also take away their dignity, as Frankl noted. A form of psychotherapy which excuses people is also a form of psychotherapy which degrades them: Our being sentenced to freedom is a prerequisite to our becoming guilty.

On the other hand, there is also the pardon, the exemption from responsibility, which is part and parcel of fate. In view of this, it is the task of psychotherapy to resolve the patients' unjustified feelings of guilt in order to restore their sense of dignity.

An example: A man came for therapy who was ashamed to even tell me what his problem was. He felt strongly attracted by children about whom he had sexual fantasies. This happened especially at the meadows along the Isar River in Munich where, during summer, many children run around in the nude. He was afraid he might give in to this urge and assault some child. This bothered him so much that he did not go to the river at all and even avoided all places where he might suddenly be alone with children playing. But the fact was that nothing had ever really happened. That man had absolute control over himself, but he felt guilty because of his abnormal thoughts and fantasies.

This is the issue where I intervened and relieved him of every shred of guilt. Feelings and compulsive thoughts belong to the circumstances of fate. They are not freely chosen but suddenly come up, wherever they may have come from. The man was in no way guilty for having these pedophile tendencies or for having the anxious hyperreflections associated with them. What he alone was responsible for, was within the area of his freedom—that of deciding between giving in to his tendencies or resisting them.

Within his area of freedom, however, he had always chosen to resist. Thus he behaved with responsibility, and that is certainly the kind of behavior which we can recognize as praiseworthy. I was therefore able to tell him: "You do not have any reason to be ashamed. On the contrary, you should be proud of yourself. You are in fact a respectable man, and your tendency to have sexual fantasies does not alter that fact. The only question now is how you can manage your emotional turmoil better, and there are psychotherapeutic methods which can help you."

I thought about a combination of paradoxical intention and dereflection, but surprisingly these turned out to be unnecessary. My explanation that he was basically respectable and that he was free of all guilt, had such a positive effect on him that he felt relieved of the problem and gradually overcame it completely. He even went to the meadows along the Isar River again, and later he told me that at the sight of children playing he only had a deeply satisfying feeling of his acceptance of himself.

How different is this behavior from that of the young man I mentioned at the beginning of this chapter, whose unspeakably brutal behavior took place on the pretext of having to abreact his feelings! That man was not tormented by feelings of guilt after he had kicked an innocent victim in the face. But he should have felt guilty because, in spite of all that went on before his assault, he was still fully able to think and was consequently free to choose how he responded. He wantonly chose a negative behavior. If any form of psychotherapy can reach him, it would be one which could show him these connections.

It is not the intention of those practicing logotherapy to put blame onto patients; nor are they interested in exonerating them of guilt. Rather, logotherapists are concerned with insight into just how far we are free and hence responsible compared to how far we are a plaything of fate and hence not responsible or guilty. Which possibility is preferred is an open question.

Which would you prefer: being run down by a car while walking unsuspectingly on the sidewalk, or being the driver of the car who, in a moment when you paid no attention, runs down an innocent pedestrian? If you are the victim, you have the pain—but at least you do not have any guilt. The car from behind was your fate. On the other hand, if you are the negligent driver you do not suffer any physical pain—but you do have a suffering of a different kind. Your failure occurred within your area of freedom. It is a difficult choice. It reminds me of the saying, "The mother of the murdered son can sleep, but not the mother of the murderer."

These considerations have applications in therapy. Some of my patients pay attention mainly to the circumstances of fate, and others primarily to the area of their freedom.

Some depressed people are in sheer despair about their depression. And others think about what they can do about it in spite of feeling depressed. The former perceive their fate, the latter perceive that amount of freedom which their fate just barely allows.

Some people constantly live in a past filled with sorrowful memories from which spring the complaints of the present. And others use the sorrowful memories of their past to renew and transform their present. The former use up their energy in coming to terms with fate because the past, in its immutability, belongs to the circumstances of fate. But the latter increase their energy in grappling with the circumstances of fate—energy which they can use to shape their present area of freedom.

Within the area of fate, there is not a single possibility available to us because, by definition, we do not have any choice within that area. But in the area of freedom there are as many possibilities as there are stars in the sky, and for every single situation and every single moment we can pick one or another. But when we have chosen, we have obliterated all other possibilities of that same situation, and that exact pattern of opportunities will never return. Certainly there will be new situations with new possibilities as long as we live, but the starry sky of a particular moment passes away when we make just a single star our concrete choice.

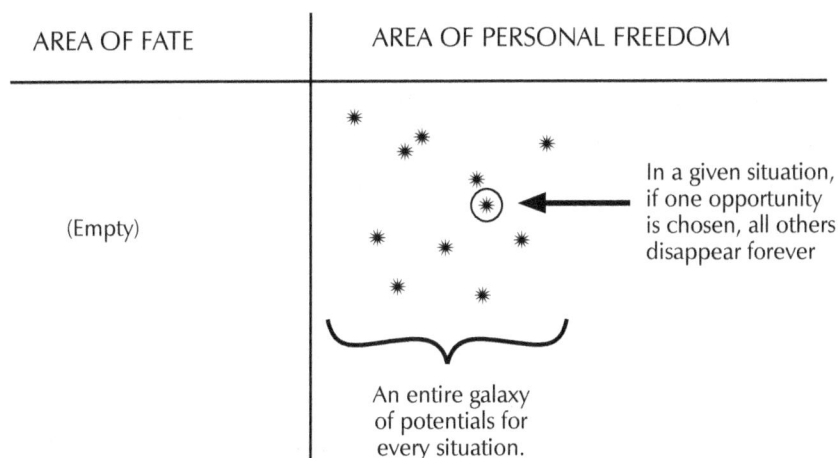

AREA OF FATE	AREA OF PERSONAL FREEDOM
(Empty)	An entire galaxy of potentials for every situation.

In a given situation, if one opportunity is chosen, all others disappear forever

For instance, someone getting up on a Sunday morning has a number of opportunities for spending it. If the decision is made, for example, to visit an art exhibition then all the other opportunities for that morning vanish. Never in a million years will the same constellation of choices be available as on that specific Sunday morning. Neither can that decision ever be reversed of having visited the exhibition. That visit belongs *instantly*—from that moment—to a solid and unexchangeable part of that person's life. If the person concerned had collapsed after arising, then that area of freedom would no longer have been available and fate would have taken over. The individual may have been left lying on the floor or perhaps taken to the hospital. In that case, there would have been no personal opportunity for choice.

Thus, the area of fate and the personal area of freedom are often mixed together (just as the diagnostic systems for psychological disturbances really are!). But for that very reason it is important to distinguish the two areas from each other and to concentrate on the area of freedom that is available to us.

Patients who do this have a big advantage over those who do not. Those who look at the circumstances of fate are looking at emptiness. They live in a world which is cemented shut and in which there is nothing to remove and nothing to change. On the other hand, those who look at their area of freedom, however small it may be, see the many possibilities of the situation and, among those, the one that is most meaningful.

Viktor Frankl has called the *conscience* our "meaning organ," which is always able to intuit the hidden or obscured but ever-present meaning of a situation. On the basis of our drawing, we can also call the conscience the organ to help us find the brightest star in the starry sky of the moment. Our conscience helps us in finding the most meaningful choice out of all the possibilities present in our area of freedom. The real advantage for those people who primarily perceive their area of freedom is that they have the chance to feel satisfied. For when we can say that we have done everything possible within our area of freedom, especially what has been "meaningfully possible," then for us this is good. Then we can be satisfied with ourselves, regardless of what our fate may now seem to be. The feeling "it is good" is, in the last analysis, the awareness that "I have done everything that is possible and meaningful." We do not get this awareness if we keep our eyes on the circumstances of fate, because fate will always provide us with a reason to be dissatisfied with something or other.

THE FIVE BEARS

To help my patients to push forward to this experience of "it is good" in spite of their own personal limits and needs, I developed five humorous picture cards which I gave the participants in my group to take home with them. It was a post-therapy group; most participants had long periods of illness behind them. Two women had been diagnosed as incurable before I saw them. Prior to joining this group, all participants had received individual therapy from me and had become relatively stable again but they were still faced with the shambles of their life left by their illnesses.

We talked about the ideas I have just discussed, and the patients expressed the wish of having something in writing which would remind them, in times of crises, to focus on the present possible meanings of their lives. The idea came to me to adapt for adults five picture cards [see next page] which were used effectively in a therapeutic program for children. They represent five stages of an ideal response pattern for actual life situations that can bring about a constructive rethinking of a situation.

1. What is my problem? The first card asks: "What is my problem?" This is not a uniquely logotherapeutic question, but is rather the psychological question asked by everyone who in some way does not feel good. It concerns our psychological dimension, because a problem is in reality always an emotional problem caused by sadness, fear, anger, desire, disappointment, or other crisis. It is the emotion associated with the actual situation, and not the situation as such, which causes the problem. For example, if you have been divorced and think: "Great! I am rid of my partner," then the divorce is not a problem. It becomes a problem when you regret losing the other person, or when you cannot stand the loneliness, or when you now hate the other person. Similarly, when you lose your job and think: "I can finally have a rest!" then unemployment is not a problem. It becomes a problem when you experience feelings of inferiority, fear of the future, and so on. Our first bear is standing in front of a stop sign, which is the emotional barrier that is holding him back on his path through life. To move forward, it is necessary to discern the problem.

2. Where is my area of freedom? After he has clarified the problem, the bear on the second card turns in a new and logotherapeutic direction: In addition to the psychological dimension, he allows the spiritual dimension to come through. This spiritual dimension goes beyond all stop signs and barriers and allows a certain area of freedom within one's inner attitude towards the problem, towards the emotions, and towards the given situation. "Where is my area of freedom?" Patients who look for their freedom will find it.

3. What are my possible choices? When individuals find their freedom, they have the entire starry sky of possibilities spread out in front of them. The bear on the third card is asking himself about these possibilities. Emotion is no longer determining the issue. Here cognition has its say, and cognition has a wealth of ideas, releasing our whole creativity. When we explore our possible choices, we will find many more than we suspected, even in difficult life situations. But knowing the various possible choices is not enough.

4. Which choice is most meaningful? Our spiritual dimension must raise its voice, the voice of our conscience as the human "sense organ," which senses meaning. It would be easy for emotion or even cognition to make the wrong decision, a decision against meaningfulness. This would occur if the emotions were chosen according to the principle of blindly "wanting to act out," or if the cognitions were chosen according to the principle of the greatest possible advantage for ourselves, the principle of blindly calculating without reference to values. The conscience, however, is self-transcending. It allows us to rise above ourselves and see the world in which we live, and to see the "one right thing to do" in the here and now. Only our conscience can sense *which one is the most meaningful* choice of all possibilities.

5. I want to actualize this one! After we know that, there is only one more choice: whether to follow our conscience. The bear on the fifth card is speaking for following our conscience, with the intention of actualizing what we know.

You may be wondering whether the original problem has thus been solved. It is certainly not the same problem it was at the beginning. Clients who have inwardly followed the path of the bears have left the stop sign behind them. They may still be suffering emotionally somewhat, but they know where they ought to go and their pathway is open.

I also gave these cards to my patients because I wanted to bring some humor into our serious discussions. Logotherapy appeals—with good therapeutic reason—to our sense of humor.

The clients used the cards in various ways. Some put them up on the shelf above the fireplace and looked at them every day. Others took them out of the drawer only when they were bothered by a problem. One woman gave them as a gift to her daughter, who went through stressful school tests. With the help of the bears, she succeeded in staying calm and getting one requirement finished right after the other. Since the group sessions have ended, every client without exception has told me at some time his or her own personal "bear story"—how they were able to help themselves in critical situations by referring to the questions on the cards.

I should like to read to you one of the most beautiful of these bear stories and, by doing so, return to our theme of human dignity in psychotherapy. The story, which I tell with the client's permission, is a touching documentation of "humanity," which we psychotherapists can only regard with respect and admiration. She wrote:

> I have suffered from a series of symptoms. When one disappeared, the next one came. You, Dr. Lukas, were the ninth therapist who tried to help me. I have often spoken of how sad my past life had been. I have been given interpretations for my conditions and diagnoses have been produced. I was narcissistic, infantile, my child-ego dominated me. Then you worked with me differently. You taught me to take my symptoms less seriously. You helped me to have courage and self-confidence. With you, I have become much more relaxed.

> But there is something I have never talked about. Not with a therapist, not even with you. I don't know why myself. It is something that has never given me any peace, as long as I can remember. I get too little love. People don't love me. No

one loves me as much as I want and need. Love! Why has love been closed off to me? Oh, God, just why? I have never told this to anybody, but it is the only thing that really hurts me. Everything else is almost just an afterthought. No, that's not so. Or is it? After having had so much therapy I should finally understand myself, but I have become even more unknown to myself.

Then, the other day, I took out the bear cards again. I was alone at home, and it was nighttime. I cried about the first card. Then I looked at the second card. My area of freedom… I couldn't think of anything. But there must be something! Then I had the thought: What am I waiting for? If I can't have love, then I can be love. *Be love*….

The thought seemed strange. And entirely new. How is it when love is inside a person, when love radiates from someone? Once, you said something about having and being. Having, you said, is something you can lose, but being cannot be lost, even when it is past being. I looked at the third card, and now I knew what you meant by the "starry sky of possibilities." All at once I had an incredible number of ideas. All those people I see every day, I could be friendly to them, much nicer than before. They could feel love in my presence. Is that really possible?

Permeated through and through with love—what an idea! Then I made plans and pictured it all. How I would go right up to people without hesitating, how I would invite my friends over, and how everyone would thank me for the evening. But the fourth card made me serious. My conscience was really tough on me. "You are filling yourself full of illusions," it told me. "It is not meaningful to try to buy affection. If you want to love, then you have to take people as they are. Without expecting something in return. For example, the old woman on the fourth floor who is always so rejecting. Give her some flowers and just swallow her unfriendliness; then you can love!" Believe it or not, that's what my conscience said.

The next morning I went to the florist and bought a bouquet of spring flowers. I took it upstairs to the old lady. She did not say a word, just looked at the flowers and looked at me. Then I felt that, from now on, things will be different. I am not going to complain any more that I get too little love. That is not the issue at all, getting is not the issue. There was just too little love in me, and that I can change. I change it a little bit every day. I take the fifth card with me in my handbag, wherever I go. Some day or other I am just happy. It is not the happiness I dreamed about, but it is a good happiness. Yes, finally it is good."

This woman's letter woke me up to an idea which might be generally true. It might lead to a breathtaking theory if we were to follow it out. Let us assume that there really are people who intensely concentrate on the causes of their fate. And that, on the other hand, there are people who are quicker to see their area of freedom. Wouldn't that mean that the former also more frequently talk about the causes of their fate, because we talk about whatever we are concerned with?

Now, depending on whether the patients are oriented more toward the circumstances of fate or toward their area of freedom, wouldn't that determine how much they talk in our sessions about such things as environmental influences, mistakes by parents, or their illnesses or accidents, which then provide the basis of our psychological interventions with them? This would mean that two patients with a similar background might tell two different stories. One of them might tell the interviewer how he had been ignored by his mother too much, or how he was shocked when his dog was run over by a car. In other words, he would emphasize the degree to which he was at the mercy of his circumstances. On the other hand, the second patient might bring up that her mother let her decide on her profession, or that she had always liked animals—in other words, that she was able to participate in deciding what would happen.

For three quarters of a century, psychologists have taken at face value what clients have said about events in their lives, have reconstructed clients' life histories on the basis of what was said, and consequently have drawn conclusions about their current states. But couldn't the truth be rather that both the selection of the reported life events as well as the description of how the client is currently doing represent simply and solely the degree to which the person's attention is focused on the circumstances of fate? Is it possible that these self-reports signify the extent to which the clients do not feel free, although there actually were areas of freedom for them?

Is emotional illness, or let us say it more carefully, neurotic illness nothing but a dead-end street of the mind, a chronic concentration on what is unchangeable or, as the case may be, an inattention to what is changeable? If that were so, we could solve the contradiction between the assertion of innumerable psychology textbooks, that neurosis results from early childhood frustrations, privations, and inadequate parental models, and the fact that millions of people all around the world have had a bad or difficult childhood and still have matured into completely normal adults.

It is obvious that those who do not make responsible use of their freedom—because they are not even aware of it—will fail in their adult life, just as they will fail when they try to look back only upon the facts of the past. They overlook the chances they have in their present life and the chances their childhood concealed. They only notice what the environment inflicted on them because they have not identified themselves as persons who themselves respond to "inflictions of all kinds" and freely respond according to their own choices, as the persons who—in spite of everything—they truly are.

Human dignity is something that belongs to every person: even the poorest, the sickest, the most "useless" person. Psychotherapy is something that we should be able to apply to the poorest, the sickest, the most "useless" person. If we want to merge the two, we will have to operate within the area of our last possession, which absolutely cannot be taken from us except by death or loss of mind function. And this possession is our spiritual freedom. Logotherapy is the only therapy which has succeeded in fully integrating spiritual freedom in its medical and psychological concept of the human being. This is why logotherapy deserves to be called a psychotherapy worthy of human dignity.

BIBLIOGRAPHY

[1]Viktor E. Frankl, *Der Mensch vor der Frage nach dem Sinn*, Piper, München, 7th ed. 1989

[2]Viktor E. Frankl, "Der unbedingte Mensch" in *Der leidende Mensch*, Piper, München, new ed. 1990

[3]Viktor E. Frankl, *Ärztliche Seelsorge"* Fischer TB, Frankfurt, 4th ed. 1987

[4]Viktor E. Frankl, "Zeit und Verantwortung" in *Der Wille zum Sinn*, Piper, München, new ed. 1991

[5]Elisabeth Lukas, *Suicidprophylaxe*, Stuttgart, Darmstadt, 1983

[6]Viktor E. Frankl, "Argumente für einen tragischen Optimismus" in *Sinn-voll heilen*. Herder, Freiburg, 1983

[7]Viktor E. Frankl, *Die Sinnfrage in der Psychotherapie*, Piper, München, 3rd ed. 1988

[8]Viktor E. Frankl, *Psychotherapie für den Laien*, Herder, Freiburg, 13th ed. 1989

[9]Viktor E. Frankl, "Homo patiens: Versuch einer Pathodizee" in *Der leidende Mensch"* Piper, München, new ed. 1990

[10]Viktor E. Frankl, *Der leidende Mensch*, Piper, Munchen, new ed. 1990

www.ingramcontent.com/pod-product-compliance
Lightning Source LLC
Chambersburg PA
CBHW020530270326
41927CB00006B/513